ten dollar DINNERS

ten dollar DINNERS

140 Recipes and Tips to Elevate Simple,
Fresh Meals Any Night of the Week

Melissa d'Arabian

with Raquel Pelzel

Photographs by Ben Fink

Clarkson Potter/Publishers
New York

Published in the United States by Clarkson Potter/Publishers, an imprint of the
Crown Publishing Group, a division of Random House, Inc., New York.
www.crownpublishing.com
www.clarksonpotter.com

CLARKSON POTTER is a trademark and POTTER with colophon is a
registered trademark of Random House, Inc.

Library of Congress cataloging-in-publication data is available upon request.

ISBN 978-0-307-98514-9
eISBN 978-0-307-98515-6

Printed in the United States of America

Book and cover design by Ashley Tucker
Cover photography by Ben Fink

10 9 8 7 6 5 4 3 2 1

First Edition

Philippe, Valentine, Charlotte, Margaux, and Océane:
You made this happen, and you make this matter.

contents

introduction

I am so proud to bring my first
cookbook to your kitchen, because it
will help you save money (and lots of it)
and encourage you to think about
cooking in a different way.

I see my recipes as part of a bigger story that shows you
how to eat well, be a responsible consumer, and spend with
purpose. Saving money can be incredibly empowering—
especially when you know that you're putting healthy dinners on the table for your family every night of the week.

I believe that a budget meal can also be an enticing one:
delicious, fresh, exciting, and made without compromise.
At its heart, that is what my Food Network show, *Ten
Dollar Dinners*, and my *Ten Dollar Dinners* cookbook are
all about: the celebration of smart cooking and saving
along the way. So if you think that budget food is only
about meat loaf and rice and beans, think again. On these

pages, you'll find recipes that call for shrimp, wild mushrooms, and sirloin steak (as well as creative ways to dress up meat loaf and rice and beans!).

I learned how to be a smart cook and shopper because I grew up with a coupon-cutter mentality and on a shoestring budget. My mom raised me on her own *and* while she was putting herself through college and medical school. To say that money was tight would be an understatement. I remember one time when we had a jar of pickles in the refrigerator, and that was it. My mom, my sister, and I stayed up until the wee hours of the morning making candles to sell at the local dime store so we could buy groceries. Waste was never a temptation in our house. That said, my mom still wanted to teach me the joy of hosting others, something we rarely had the budget to do. When I was five Mom invited her girlfriends (and their daughters) and my friends (and their moms) over for a ladies' holiday cookie and hot cocoa party at our home in Tucson, Arizona. Even though we had no extra cash to be throwing a party, we still managed to put together a beautiful celebration on a tight budget. We decorated the Christmas tree, ate cookies, drank hot cocoa, and sang songs around the piano. It was simple and lovely. That single experience taught me how beautiful it is to cook for people and to bring joy to loved ones by creating something welcoming. My mom passed away when I was twenty years old, and to this day, I still hold our holiday cookie and cocoa memory close to heart—in fact, every December I now host a mother-daughter holiday tea with my four girls and their friends and their mothers.

My path to being the mom of four girls and hosting my own television show was circuitous, to say the least! After graduating from the University of Vermont, I went to Georgetown University and earned an MBA, which led to a career in finance and strategy. My job eventually landed me in France. I fell in love with the food markets in Paris: the cheese shops and boulangeries, the butchers and outdoor produce stalls. I was living there when I made the leap from relying on recipes to letting beautiful ingredients drive a meal.

I lived in France for four years and met my future husband and father of our gorgeous girls there. We married in the small village where he grew up in the south of France and eventually moved back to the United States. Before I knew it, we were parents to four little girls, and I found myself streamlining our expenses (just like my mom had to do) so we could survive on a single income. Shopping and cooking for four hungry toddlers and a husband with decidedly sophisticated tastes on a strict budget became a challenge, a game, and something I was hardwired to do.

I started teaching other women strategies for saving money while cooking delicious homemade meals. The most requested topic was how to make homemade yogurt—because we went through a *lot* of yogurt, and I quickly discovered that I could save hundreds of dollars a year just by making it myself. I decided to set up a handheld video camera in my kitchen and shoot a demo of me making yogurt that I would e-mail to my stay-at-home-mom group. That was the video that landed me a spot on *The Next Food Network Star.*

On the show, when we were down to three finalists, only one of whom would get their own program, the challenge was to make the "ultimate dinner party" for an incredibly esteemed group of judges (Bobby Flay, Rick Bayless, Masaharu Morimoto, and Marcus Samuelsson, to name a few). Our budget was sky's-the-limit *huge.* You know what dish stole the show (and sealed my fate)? My humble Potato-Bacon Torte (page 348), a country-style savory pie that cost me about fifty cents a serving to make. These chefs were being treated to the best that money could buy and they chose my simple and downright cheap potato pie over the other contestants' pricier dishes! It concreted my philosophy that a delicious meal doesn't have to be expensive to satisfy even the most esteemed taste buds. That is the power of *Ten Dollar Dinners*.

I want my recipes to be clever examples of a bigger story, a celebration of resource responsibility and spending with purpose. Saving money can be incredibly empowering, and it feels good to know we are spending wisely. I have hundreds of savings strategies to share, and if I could personally go shopping with each one of you—walking you through the grocery store and unveiling bargains and tips—then cook in your kitchens, I would. But instead, I offer this book, which I hope gets you as excited about cutting your grocery bill as I do about cutting mine.

I consider myself the luckiest cook in the world. I have my very own test kitchen "staffed" by my daughter-chefs and the world's most supportive husband. We don't overspend and we love food that nourishes our bodies and our souls. I believe in the power of the family meal and making them happen as often as possible. I hope that with this cookbook, you will find many fantastic recipes and mealtime strategies that help you get dinner on the table and guide you to living and eating better.

Melissa d'Arabian

making
ten dollar dinners
work for you

This book is about serving delicious food to your family and friends (and yourself) and how to do that while saving money. Some of that happens when you're out grocery shopping: looking for manager's specials, markdowns, and advertised weekly deals (boneless chicken breasts when they're on sale can be half their usual price). However, grocery-store cash-register success stories are only part of the big picture. The other part happens at home. A combination of smart recipes, ingredient-management strategies, and cost-saving tips adds up to less waste and more economy in the kitchen (for example, use cabbage to bulk up fennel, water adds volume to chicken broth, and stretch shrimp with inexpensive and filling beans or pasta).

Cooking on a budget should feel great—I feel empowered knowing that I spend my family's resources wisely and still cook fantastic meals. What I hope you will take away after reading this book is that you can serve exciting, fresh, and tasty food without sacrifice.

Recipe costs are calculated according to how much of each ingredient is used, not by the price of the entire package of the ingredient. The cost of a cup of sugar, for instance, counts toward the total cost of the recipe you're making, even if you bought the sugar two months ago and it is sitting on your shelf. Pantry ingredients such as sugar and flour are generally good budget bets, not because they don't "count" but because they are usually inexpensive commodity items bought in large quantities that last a long time. Often-used long-lasting items also save money (as long as you use the item before it can spoil!) because larger packaged ingredients are often cheaper per ounce or per cup.

Some of you may already have a complete pantry outfitted with the staples. However, for those of you setting up a kitchen for the first time, it's smart to stock your pantry over the course of several weeks so you're not facing a hefty grocery bill the first time you go to the store. Focus on the least expensive recipes in this book to build your arsenal of ingredients, and stock up according to what is on sale (make a copy of my list of pantry staples on pages 26–27 to bring with you to the store). Before you know it, you will have a kitchen full of basic essentials ready to support your ten dollar dinner efforts.

Being conscious of your buying choices is a game as much as it is a lifestyle. Once you see how much money you can save by making informed buying decisions, you'll be scoping out deals and bargains like a pro and saving a ton while you're at it.

How to Use *Ten Dollar Dinners*

Here is my promise: you can eat a delicious meal for ten dollars. Not one dish, but a *meal*. A ten dollar dinner is a main dish plus two other dishes (maybe a side dish and a dessert, or an appetizer and a salad). If you choose a pricier main dish, then you compensate by serving two other less-expensive dishes.

To help you plan your own ten dollar dinner menus, see the convenient scale that appears with each recipe that tells you approximately how much each dish will cost: downright cheap, middle of the road, or pricey. (See my recipe cost index on page 355.)

Throughout the book and as a companion to each recipe, you'll see five dots with the serving information. The shaded dots relate to the costs of the recipe, with one shaded dot being the least pricey.

- If you choose a high-range main dish, then to balance the cost, you need to choose two complementary low-range menu items.

- If you choose a low-range main dish, then you have more flexibility in choosing your two complementary dishes.

- If you're in a cash crunch and need to build the cheapest dinner possible, choose three low-range options.

- If you're hosting a dinner party and want to pull out all the stops, pick all mid- and high-range recipes (knowing that you'll extend your ten dollar budget by only a few bucks).

The dots that accompany each recipe help keep the guesswork out of the *Ten Dollar Dinners* equation. Splurge on one course, save on another, and feel confident about creating a menu that satisfies your craving and your budget.

strategies for saving

Eating well on a budget is about saving money at the supermarket and using what you have at home to your best advantage. Here are ten ways to get started—incorporate them into your shopping and meal planning and they will pay off handsomely!

The *Ten Dollar Dinners* Top 10 List

1 Try a clear-the-pantry week. This is a great plan for when you need a quick hit of major savings (such as after the holidays or an unexpected expense). When I do this, I easily uncover hundreds of dollars I didn't need to spend! Remember that your "pantry" includes your freezer, so you can defrost frozen bags of soup, meatballs, or packages of chicken that you have stowed away for a rainy day. Take a tour of your kitchen pantry and write down the major ingredients lurking around. Use this list to create a menu for the week. It's a fun challenge to see how long you can go without buying new food items (beyond the few necessary perishables, such as milk and eggs).

2 Incorporate bean night once a week. Dried beans are super cheap (and canned beans are inexpensive, too), incredibly healthy, and delicious! This frugal protein can easily be turned into dinner and will save you so much money compared to serving chicken or beef. By the way—"bean" night can mean any inexpensive protein such as whole-grain pasta, eggs, lentils, or other legumes.

3 When entertaining, fit inexpensive proteins into the first course. Buffets always tempt diners with delicious yet cheap-to-make items at the front with the pricey showstoppers, such as prime rib, at the end of the line. I follow their lead when entertaining. Starters like White Bean Tapenade Crostini (page 38) or Lentil and Celery Salad (page 97) are cheap to make, delicious, and satiating, so a pricier yet smaller second course like Shrimp Scampi Linguine (page 272) will seem incredibly satisfying and plentiful.

4 Splurge smart in the produce aisle and make a fresh vegetable the star of a dish. Buying just a handful of a pricier vegetable is a smart way to add a touch of luxury to dinner without breaking the bank. Just a few ounces of expensive wild mushrooms is enough to make an impact. Buying a small portion of pricier fresh produce—perhaps a small amount of baby arugula or a beautifully bumpy heirloom tomato—allows you to treat yourself without blowing your budget.

5 Stretch expensive ingredients alongside inexpensive ones. Bulking up pricey ingredients with less expensive ones is a great trick for serving shrimp (or other pricey proteins) while not overspending at the market. Beans, rice, pasta, and cheap vegetables such as cabbage are great for making a small amount of costly fennel or leeks seem plentiful and abundant.

6 Use the bulk aisle in surprising ways. Buying large quantities in the bulk aisle will save money, but it's only half the story—you can also buy *small* quantities in the bulk aisle. A handful of hazelnuts from that aisle will set you back only twenty or thirty cents—toast, chop, and sprinkle over green beans or in a cheap lettuce salad and you have a fancy restaurant-worthy dish.

7 Keep flavor enhancers in the freezer. Bacon, fresh ginger, nuts, grated cheese and even leftover wine (for cooking) keep exponentially longer in the freezer than in the fridge. Store in resealable freezer bags so you can easily add just enough to brighten, deepen, or add a textural component to a recipe.

8 Take an inexpensive "standby" favorite dish and give it an ethnic makeover. Meat loaf, meatballs, chicken soup, and chili are all crowd-pleasing recipes that easily can take on a flavor boost from ethnic ingredients. Cilantro, curry powder, chipotle chiles in adobo sauce, coconut milk, and salsa are all ingredients that are easy add-ins to change the taste of a dish just enough to refresh it and give it new energy.

9 Never throw away a source of free flavor. Ingredients that give you double the mileage are pure gold for budget cooks. Lemon offers lemon juice and lemon zest. I make good use of squeezed lemon halves and freeze them in a resealable freezer bag to zest another time; I also often dry lemon zest in a low-temperature oven and store the dried zest in a glass jar or spice shaker. Buy shrimp with the shells on and make a quick shrimp stock from the shells. Buy celery with the leaves still attached—they're a great substitute for parsley. Beets with beet tops, fennel and its fronds, Parmesan rinds (add to pasta sauce or broth for a rich, nutty taste), and even mushroom stems (they add tremendous depth to vegetable broths) are all great sources of flavor for which you don't have to pay an extra dime.

10 Once a week quickly tally your perishables and create a five-minute menu plan. The most expensive ingredient is the one you throw away. So take a few seconds to check through your crisper drawers and see what's lurking in the back of the fridge. Let your inventory review drive your week's menu. If all you have are odds and ends, make an anything-goes soup or pasta sauce! Your menu plan doesn't have to be fancy to be effective.

Store Pricing Secrets You Need to Know

Along with my top ten tips for saving, every budget shopper should be aware of how their grocery store moves product. Here are two pricing strategies often used in major supermarkets.

loss leaders: Every week in major grocery store chains, there is usually one beef, one chicken, and one pork cut on sale for 50 to 75 percent off its normal price. The objective of a loss leader is to get shoppers in the door of a supermarket, and though the store may take a hit on this one item, they know that you will also likely buy the rest of your groceries while you're in the store (and make up the cost). I like to stock up on a few packages of these loss-leader meat items because meat freezes so beautifully. (By the way, wine is also sometimes a loss leader.)

manager's special: When an item is about three days before its sell-by date, it often goes on manager's special (look for the big orange sticker). If you see bread or dairy on manager's special, grab it—it's often a great deal at up to 50 percent off (or more!).

Note: the one thing I do not buy on manager's special is meat, for two reasons: if you buy meat that has turned south, and you don't realize it until after you've cooked it, you lose the cost of not only the meat but also the other ingredients; second, you're stuck without dinner! Don't forget that meat is often a loss leader, meaning it's often marked down by 50 percent anyway—so why take such a risk for the exact same discount?

the ten dollar dinner pantry

Saving Starts at Home

Saving money at mealtime starts in your kitchen. Although keeping your budget radar attuned to deals in the supermarket is incredibly important, pantry management is a critical part of saving money.

The pantry is your wingman in the kitchen—it's where you turn for your everyday resources. A useful pantry should present you with options, meaning it contains ingredients your family loves and that you cook with often. You save money because pantry ingredients are often cheap to begin with, and since you use the ingredient a lot, you can buy it in large quantities when the prices are low without worrying about it going to waste.

Your pantry will probably look a little different from my pantry. That's the way it should be. Really think about the foods your family loves the most, and that should be what is in constant supply in your cupboards, refrigerator, and freezer.

Pantry Snapshot
a list of must-haves

This is a list of ingredients that I always have in my pantry (which includes my dry storage, refrigerator, and freezer). Scan or make a photocopy of this page and add or cross out items to customize it for your house.

DRY STORAGE

- All-purpose flour
  (I prefer unbleached)
- Baking powder and baking soda
- Beef and chicken broth
  (small containers of stock concentrates, or bouillon cubes)
- Bread crumbs
- Canned fruit
  (mandarin oranges, crushed pineapple)
- Canned whole peeled tomatoes, tomato paste, and tomato sauce
- Cocoa powder
- Cornstarch
- Dried beans and legumes
  (black beans, lentils, at least one white bean variety)
- Dried fruit
  (apricots, prunes, raisins)
- Dried herbs and spices
  (basil, black pepper, cardamom, cayenne, chili powder, ground cinnamon, ground coriander, ground cumin, herbes de Provence, oregano, paprika, crushed red pepper flakes, rosemary, thyme)
- Hot sauce
- Jarred salsa

- Kosher salt
  (I prefer kosher salt because I can add it by the pinch and to taste; if using table salt, halve the quantity called for in the recipe)
- Long-grain white rice and brown rice
- Oil
  (I use a cheaper olive oil for cooking and a fancier bottle for drizzling and salads; sesame oil; and vegetable oil for my neutral-flavored oil)
- Old-fashioned rolled oats
- Pasta
  (whole-grain and a variety of dried shapes)
- Semisweet mini chocolate chips
- Smooth peanut butter
- Soy sauce
- Specialty grains and starches
  (bulgur, couscous, polenta, quinoa)
- Sweeteners
  (confectioners' sugar, granulated sugar, honey, light or dark brown sugar, maple syrup)
- Vinegar
  (apple cider, balsamic, distilled white, red wine, white wine)
- Wine
  (red and white)

FRESH PRODUCE

- Apples
- Bananas
- Bell peppers
  (sweet red, orange, or yellow)
- Citrus fruit
  (lemons, limes, and oranges are great
  for eating, juicing, and zesting)
- Fresh herbs
  (it's most economical to grow your own
  in a garden or window box container)
- Garlic
- Hardy vegetables
  (since they last a while, buy what's on
  sale to keep the crisper drawer stocked:
  broccoli, cabbage, carrots, cauliflower,
  celery, parsnips, radishes)
- Leafy greens
  (kale and spinach are great both raw
  and cooked)
- Onions
  (scallions and yellow onions)
- Potatoes
- Tomatoes
  (only when they're reasonably priced;
  otherwise used canned)
- Zucchini or yellow summer squash
  (when in season)

REFRIGERATOR

- Butter
  (unsalted)
- Capers
- Cheese
  (Cheddar, mozzarella, Parmesan)
- Condiments
  (ketchup, mayonnaise, mustard)
- Cream cheese
- Eggs
- Jam
  (apricot, marmalade, and raspberry)
- Milk
  (whole, low-fat, or skim)
- Olives
- Plain yogurt
- Sour cream

FREEZER

- Bacon
- Beef
  (ground, large roasts like chuck for
  braising, sirloin steaks)
- Bread
  (sandwich bread and baguettes)
- Chicken
  (boneless breasts, drumsticks, thighs)
- Ice cream
- Nuts
  (pecans or walnuts)
- Peas
- Pork
  (loin divided into cubes, boneless chops,
  and roast)
- Puff pastry
- Spinach
  (chopped leaf)

appetizers & snacks

Small Bites to Start Things Off

Entertaining—whether it involves work colleagues, PTA parents, or simply keeping your kids busy while you prepare dinner— is a lot easier to do when there is something tasty on the table.

It always pays off to have a baguette tucked away in the freezer for just this occasion (buy them from your supermarket's day-old rack to pay half price). I use the time while it warms in the oven to whip up a spread, a seasoned butter, or a dip that takes barely a minute to make. For family nights or on weekends, when I want something on the counter to snack on throughout the day, I bake a quick tart or tortilla, both of which can be enjoyed warm, at room temperature, or cold. Of course there are times when I want the appetizer to be more of a polished affair; that's when I don't hold back and pull out the fancy hors d'oeuvres like California-Style Bruschetta (page 49) or Pork Rillettes (page 43). Whether you're looking for a low-maintenance snack or a more refined first course, these satisfying small bites leave a thoughtful and welcoming first impression.

Toasted Baguette with Garlic Confit

If he got his way, my husband the Frenchman would eat a baguette for every meal and as a snack in between! This simple and thrifty starter makes him incredibly happy. The garlic is slowly poached in olive oil, rendering it tender, mild, and nearly buttery in texture when spread on bread. Philippe likes to dip bread in the garlic-infused oil, but I always make sure to squirrel away some of the fragrant oil for a dinner down the road—it's unbelievable tossed with pasta, fresh tomatoes, black pepper, and grated Parmesan.

serves 4

preparation time:
15 minutes

cooking time:
50 minutes

20 garlic cloves

3 tablespoons unsalted butter

1 sprig fresh rosemary

1 teaspoon kosher salt

¾ to 1½ cups olive oil

Cooled crostini (page 38)

Balsamic vinegar, for serving (optional)

1 Place the garlic, butter, rosemary, and salt in a small saucepan. Add enough olive oil to cover the garlic and cook over low heat until the garlic is very tender (a paring knife will easily slide through a clove), about 45 minutes, occasionally swirling the oil and garlic cloves (note that the garlic will turn toasty brown).

2 Strain the garlic mixture through a fine-mesh sieve set over a medium bowl. Discard the rosemary and turn the garlic out into a small dish. Pour the excess oil into another small dish.

3 Place the bread slices on a hot grill or grill pan and toast until golden on both sides, about 4 minutes total. Transfer the bread to a plate and serve with the garlic and the oil. If you like, just before serving, you can add a few drops of balsamic vinegar to the oil—don't stir, just let the vinegar sit in droplets.

deals, dollars & sense : freezing baguettes

I always keep a baguette half or two in the freezer. Pop it in a hot oven for a few minutes to crisp up and you have the perfect "fresh baked" side for salad, soup, or bruschetta. (Keep your eye on the day-old bread rack at the market and bring home a few just for this purpose!)

Grilled Bread con Tomate with Crispy Ham

One of the first trips that my husband and I took together was to Barcelona, where we ate pan con tomate, bread with tomatoes, at the start of nearly every dinner. The simple appetizer of bread brushed with olive oil, then grilled to charred perfection and rubbed with raw garlic and a tomato, quickly became one of my favorite Spanish foods. In Spain, a thin slice of Serrano ham is often served on the side. My budget-friendly solution is to take deli ham and fry it, to draw out its salty-caramelized, meaty taste.

serves 4

preparation time:
15 minutes

cooking time:
8 minutes

½ baguette, thinly sliced on a bias

4 tablespoons olive oil, plus extra for drizzling

2 garlic cloves, halved

5 thin ham slices, quartered

2 plum tomatoes

½ teaspoon kosher salt

1 Preheat a grill pan over medium-high heat (you can also use a charcoal or gas grill). Brush both sides of the bread with 3 tablespoons of the olive oil. Place the bread slices on the grill (you may need to do this in two batches) and toast until golden with grill marks on both sides, about 4 minutes total. Transfer the bread to a plate, rub one side of each slice with half a garlic clove, and set aside.

2 Heat the remaining 1 tablespoon olive oil in a large skillet and fry the ham until crisp on both sides, 1 to 2 minutes per side. Use tongs to transfer the ham to a paper towel–lined plate and set aside.

3 Slice off the top of both tomatoes and rub the tomato, cut side down, on each slice of bread. Drizzle with olive oil, sprinkle with the salt, and top with a piece of crispy ham. Serve.

Olive Butter

Seasoned butter made with marinated olives couldn't be easier: chop, mix, and chill, and you have a delicious low-cost spread that tastes like big money. It's a briny complement to toasted crostini or oven-warmed bread. The next time you pass your supermarket's olive or salad bar, buy a small amount of olives and try this recipe!

● ● ○ ○ ○ ○

serves 4

preparation time:
5 minutes (plus time for the butter to chill)

cooking time:
5 minutes

½ cup marinated and pitted olives, roughly chopped

1 stick unsalted butter, at room temperature

¼ teaspoon kosher salt

1 baguette or country-style loaf

1 Preheat the oven to 350°F. Place the olives, butter, and salt in the bowl of a food processor and pulse to combine, scraping down the sides of the bowl as needed, until the mixture is semismooth with no chunky olive pieces. Scrape the butter into a small bowl or ramekin, cover with plastic wrap, and refrigerate.

2 Place the bread in the oven and warm just until the crust is crisp and hot to the touch, 3 to 5 minutes. Remove the bread from the oven and serve whole or sliced with the chilled butter.

10 flavored butters

Fast, Cheap, and Easy Softened butters mixed with fresh herbs, onions, spices, citrus, or other boosts (such as olives) are fantastic to have in the refrigerator or freezer. They add an extra layer of flavor to anything from steamed green beans to grilled chicken, sautéed fish, or biscuits. They're simple to prepare: mix room-temperature butter and a generous pinch of salt with any of the following seasonings and pack it into a small bowl or ramekin (or shape into a log on a piece of plastic wrap, wrap tightly, and refrigerate or freeze for future slicing). Store in the refrigerator for up to a few days (if the butter has garlic or onions in it, its flavor will get more pungent as it ages). Here are ten of my favorite seasoned butter mix-ins:

- Lemon zest + minced garlic
- Orange zest + chopped fresh rosemary
- Minced shallots + chopped fresh tarragon
- Chopped fresh basil + herbes de Provence
- Chopped fresh cilantro + ground cumin
- Chopped fresh chives + chopped capers
- Chopped fresh parsley + minced garlic + crushed red pepper flakes
- Lime zest + smoked paprika
- Lemon zest + chopped anchovies + minced garlic
- Grainy mustard + minced shallots

Caprese Tartlets

A mozzarella, basil, and tomato salad turns into the cutest handheld tartlet when layered into toasted bread cups. Instead of making time-consuming individual tartlets from pastry dough, I take white bread, flatten it with a rolling pin so it gets almost doughy, and then press each slice into a muffin cup. After a brush with olive oil and a short trip into the oven, they become thin, crisp, golden-brown shells, perfect for mozzarella cheese and a juicy tomato slice.

● ● ● ● ● ●

serves 4

preparation time:
15 minutes (plus 30 minutes to cool)

cooking time:
13 minutes

8 slices white bread, crusts removed

¼ cup olive oil, plus extra for drizzling

3 tablespoons cream cheese, at room temperature

1 teaspoon garlic powder

2 teaspoons finely chopped fresh basil plus 8 leaves, stacked, rolled, and thinly sliced

Kosher salt

Ground black pepper

2 plum tomatoes, thinly sliced crosswise

4 ounces mozzarella, sliced into 8 small pieces

Balsamic vinegar, for drizzling (optional)

1 Preheat the oven to 375°F. Place the bread on a cutting board and use a rolling pin or the underside of a large spoon to flatten the bread slices until they are very thin and almost doughy. Brush both sides of the bread with the olive oil and press the slices into the cups of a muffin tin to form shells. Set aside.

2 Stir together the cream cheese, garlic powder, the 2 teaspoons chopped basil, ½ teaspoon salt, and ¼ teaspoon pepper until smooth. Divide the cream cheese mixture among the bottoms of the bread cups and bake until the tartlets are

more salad tartlets

These tartlets are so sweet and picturesque—why stop with Caprese? Here are a few more ideas for ways to fill up bread tart cups (if a savory filling is especially saucy, create a cushion using shredded lettuce so the bottom of the cup doesn't get soggy and fall apart):

- Crumbled feta cheese, chopped tomatoes, and olives
- Creamy Cheese (page 39) and fried ham
- Lentil and Celery Salad (page 97)
- Chopped Salad with Chicken, Salami, and Mozzarella (page 101)
- Crumbled blue cheese, finely chopped romaine, and crispy bacon
- Fruit Salad with Lemon-Mint Syrup (page 288)

golden and crusty, 12 to 13 minutes. Remove the muffin tin from the oven and set aside to cool for 10 minutes before removing from the pan (use your fingers) and placing them on a wire rack to cool completely.

3 Place the tomato slices on a large plate and season with a few generous pinches of salt. Set 1 slice mozzarella in each bread cup and then cover with 1 or 2 slices tomato. Season with salt and pepper, drizzle with olive oil and balsamic vinegar (if using), and finish with the ribbons of fresh basil.

deals, dollars & sense: fresh bread crumbs

I freeze bread crusts and bread heels in a resealable bag to make fresh bread crumbs. Since ends and crusts have more heft to them than the interior crumb, they don't need to be toasted before using.

White Bean Tapenade Crostini

Tapenade is an olive-based spread served frequently throughout the Mediterranean. There is much (spirited!) debate about what makes a truly great tapenade: should it include garlic, or anchovies, or capers, or just olives? My husband is the best tapenade maker of the family, and over the years we have developed some twists on the classic. This is my favorite version, made with white beans for added body, protein, and creaminess. Combined with olives, capers, fresh lemon, and garlic, it's easy to love.

● ● ○ ○ ○

serves 4

preparation time:
15 minutes

cooking time:
10 minutes

for the crostini

- 1 tablespoon olive oil
- 1 tablespoon vegetable oil
- ¼ teaspoon kosher salt
- ¼ teaspoon ground black pepper
- 1 baguette, thinly sliced on a bias

for the tapenade

- ½ cup pitted black olives
- ½ cup pitted green olives
- ¼ cup brine-packed capers, rinsed
- Zest of 1 lemon plus 1 tablespoon of juice
- 1 garlic clove, finely minced or pressed through a garlic press
- 2 tablespoons olive oil
- ½ teaspoon kosher salt
- ¼ teaspoon ground black pepper
- ¾ cup cooked white beans

deals, dollars & sense: olives

Most grocery stores have an olive bar or a salad bar with several varieties of olives. Buying olives in small quantities, limiting your purchase to just what you need—perhaps ½ cup—is enough to dress up a salad or pasta dish or make a spread or a compound butter, yet doesn't break the bank.

1 **To make the crostini:** Preheat the oven to 350°F. Mix the olive and vegetable oils, salt, and pepper in a small bowl. Place the baguette slices on a rimmed baking sheet and brush with some of the oil mixture. Set in the oven and bake until golden brown, 8 to 10 minutes. Remove from the oven and set aside.

2 **To make the tapenade:** Place the black and green olives, capers, lemon zest and juice, garlic, olive oil, salt, and pepper in the bowl of a food processor and purée until nearly smooth. Add the beans and pulse until the beans are broken up and the mixture is rough textured, about 4 pulses. Scrape the mixture into a bowl and serve with the crostini.

Creamy Cheese and Basil Crostini

When I entertain, my strategy often begins with a baguette and a flavorful filling to spread on top. This topping uses puréed cottage cheese (an alternative to pricey ricotta) and tastes fresh and light thanks to a pinch of lemon zest and fresh basil. For a real treat, halve a few thin sheets of ham and drape them over the topping; thinly sliced juicy summer tomatoes are also an incredible topper.

● ●

serves 4

preparation time:
12 minutes

cooking time:
none

¾ cup 4% cottage cheese

1 to 2 tablespoons milk, if needed

Zest of ¼ lemon

½ teaspoon kosher salt, plus extra for serving

Cooled crostini (page 38)

½ tablespoon extra-virgin olive oil

8 fresh basil leaves, stacked, rolled, and thinly sliced

1 Place the cottage cheese in the bowl of a food processor and purée until completely smooth. Scrape it into a medium bowl. The texture should be slightly thicker than whipped cream cheese—if it's too thick, add the milk to thin it out. Stir in the lemon zest and salt.

2 Set the crostini on a platter and spread the cheese mixture over each piece. Drizzle each with a few dots of the olive oil and a sprinkle of salt. Finish with the basil and serve.

Smoked Tuna Spread

I keep my kitchen stocked with a few low-cost, nonperishable proteins that I count on for their ease and speed. Canned tuna is an absolute must for the cupboard because it's so versatile. In this spread, I mix tuna with a few other pantry staples, including mayonnaise, sweet relish, and dried dill for a sophisticated-tasting spread that takes only ten minutes to make. Liquid smoke is a specialty ingredient worth buying since all it takes is a few drops to make a smoky impact (one small bottle lasts a long time).

● ○ ○ ○ ○ ○

serves **4**

preparation time:
10 minutes

cooking time:
none

3 tablespoons mayonnaise

2 teaspoons fresh lemon juice

1 teaspoon sweet relish

½ teaspoon dried dill

¼ teaspoon liquid smoke

   5-ounce can oil-packed light tuna, drained

1 celery stalk, finely chopped

1 scallion (white and green parts), finely chopped

   Kosher salt, if needed

   Fresh bread or crackers, for serving

Stir the mayonnaise, lemon juice, relish, dill, and liquid smoke together in a medium bowl. Add the tuna, celery, and scallion and stir until well mixed. Taste and add a pinch of salt if needed. Serve with fresh bread or crackers.

deals, dollars & sense: smoky swap-outs

Liquid smoke adds a great smoky quality. But if you don't have any, use one of these other smoky ingredients: smoked paprika, a little bacon fat (or even chopped crispy bacon if the texture won't cloud the recipe), a splash of liquid smoke, chipotle chile powder, or chopped canned chipotle chiles (or even the adobo sauce they're in).

Swapping Ingredients

Knowing how to swap out ingredients you don't have for ones you do is critical if you're looking to keep your grocery list modest and cheap. You never want to feel like you're stuck having to buy an expensive ingredient (unless you're excited to try it, of course). I'm here to tell you that there is almost always an alternative.

The key to swapping is to substitute a similar ingredient that exhibits the same flavor function as the item called for in the recipe: acid, sweetness, spice, tang, smokiness.

Here are a few swap ideas to get you thinking.

- For **wine** think about chicken broth, vermouth, water with a little tomato paste or a splash of wine vinegar, or citrus juice.
- For **Parmesan cheese** any similarly dry, crumbly texture (such as Pecorino, an aged Cheddar, or feta) or a cheese with a nutty quality (such as Gruyère) works well.
- **Soft cheeses** with a good melting quality are generally happy to sit in for one another. Try a young Cheddar (not aged, crumbly Cheddar), mozzarella, Monterey Jack, and Swiss.
- **Tender herbs** such as basil, cilantro, chives, mint, parsley, scallions, and tarragon all substitute well for one another (if using dried herbs, use half as much; a little chopped fresh parsley is a good addition to dried herbs to give them a fresh taste).
- **Hardy herbs** such as oregano, rosemary, and thyme (and even parsley) can be used similarly (if using dried herbs, use half as much).
- **Acidic ingredients** including lemon juice, lime juice, orange juice, and vinegar can often be swapped for one another.

Pork Rillettes

When I crave a bite of something meaty, rich, and comforting, I reach for rillettes, a deliciously decadent spread made from cooked and shredded meat. I load up on crocks of duck and pork rillettes from the best pâté makers in France when visiting my in-laws, but when my stash runs out, I make my own pretty great version that costs less than one-tenth the price! This is an ideal make-ahead appetizer for company—just pull out the crock of rillettes from the fridge and serve with good bread (or crackers in a pinch) and perhaps some grainy mustard and pickles.

● ●

serves 4

preparation time:
15 minutes (plus 40 minutes to chill)

cooking time:
7 minutes (4 hours to make the Slow Cooker All-Purpose Pork Shoulder on page 178)

8 tablespoons unsalted butter, at room temperature

1 shallot, finely chopped

¼ teaspoon kosher salt, plus extra, if needed

1 garlic clove, finely minced or pressed through a garlic press

2 tablespoons dry white wine or dry sherry

1 cup cooked pork shoulder (page 178), finely shredded

¼ teaspoon ground black pepper

Grilled baguette slices (page 33), toasted crostini (page 38), or crackers, for serving

1 Melt 1 tablespoon of the butter in a small skillet over medium heat. Add the shallot and salt and cook until soft, stirring occasionally, 4 to 5 minutes. Stir in the garlic and cook until fragrant, 1 to 2 minutes, then pour in the wine and simmer until it has completely evaporated. Scrape the shallot mixture into a small bowl or ramekin and chill in the refrigerator for 10 minutes.

2 Place the pork and the remaining 7 tablespoons butter in a medium bowl and stir to combine. Stir in the cooled shallot mixture and the pepper. Taste and add salt if needed. Scrape into a small crock or ramekin, cover with plastic wrap, and chill for at least 30 minutes before serving with the sliced baguette. The rillette can be refrigerated for up to 5 days.

deals, dollars & sense: leftover wine

If you have a little leftover wine in the bottle, don't pour it down the drain. Fill an ice cube tray half-full with wine and then freeze (if you fill all the way, the alcohol won't freeze). Once frozen, transfer the cubes to a resealable freezer bag. The next time you need to deglaze a pan or make a quick pan sauce, toss in a few cubes for an extra layer of flavor that didn't cost you an extra dime.

Simple Tomato Tart

When I lived in Paris, I used to eat tomato tarts all the time. Parisians treat tomato tarts like omelets: easy to make, delicious, and comforting at the end of a long day. Plus they're also refined and elegant. At home, I sometimes whip up one of these tarts to have on the counter for snacking throughout the day, or for impromptu entertaining (everyone will think you're so fancy!). It's absolutely perfect paired with a simple Parisian Café Salad (page 90) on the side.

● ● ● ○ ○ ○

makes one 9-inch tart

preparation time:
15 minutes

cooking time:
25 minutes

2 medium tomatoes, thinly sliced

1 teaspoon kosher salt

1 sheet thawed puff pastry, from a 17.3-ounce box

1½ teaspoons Dijon mustard

¼ teaspoon dried rosemary

¼ teaspoon dried thyme plus a squeeze of lemon juice

¼ teaspoon ground black pepper

1 tablespoon olive oil

1½ tablespoons grated Parmesan cheese

1 Place the sliced tomatoes in a single layer on a paper towel–lined baking sheet. Sprinkle with the salt and use a paper towel to blot the moisture from the top of the tomatoes every few minutes.

2 Meanwhile, prepare the tart crust. Adjust an oven rack to the lowest position and preheat the oven to 450°F. Spray a 9-inch fluted tart pan (preferably with a removable bottom) with nonstick pan spray and set aside.

3 Place the puff pastry on a cutting board and unfold it. Arrange it on the board so it looks like a diamond rather than a square. Use a rolling pin to gently roll it from the center out toward the edges until it is ¼ to ⅛ inch thick and slightly larger than the tart pan. Gently drape the dough over the rolling pin and lay it in the pan, lifting and fitting the dough into the corners and sides of the pan. Press the dough into the pan and press off any excess dough from the sides. Use a pastry brush or your fingers to smear the mustard over the bottom of the crust. Use a fork to prick the bottom of the crust all over.

4 Arrange the tomatoes in the crust so they overlap slightly, saving the 6 smallest slices for the center of the tart. Sprinkle the rosemary, thyme, and pepper over the tomatoes, then drizzle with the oil. Sprinkle the Parmesan over the top and bake the tart until the edges are golden brown and the tomatoes are tender, about 25 minutes. Remove from the oven and cool slightly before slicing and serving.

Crispy Kale Chips

Kale has long been one of my favorite winter greens; it's just so darned cheap! I love it sautéed, braised, or chopped into Kale and Crispy Bacon Salad (page 109). In this recipe, I toss it with some olive oil and salt and then bake the leaves until they're crisp and brittle, creating wonderfully tasty and healthy veggie chips. My husband, kids, and I love snacking on these, and since kale is so good for you, you can feel good about eating more than your fair share.

● ● ● ● ● ●

serves 4

preparation time:
15 minutes

cooking time:
20 minutes

Bunch of kale, washed and thoroughly dried

2 tablespoons olive oil

Kosher salt or sea salt

1 Preheat the oven to 275°F. Place the kale leaves on a cutting board and remove the tough ribs so you end up with 2 long and slender leaves for each single original leaf. Stack the leaves into 2 piles and slice each pile crosswise into 1½-inch pieces. Place them on a rimmed baking sheet in an even layer so the kale doesn't overlap. Drizzle with the olive oil, add a generous pinch of salt (take care not to oversalt; the kale shrinks as it bakes and the salt will concentrate), toss to combine, and then rearrange in an even layer.

2 Bake the kale leaves until they are crisp, about 20 minutes, turning them over halfway through cooking. Remove from the oven, transfer to a large bowl, and serve.

California-Style Bruschetta

In this recipe I combine two ideas: the beautiful flavors of bread topped with tomatoes like an Italian bruschetta and the cilantro-lime duo that has become ubiquitous in Southern California cooking. To stretch the tomatoes I mix in some creamy-tender white beans to the salsa-style sauce. The result is both familiar and surprising, and definitely delicious.

● ● ● ● ● ●

serves 4

preparation time:
15 minutes

cooking time:
12 minutes

2 tomatoes, halved, seeded, and chopped

½ teaspoon kosher salt, plus extra, if needed

Pinch of sugar

¾ cup cooked cannellini beans

Juice of ½ lime

1 tablespoon finely chopped fresh cilantro

4 tablespoons olive oil

3 tablespoons unsalted butter

1 baguette, thinly sliced

1 garlic clove, halved

1 Place the tomatoes in a medium serving bowl and stir in the salt and sugar. Mix in the beans, lime juice, cilantro, and 1 tablespoon of the olive oil. Taste and add more salt if needed, then set aside.

2 Melt 1½ tablespoons of the butter with 1½ tablespoons of the olive oil in a large skillet over medium-high heat. Place half of the bread slices in the pan and cook until golden brown on both sides, 4 to 6 minutes total. Remove the toasted bread from the pan and set aside. Add the remaining 1½ tablespoons butter and 1½ tablespoons oil to the pan and repeat with the remaining bread slices. While the bread is still warm, rub one side of each slice with the garlic. Spoon some of the bean-tomato mixture on top of each fried bread slice and serve.

Spanish Tortilla

An appetizer wins extra points with me if it has temperature flexibility, meaning I can serve it hot, cold, or at room temperature. A thick Spanish tortilla made with eggs, layers of tender-cooked potatoes, peppery chorizo, and sweet caramelized onions absolutely fills that requirement. Besides being an all-star party bite, it's also excellent for picnics, potlucks, or a casual dinner, perhaps with a small green salad alongside. For party-perfect clean-edged pieces, refrigerate the whole tortilla after baking but before slicing. Cut it into wedges while it's cold and then place the slices on a baking sheet and warm in a 300°F. oven.

● ● ● ○ ○ ○

serves 4

preparation time:
20 minutes (plus 10 minutes to rest)

cooking time:
30 minutes

1½ pounds russet potatoes, peeled and thinly sliced

2 tablespoons olive oil

½ large sweet onion, such as Maui or Vidalia, thinly sliced into rings

1 teaspoon kosher salt

½ teaspoon ground black pepper

¼ pound dry chorizo or salami, thinly sliced

2 garlic cloves, finely minced or pressed through a garlic press

6 large eggs

⅔ cup whole milk

3 scallions (white and green parts), trimmed and finely chopped

1 cup grated Cheddar cheese

deals, dollars & sense: buying potatoes

Even though potatoes are cheap, there are opportunities to save even more money. Always look at the per-pound price of loose potatoes compared to bagged potatoes—often you can get five pounds of bagged potatoes for the cost of two pounds loose—that's about three free pounds! If you're feeding a lot of mouths, definitely consider the enormous ten-pound bags. All three of these options are usually right next to each other at the store; it takes only a second and some quick math to figure out the savings.

1 Preheat the oven to 350°F. Bring a large pot of water to a boil over medium heat. Add the sliced potatoes and cook until they are just tender, about 8 minutes. Drain and set aside.

2 In a medium nonstick skillet, heat the olive oil over medium heat. Add the onion, season with ¼ teaspoon of the salt and ¼ teaspoon of the pepper, and cook the onion until it is soft and starting to caramelize, about 5 minutes, stirring occasionally. Mix in the chorizo and garlic and cook until the sausage begins to brown, 2 to 3 minutes. Turn off the heat.

3 In a large bowl, whisk the eggs until they are pale yellow in color, about 1 minute. Whisk in the milk, scallions, cheese, the remaining ¾ teaspoon salt, and the remaining ¼ teaspoon pepper. Stir in the chorizo mixture, add the

recipe continues

potatoes, gently stir to combine, and pour the mixture back into the pan. Place the pan in the oven and bake until the eggs are set and no longer watery in the center, about 15 minutes. Remove from the oven and let the tortilla rest in the pan for 10 minutes.

4 Place an upturned plate over the pan (make sure the plate is larger than the pan), carefully invert the tortilla onto the plate, and then slide the tortilla onto a cutting board. Slice the tortilla into wedges and serve warm or at room temperature.

food for sharing

Perfect Dishes to Give Spanish Tortilla is a great offering to new moms, new neighbors, or house-guests. I have even been known to make it on a lazy weekend morning and leave it on the counter for my family to snack on. Here are a few other dishes to give for any occasion.

- Simple Tomato Tart (page 45)
- Garlic Confit (page 33) with a fresh baguette
- Fennel-Onion Quiche (page 208)
- Potato-Bacon Torte (page 348)
- Pork Rillettes (page 43)
- Easy Scones (page 339)
- Cinnamon Buns (page 345)

- Classic Apple Tart (page 291)
- Buttery Shortbread (page 309)
- Orange Marmalade and Raspberry Jam Pochette Cookies (page 313)
- Citrus Butter Cookies (page 311)
- Double Chocolate Pound Cake (page 304)
- Black Bean Brownies (page 314)

Zucchini Carpaccio

Thin ribbons of zucchini softened with lemon juice and loosely arranged on a plate make a graceful starter. I'll sometimes eat a whole plate of this for dinner. Fresh thyme and thin shards of Parmesan cheese give it an herby nutty quality that is at once bright and soft-spoken. This is lovely as a side dish to a simple protein like Thyme and Lemon–Infused Fish en Papillote (page 117) or Pork Loin Milanese (page 174). It is also an excellent choice for al fresco dining.

● ● ○ ○ ○ ○

serves 4

preparation time:
15 minutes (plus 15 minutes to marinate)

cooking time:
none

2 medium zucchini

3 tablespoons olive oil

Juice of ½ lemon

2 teaspoons finely minced fresh thyme

¼ teaspoon kosher salt

¼ teaspoon ground black pepper

Wedge of Parmesan cheese, for shaving

1 baguette, thinly sliced

1 Trim the ends off the zucchini and use a vegetable peeler to shave them into very thin, long slices, discarding the slices that are mostly dark green skin. Arrange the ribbons on a platter in a delicate mound.

2 Whisk the olive oil, lemon juice, thyme, salt, and pepper together in a small bowl and pour over the zucchini slices. Set aside for 15 minutes to 1 hour.

3 Use a vegetable peeler to shave thin slices of Parmesan over the zucchini. Serve with the sliced baguette.

Caramelized Onion Pizzettas

On movie nights at our house, we often cook up mini personalized pizzas. The girls top their dough with whatever strikes their fancy (olives for eyes, pepperoni for rosy cheeks, or plain cheese) while Philippe and I top ours with more refined choices, such as caramelized onions. It always wows me that all it takes to transform a humble onion into the most buttery and sublimely sweet caramelized onion is a skillet and a little time. This combination of caramelized onions and Parmesan cheese makes for one of my all-time favorite pizzas. This recipe easily serves four as a small meal or eight as an appetizer.

● ●

makes **4** **pizzettas**

preparation time:
10 minutes

cooking time:
1 hour, 10 minutes

2 tablespoons unsalted butter

2 tablespoons olive oil, plus extra for rolling dough and greasing the baking sheets

3 yellow onions, halved and thinly sliced

1 teaspoon finely chopped fresh thyme or ½ teaspoon dried plus a squeeze of lemon juice

¼ teaspoon kosher salt

1 pound homemade or store-bought pizza dough

½ cup grated Parmesan cheese, plus extra for serving

1 Melt the butter with the olive oil in a large skillet over medium heat. Add the onions and cook, stirring often, until they soften, about 5 minutes. Stir in the thyme, reduce the heat to low, cover, and cook until the onions are very nutty brown and sticky, 40 to 45 minutes, stirring every 5 minutes. If the onions start to stick to the bottom of the pan, splash with a little water to scrape up any browned bits. Stir in the salt, turn off the heat, and set aside.

2 While the onions caramelize, prepare the dough: Adjust two oven racks to the upper-middle and lower-middle positions. Preheat the oven to 450°F. Drizzle a little olive oil on a cutting board. Place the pizza dough on the oiled part of the cutting board and divide into quarters. Tuck the corners of the dough under and place each quarter on a large plate. Rub a little olive oil on top of each round, cover with a kitchen towel, and set aside for 30 minutes.

3 Lightly oil 2 baking sheets. Coat the cutting board with about ½ teaspoon oil. Place one round of dough on top and turn it over so both sides have a lightly oiled surface. Use a rolling pin to roll the dough into a 6- to 7-inch circle about 1/16 inch thick. Transfer the dough to the oiled baking sheet. Repeat with the 3 remaining pieces of dough (you should be able to fit 2 pizzas on each baking sheet).

recipe continues

4 Divide the caramelized onions among the 4 pieces of dough. Sprinkle each with 2 tablespoons Parmesan and bake until golden brown, 18 to 20 minutes, rotating the baking sheets from the top rack to the bottom rack and vice versa midway through baking. Remove the baking sheets from the oven, sprinkle with a little more Parmesan, and serve whole or sliced.

deals, dollars & sense: pizza dough

There are lots of places to look for pizza dough, including the freezer section at your supermarket, the dairy aisle for ready-to-roll dough, and even your local pizzeria, where the manager will probably be more than happy to sell you a ball of dough for next to nothing. Refrigerated-in-the-tube pizza dough is an option too, especially when it's on sale for a buck. I like to buy a can or two to have on hand—it's especially great for grilled pizza.

Corn and Black Bean Pico

I grew up in Tucson, and many meals began with humble chips and salsa. I still love serving this crowd-pleaser at parties and dinners. Instead of simple salsa, I go for a protein- and fiber-loaded pico with black beans and corn, plus tomatoes, cilantro, and spices. A hearty starter not only whets people's appetites but fills them up a bit, so guests walk away feeling satisfied and happy. I use frozen corn and canned tomatoes, but if you're making this in the summer when both are at their peak (and cheap), then feel free to substitute fresh (blanch the corn for a minute or two to sweeten the kernels and soften the starch).

makes **3½ cups**

preparation time:
10 minutes (plus 30 minutes to rest)

cooking time:
none

¼ red onion, finely chopped

1 cup frozen corn (about ½ pound)

1 cup cooked black beans

¼ cup roughly chopped fresh cilantro

¾ cup canned tomatoes with green chiles

Juice of 1 lime

½ to ¾ teaspoon kosher salt

¼ teaspoon ground black pepper

¼ teaspoon ground cumin

⅛ teaspoon cayenne pepper (optional)

Tortilla chips, for serving

Place the onion in a fine-mesh sieve and rinse under cold water. Shake the onion to remove as much water as possible and place in a medium bowl. Add the corn, black beans, cilantro, tomatoes, lime juice, ½ teaspoon of the salt, and the pepper, cumin, and cayenne (if using). Stir to combine and set aside for 30 minutes to let the corn thaw and the flavors come together. Taste with a chip and add more salt if needed. Serve.

Bacon Deviled Eggs with Tuna Tartare

I first heard of this starter, tuna tartare–topped deviled eggs, at one of my favorite restaurants outside Seattle. Tuna on top of deviled eggs? I was immediately intrigued, meaning I had to order it! It was absolutely phenomenal, with only the tiniest bit of chic sushi-quality tuna, elevating homey deviled eggs to new heights. This is a great example of how to stretch an indulgent, high-impact ingredient.

● ● ● ● ●

serves 4

preparation time:
15 minutes

cooking time:
20 minutes

for the deviled eggs

6 large eggs

1 teaspoon vegetable oil

1 bacon strip, chopped

½ small red onion, finely chopped

½ teaspoon kosher salt

2½ tablespoons mayonnaise

1 tablespoon sour cream

1 **To make the deviled eggs:** Place the eggs in a large pot of water and bring to a boil. Cover, turn off the heat, and let sit for 15 minutes. Drain and run under cold water to cool.

2 While the eggs cool, heat the oil in a small skillet over medium heat and add the bacon, cooking until it starts to render, about 2 minutes. Stir in the onion and ¼ teaspoon of the salt and cook until the onion starts to soften, about 3 minutes. Reduce the heat to medium-low and cook, stirring often, until the bacon is very crisp and the onion is browned and soft, 8 to 10 minutes more. Transfer the bacon and onion to a small plate and set aside.

3 Remove the eggs from the water and peel them. Halve the eggs lengthwise and pop the yolks out into a medium bowl. Place the whites on a platter. Add the mayonnaise, sour cream, and the remaining ¼ teaspoon salt to the yolks and, using a fork, mash and stir them together until smooth and creamy. Scrape the cooled bacon mixture into the yolk mixture and stir to combine, then transfer it to a quart-sized resealable bag. Push the mixture down into the bottom of the bag, snip off one corner, and squeeze the deviled filling into the whites (a small spoon works fine, too).

4 **To make the tuna tartare:** Place the tuna on a cutting board and, using a very sharp knife, chop it into small cubes. Whisk the oil and soy sauce together, add the tuna, and toss to combine. Sprinkle with chives and gently toss to combine. Set a few cubes of tuna on top of each deviled egg and serve.

for the tuna tartare

¼ pound fresh sushi-grade tuna

½ teaspoon sesame or vegetable oil

½ teaspoon soy sauce

2 teaspoons finely chopped fresh chives

Crispy Sardines with Fried Capers and Parsley

Barcelona is known for its tapas culture, so it's no surprise that I call on its small plate–type appetizers for inspiration. Fried fresh sardines are a delicacy I adored when I was in Spain, but fresh sardines can be hard to find. I was inspired to create a recipe with canned sardines, and the results were incredible. Add some flash-fried capers and a squeeze of lemon and I could be in Barcelona, standing at a tapas bar enjoying a barrage of little bites. To give the parsley a slightly salty flavor, swish it in salted water.

● ● ○ ○ ○

serves 4

preparation time:
12 minutes

cooking time:
3 minutes

- 1 tablespoon brine-packed capers
- ¾ teaspoon kosher salt
- 4 sardines from a 3.75-ounce tin
- ⅓ cup vegetable oil
- 1½ tablespoons all-purpose flour
- ½ bunch of fresh flat-leaf parsley, with stems
- ½ lemon, sliced into 4 wedges

1 Place the capers in a fine-mesh sieve and rinse. Turn them out onto a paper towel–lined plate and set aside. Dissolve ½ teaspoon of the salt in ½ cup water and set aside. Remove the sardines from their tin and place them on a paper towel–lined plate. Heat the oil in a small skillet over medium-high heat.

2 Mix the flour with the remaining ¼ teaspoon salt and lightly coat both sides of the sardines with the flour mixture. Place the sardines in the hot oil and fry on both sides until golden brown, 2 to 3 minutes total. Place a fresh paper towel on top of the plate. Using a frying spider or a slotted spoon, transfer the sardines to the paper towel–lined plate and set aside. Add the capers to the pan (step back, as they'll sizzle and may splatter) and fry until they're crisp and have burst, 10 to 15 seconds. Transfer back to the paper towel–lined plate.

3 Holding the parsley by the stems (like a bouquet), dunk the leaves into the salted water. Swish the leaves around and then twist off the stems. Divide the parsley leaves among 4 plates. Top each with a sardine and some capers. Squeeze the lemon over the fish and salad and serve.

// 2 //

soups

A Meal in a Bowl

I fell in love with soup in college, when
I was studying abroad and living with
a family in France.

Every night they began their meal with a silky vegetable soup (see my version on page 75). I found the routine homey, comforting, and elegant all at once. While we don't eat soup every day at my house, I do try to have some in the fridge or a few varieties in the freezer.

Soup is cheap to make, packed with nutrition, and a quick meal in a bowl, perfect for busy weeknights or a weekend lunch with friends. Brothy soups can be a lovely start to a meal (add crusty bread and you have a light meal), while hearty chilis and creamy soups packed with protein from beans or meat can be a meal on their own. Plus, soup recipes are so forgiving, easily adjusting to whatever ingredients are in the fridge or pantry. If I'm out of black beans, I'll use cannellini beans or pinto beans; scallions, leeks, and shallots are fine stand-ins for garlic or any color onion. Plus, serving couldn't be simpler; all I really need is a hunk of oven-warmed baguette to make my soup dinner complete.

Soupe au Pistou

This is a veggie-rich soup (photo on page 62) bulked up with pasta and enriched with a fantastic, fresh herb paste. When the hot broth and the herb paste combine, the essential oils in the herbs are released to flavor the soup. Whenever I make Soupe au Pistou I'm reminded of cold, wintry nights in Paris when my husband's childhood best friend, Nico, and his wife would come for dinner (they lived upstairs from us!) and Nico would bring his soupe au pistou, which always included white beans. Now I include beans in mine, too.

● ● ● ● ◦ ◦

serves 4

preparation time:
20 minutes

cooking time:
30 minutes

for the soup

14-ounce can whole tomatoes with juice

1 tablespoon olive oil

2 carrots, peeled and chopped

2 celery stalks, chopped

1 yellow onion, chopped

1 zucchini, quartered lengthwise and chopped

¼ pound green beans, stemmed and halved

1 garlic clove, finely minced or pressed through a garlic press

1 teaspoon dried thyme plus a squeeze of lemon juice

2 teaspoons kosher salt

¼ teaspoon ground black pepper

1 cup cooked white beans

2 cups chicken broth

1 cup small dried pasta, such as small shells

1 **To make the soup:** Empty the canned tomatoes into a large bowl. Take one tomato and split it in half; set one half aside for the pistou. Use your fingers to crush the remaining tomatoes into smaller pieces and set aside.

2 Heat the olive oil in a soup pot over medium heat. Add the carrots, celery, and onion and cook, stirring occasionally, just until the onion starts to turn golden, about 5 minutes. Stir in the zucchini, green beans, garlic, thyme, 1 teaspoon of the salt, and the pepper and cook until the thyme is fragrant, about 1 minute. Stir in the beans, crushed tomatoes and juice, and broth, and bring to a boil. Then reduce the heat to medium-low and simmer for 20 minutes.

3 Meanwhile, bring a large saucepan of water to a boil. Add the pasta and the remaining 1 teaspoon salt and cook, following the package instructions, until the pasta is al dente. Drain in a colander and set aside.

4 **To make the pistou:** While the soup and pasta are cooking, place the basil, garlic, olive oil, ½ tomato reserved from the soup, salt, and pepper in a food processor and purée until it is a runny paste. Stir 1 tablespoon of the pistou into the soup. To serve, divide the pasta among 4 bowls. Drizzle some pistou over each serving and then ladle in some of the hot soup and serve.

for the pistou

¼ cup fresh basil leaves, roughly chopped

3 garlic cloves, finely minced or pressed through a garlic press

¼ cup olive oil

¼ teaspoon kosher salt

¼ teaspoon ground black pepper

freezing and substituting fresh herbs

I love cooking with fresh herbs, and the flavor they add to a dish is often worth the money. That said, fresh herbs don't have a long shelf life so it's good to know how to make them last and how to substitute dried herbs for fresh.

- **To store fresh herbs:** Loosely wrap the herbs in a paper towel and then store in a plastic bag in the refrigerator, or place the herbs in a small jar filled with an inch or two of water (as for fresh flowers) and refrigerate.

- **To freeze fresh herbs:** Place the washed fresh herbs in a blender and purée with just enough oil to make a paste. Fill the cups of an ice cube tray one third full with the herb paste, freeze, and then pop the herb cubes out and store them in a resealable freezer bag or container.

- **To substitute dried herbs for fresh:** Use half as much dried herb as fresh (so 1 tablespoon of fresh basil equals 1½ teaspoons dried basil). To get that fresh essence, mix in fresh celery or parsley leaves, or a small pinch of chopped scallion. A pinch of lemon zest or squeeze of lemon juice can be a nice addition, too.

Orange Carrot Soup

Kid-friendly carrots are great to have around for after-school snacks or for turning into a quick side dish such as a slaw or sauté. One of my favorite recipes for carrots is this easy soup. It's creamy, citrusy, and fresh thanks to the little bit of orange zest I add along with garlic and oregano. Carrots marry well to many flavor profiles—instead of oregano and orange zest, try cumin and lime zest, curry powder for an Indian flavor, or a pinch of cinnamon and cloves for a perfect fall soup.

● ● ● ○ ○

serves 4

preparation time:
20 minutes (plus 5 minutes to cool)

cooking time:
35 minutes

1 tablespoon olive oil

5 carrots (¾ pound), chopped into ½-inch pieces

1 yellow onion, roughly chopped

1 garlic clove, smashed

2 teaspoons finely grated orange zest

2 teaspoons dried oregano

¼ cup dry white wine

1½ cups chicken or vegetable broth

2 cups water

1 teaspoon kosher salt

½ teaspoon ground black pepper

2 tablespoons sour cream

1 Heat the olive oil in a large saucepan over medium heat. Add the carrots and onion and cook until they begin to soften, about 10 minutes. Stir in the garlic, orange zest, and oregano and cook until fragrant, 1 to 2 minutes. Raise the heat to medium-high and stir in the wine.

2 Pour in the broth and water, bring to a boil, and reduce to a gentle simmer. Cook until the carrots are tender, about 20 minutes. Turn off the heat and cool 5 minutes.

3 Transfer the soup to a food processor or blender and blend until smooth (don't fill either a blender or food processor more than two thirds full; work in batches if necessary). Return to the saucepan and season with the salt and pepper. Serve swirled with a heaping teaspoon of sour cream.

Roasted Tomato Soup

I roast plum tomatoes until their flavor intensifies and becomes concentrated and wonderfully sweet. Roasting tomatoes is a great tactic not only for coaxing out the tomato's flavor (even from a fairly lackluster tomato), but for using tomatoes that may be past their prime for eating raw. A grilled cheese sandwich or panini instantly transforms this simple soup into an extra-cozy supper.

● ● ● ● ●

serves 4

preparation time:
20 minutes

cooking time:
2 hours

8 plum tomatoes, halved
lengthwise

2 tablespoons olive oil

1 teaspoon kosher salt, plus
extra, if needed

½ teaspoon ground black pepper,
plus extra, if needed

1½ cups plus 1 tablespoon water

½ yellow onion, finely chopped

2 garlic cloves, finely minced or
pressed through a garlic press

2 teaspoons herbes de Provence

1 cup chicken or vegetable broth

1½ cups water

Olive oil or sour cream, for
serving (optional)

deals, dollars & sense: plum tomatoes

When plum tomatoes are on sale, load up! Roast them and then transfer to a gallon-sized resealable plastic freezer bag to use year-round for tomato soup or for a wonderfully robust pasta sauce.

1 Preheat the oven to 275°F. Line a rimmed baking sheet with parchment paper and set aside. Place the tomatoes in a large bowl and toss with 1 tablespoon of the olive oil, the salt, and the pepper. Arrange the tomatoes on the baking sheet, cut side down, drizzle with 1 tablespoon water, and bake until their skins start to shrivel, about 1 hour. Remove the pan from the oven and carefully peel off the tomato skins and discard. Turn the tomatoes cut side up and continue to bake until they are shriveled but not dry, 40 to 50 minutes longer. Remove the pan from the oven and set aside.

2 While the tomatoes are roasting, prepare the soup base. Heat the remaining 1 tablespoon olive oil in a large saucepan over medium heat. Add the onion, reduce the heat to low, and cook until very soft, stirring often, 10 to 12 minutes. Stir in the garlic and herbes de Provence and cook until fragrant, 1 to 2 minutes. Pour in the broth and the 1½ cups water and bring to a simmer over medium-high heat. Reduce the heat to medium-low and gently simmer for 15 minutes. Turn off the heat and let the soup base cool until the tomatoes are ready.

3 Transfer the tomatoes and any accumulated juices on the sheet pan to a blender. Add the soup base and purée until very smooth (you may need to work in batches—don't fill the jar more than two thirds full). Strain the purée through a fine-mesh sieve and into a clean saucepan. Warm the soup over low heat, taste, and add more salt and pepper if needed. Serve with a drizzle of olive oil or a dollop of sour cream (if using).

taking stock of broth options

I often count on stock (made with bones) or broth (made without bones) to give extra depth to my savory recipes. Here are a few options in my order of preference:

1. **Homemade stock:** Making stock yourself is easy, cheap, and by far offers the most flavor. However, it also requires foresight! When you make a big pot of stock, portion it out into a few quart-sized resealable plastic bags or plastic containers, label, and freeze. I like to keep about two cups of stock per container. Freezing stock in an ice cube tray is also a smart idea. This allows you to toss in one-ounce cubes as you need them, great for deglazing pans and making quick pan sauces.

2. **Stock concentrates and pastes:** A small jar of stock concentrate lasts for a very long time and doesn't take up much space in the cupboard (before opening) or in the fridge (after opening). These jars are a staple in my fridge, and are my go-to when I don't have homemade stock in the freezer.

3. **Packaged cartons:** This is the priciest option, but some cooks consider it even more convenient than stock concentrates since it is ready to pour. The boxes can be bulky and the shelf life is relatively short once opened (a week to ten days) when compared to a stock concentrate.

4. **Bouillon cubes:** Convenient and cheap, bouillon doesn't have the same complexity compared to other stock options. In a pinch, though, it will pull you through.

Roasted Tomato Winter Gazpacho

On my show Ten Dollar Dinners, *I advise home cooks to use canned tomatoes in the winter because they are cheaper and taste better than the pale ones available. On a mission to bring gazpacho to my winter table, I took my own advice. To deepen the tomatoes' flavors and bring out their sweetness, I oven-roast them before puréeing with the classic gazpacho assembly of cucumbers, bell peppers, and onion. The end result is remarkably delicious! What a treat to finally be able to enjoy gazpacho year-round.*

● ● ● ● ○ ○

serves 4

preparation time:
20 minutes

cooking time:
55 minutes

- 2 28-ounce cans whole tomatoes
- ¾ teaspoon sugar
- 1⅛ teaspoons kosher salt
- ⅓ baguette, cut into bite-sized cubes (about 1½ cups bread cubes)
- ¼ cup olive oil
- 1 yellow onion, roughly chopped
- 1 cucumber, peeled and roughly chopped
- 1 red bell pepper, halved, seeded, and roughly chopped
- 3 garlic cloves, roughly chopped
- ⅛ teaspoon cayenne pepper
- 2 tablespoons sherry vinegar
- 1 cup ice cubes

1 Preheat the oven to 375°F. Line a rimmed sheet pan with aluminum foil or parchment paper and set aside. Place a fine-mesh sieve over a large bowl and empty the cans of tomatoes into the sieve. To seed the tomatoes, gently open each one and use your fingers to remove the seeds, letting them fall into the sieve. Split each tomato into two halves and lay them on the prepared baking sheet. Use a rubber spatula to press on any pulp and seeds in the sieve to extract as much tomato juice as possible. Discard whatever is left in the sieve. Pour the tomato juices into a large measuring cup and add enough water (you may not have to add any) to yield 2½ cups of liquid.

2 Sprinkle the sugar and 1 teaspoon of the salt on the tomatoes on the sheet pan and roast them until they are dry but not leathery, about 45 minutes, rotating the pan midway through cooking. Remove the sheet pan from the oven and set aside to cool slightly before using tongs to transfer the roasted tomatoes to a food processor.

3 Place the bread cubes in a medium bowl and toss with 1 tablespoon of the olive oil and the remaining ⅛ teaspoon salt. Transfer to a rimmed baking sheet and toast in the oven until golden brown, about 10 minutes. Remove from the oven and set aside.

4 Rinse the onion in a fine-mesh sieve under cold water. Add it to the tomatoes in the food processor along with the cucumber, bell pepper, garlic, cayenne, reserved tomato juices, the remaining 3 tablespoons olive oil, and the vinegar. Add the ice and process until smooth. Serve topped with some of the toasted bread cubes.

Creamy Any Veggie Soup

Managing fresh produce is a huge part of any savings strategy. Once a week, I do a quick crisper and pantry check to see if there are perishables (check onions and potatoes, too) to be used right away. I turn these veggies into a creamy or chunky soup, depending on my mood. Be sure to check out the quick soup mix-ins below for ways to add an extra flavor boost to the soup in your pot.

● ● ● ○ ○ ○

serves 4 (plus leftovers)

preparation time:
20 minutes

cooking time:
35 minutes

- 1 tablespoon vegetable oil
- 1 large yellow onion, finely chopped
- ½ teaspoon dried thyme plus a squeeze of lemon juice
- 1½ teaspoons kosher salt
- ¼ teaspoon ground black pepper
- 4 cups vegetables, such as bell peppers, broccoli, carrots, cauliflower, leafy greens, and tomatoes, roughly chopped
- 1 small potato, peeled and roughly chopped
- 1½ cups chicken broth
- 3 cups water
- 3 tablespoons heavy cream or 2 tablespoons sour cream

1 Heat the oil in a soup pot over medium heat. Add the onion and cook until it starts to soften, 5 to 6 minutes, stirring occasionally. Stir in the thyme, ½ teaspoon of the salt, and the pepper and cook until the thyme is fragrant, 1 to 2 minutes. Add the vegetables, potato, broth, water, and the remaining 1 teaspoon salt and bring to a boil. Reduce the heat to low and cook, covered, until the vegetables easily mash against the side of the pot, 20 to 25 minutes.

2 Transfer half of the soup to a food processor or blender and purée until smooth, then pour into a clean pot. Repeat with the remaining soup (leave some vegetables unblended for texture, if you like), pouring it into the same pot. Heat the soup over low heat for 2 minutes, add heavy cream or sour cream, if using, then serve.

quick soup mix-ins

- Add a dash of curry powder or smoked paprika when sautéing the onion.
- Mix dried spices or fresh herbs, such as basil, cilantro, mint, or parsley, into the sour cream for serving.
- Add 1 or 2 cups cooked beans or lentils to the soup after blending.
- Roughly tear up stale, good-quality country-style bread, toss it with some soup, and bake it in the oven dusted with Parmesan cheese for a Tuscan-style soup and bread meal.
- Stir in cooked shredded chicken and browned sausage and serve over rice.

White Bean, Leek, and Bacon Soup

If you haven't cooked with leeks before, you're in for a treat! Their deep flavor is reminiscent of onions and scallions, yet still offers a savory uniqueness. Leeks are a little pricier than onions, but since the rest of this soup is downright cheap, spend the extra buck or two in the produce aisle to make this one-of-a-kind immensely satisfying soup. Remember to thoroughly clean the leeks before cooking.

● ● ○ ○ ○

serves 4 (plus leftovers)

preparation time:
10 minutes

cooking time:
45 minutes

- 3 tablespoons olive oil
- 3 bacon strips, finely chopped
- 2 leeks, white and light green parts only, chopped
- 2 carrots, chopped
- 2 teaspoons kosher salt, plus extra, if needed
- 3 garlic cloves, finely minced or pressed through a garlic press
- ½ teaspoon celery seed
- 2 teaspoons dried marjoram
- 2 tablespoons tomato paste
- 5 cups water
- 2 cups cooked white beans (rinse under cold water if using canned beans)
- 1 dried bay leaf
  Pinch of ground black pepper

1 Heat 1 tablespoon of the olive oil in a heavy-bottomed soup pot over medium-high heat. Add the bacon and cook, stirring often, until it is very crisp, about 4 minutes. Use a slotted spoon to transfer the bacon to a paper towel–lined plate and set aside.

2 Add 1 tablespoon of the olive oil to the pot along with the leeks, carrots, and 1 teaspoon of the salt. Raise the heat to medium and cook, stirring occasionally, until the leeks are soft, 6 to 8 minutes. Stir in the garlic, celery seed, marjoram, and tomato paste and cook until the garlic is fragrant and the tomato paste has turned a deeper shade of brick red, about 2 minutes.

3 Pour in ½ cup of the water and cook, stirring and scraping any browned bits off the bottom of the pot. Add the beans, bay leaf, the remaining 1 teaspoon salt, and the remaining 4½ cups water. Bring to a boil, reduce the heat to medium, and simmer for 30 minutes. Turn off the heat and remove the bay leaf. Ladle about one third of the soup into a blender. Cover and pulse to release some heat, then purée until smooth. Pour the puréed soup back into the pot; taste for salt, adding more if necessary, and serve drizzled with a little of the remaining 1 tablespoon olive oil, sprinkled with the crispy bacon, and finished with a pinch of pepper.

A Hill of Beans

A one-pound bag of dried beans costs about $1 and cooks up four to five cans' worth of beans. Even if you buy your canned beans for a buck a pop, you get three extra cans of beans for *free* if you go for dried beans instead of precooked ones. Cooking dried beans couldn't be simpler—here's my strategy:

1. Soak the beans overnight.

2. Simmer the beans in a large pot of water until they're just tender (1 hour on average, though if they have been sitting on a shelf for a long time it could take up to 1½ hours). Don't boil the beans or use salt (both can cause the skins to slip off) and take care not to overcook them.

3. When the beans are cooled, divide them into four quart-sized resealable freezer bags. About 1½ cups of beans per bag is good—that's about how much is in a can. Freeze the cooked beans (don't forget to label the bags so you know what kind of beans are in each).

4. The next time you need beans, just pull a bag out of the freezer. Thaw first if using in a salad or for a sauté; if they're going into a soup or stew, it's fine to add them frozen.

Here are a few tricks for integrating beans into more of your meals:

• Use beans to stretch a protein. Beans are a great way to bulk up an uneaten piece of chicken or sausage from the night before. Add some rice or bulgur for a lighter-bodied dish.

• Serve beans as a side dish. Beans are filling and nutritious and are a great way to get away with serving smaller pieces of expensive protein such as salmon or steak.

• Make beans an appetizer. Serve on toasted baguette slices for crostini (page 38) or with crudités for a homemade take on hummus.

Roasted Garlic and White Bean Chili

Roasting turns pungent garlic into a mild, sweet spread you can slather on bread like butter. The downside to roasting is that it takes a fair amount of time. To get similar results in a fraction of the time, I "roast" garlic in the microwave. It works perfectly in this hearty chili (which, by the way, won me first prize at my husband's St. Patrick's Day office cooking contest—long before I had a show on the Food Network). The roasted Anaheim chiles and smoked paprika lend a fantastic smoky spice to the chili, but if you're short on time, feel free to substitute chopped canned chiles.

● ● ●

serves 4 (plus leftovers)

preparation time:
20 minutes

cooking time:
1 hour, 20 minutes

for the roasted garlic

12 garlic cloves, unpeeled

1 tablespoon olive oil

1 cup chicken broth

for the chili

3 fresh Anaheim or poblano chiles

2 tablespoons olive oil

1 large yellow onion, finely chopped

2 garlic cloves, finely minced or pressed through a garlic press

2 tablespoons all-purpose flour

½ cup dry white wine

4 cups water

2 cups chicken broth

1 To roast the garlic: Place the cloves in a microwave-safe bowl and toss with the olive oil and 1 teaspoon water. Set a cover slightly askew over the bowl (or cover with plastic wrap and make a few slits in the plastic to vent) and microwave until the garlic is soft, about 1½ minutes. Set aside to cool and keep covered. Once cool, remove the cover and squeeze the garlic cloves out of their skins and into a food processor or blender. Add the broth and process until smooth. Set aside.

2 To make the chili: Preheat the broiler to high. Line a rimmed baking sheet with aluminum foil and place the Anaheim chiles on it. Broil until charred on all sides, turning often, 10 to 15 minutes. Transfer to a medium bowl, cover with plastic wrap, and set aside until cool enough to handle. Peel away the skin from the peppers and then stem, seed, and finely chop. Set aside.

3 Heat the olive oil in a large skillet over medium heat. Add the onion and cook, stirring often, until deep golden brown and caramelized, about 20 minutes. Stir in the garlic and cook until fragrant, about 2 minutes. Mix in the flour and cook, while stirring constantly, for 3 minutes. Raise the heat to high and pour in the wine, stirring it into the onion mixture and scraping up any browned bits stuck to the bottom of the

pan. Bring to a simmer and then add the chopped roasted chiles, water, broth, cooked chicken, chili powder, cayenne, beans, salt, and pepper. Bring the mixture to a simmer.

4 Stir in the roasted garlic purée and cook until the chili has thickened slightly, about 25 minutes. Add the spinach and continue to cook for 5 minutes longer. Stir in the paprika, taste for seasoning, and serve in bowls with a dollop of sour cream and a sprinkle of cheese.

1 to 2 cups shredded cooked chicken

2 teaspoons chili powder

¼ teaspoon cayenne pepper

1½ cups cooked navy beans

2 teaspoons kosher salt

1 teaspoon ground black pepper

10-ounce box frozen chopped spinach, thawed, liquid squeezed out

¾ teaspoon smoked paprika

2 tablespoons sour cream

½ cup grated Monterey Jack cheese

Slow Cooker Tortilla Soup

This Mexican-inspired chicken, tomato, and bean soup practically cooks itself. I pile the ingredients into a slow cooker while I'm off doing far more glamorous things (like working, picking up dry cleaning, or dropping off a forgotten lunch at school!). My weekday cheat is to use tortilla chips instead of fresh tortillas. My favorite kind is the better-for-you baked white tortilla chips with a hint of lime, but any kind will do. If I'm feeling fancy, I'll add cubed avocado and sour cream before serving. If you have leftover cooked rice in the fridge, a spoonful in the soup is a nice touch, and for a less spicy flavor remove the jalapeño seeds and ribs.

● ● ● ○ ○

serves 4

preparation time:
10 minutes

cooking time:
3 to 8 hours (depending on whether you set the slow cooker to high or low heat)

3 chicken thighs, skin removed

10-ounce can diced tomatoes with green chiles

1½ cups cooked black beans

1½ cups chicken broth

1½ cups water

1 yellow onion, finely chopped

3 garlic cloves, finely minced

1 jalapeño, finely chopped

½ teaspoon ground cumin

½ teaspoon chili powder

Juice of ½ lemon

20 tortilla chips

3 tablespoons finely chopped fresh cilantro

½ cup shredded Monterey Jack cheese

1 Place the chicken, tomatoes (and juices), beans, broth, water, onion, garlic, jalapeño, cumin, and chili powder in a slow cooker. Cover and cook on high for 3 to 4 hours or on low for 6 to 8 hours.

2 Uncover the slow cooker and use tongs to remove the chicken from the pot. Once cool enough to handle, remove the meat from the bones and shred, then return the meat to the pot. Stir in the lemon juice. Crumble a few tortilla chips into each bowl and cover with some soup. Serve sprinkled with cilantro and grated cheese.

Quick Black Bean Chili

A basic chili that is quick to make and easy on the wallet should be in every home cook's repertoire. This chili happens to be vegetarian, too. I love making this chili for game days. Even if there are big-time meat lovers in the crowd, something about the way the black beans mingle with the tomatoes and the chili powder makes it extra satisfying and indulgent—especially topped with tasty sour cream, cheese, and scallions.

● ● ●

serves 4

preparation time:
10 minutes

cooking time:
40 minutes

- 1 tablespoon olive oil
- 1 yellow onion, finely chopped
- 1 red bell pepper, halved, seeded, and chopped
- 3 garlic cloves, finely minced or pressed through a garlic press
- 28-ounce can crushed tomatoes
- 15-ounce can tomato sauce
- ½ cup vegetable broth (or chicken broth)
- 2 cups cooked black beans
- 2 tablespoons chili powder
- 1 teaspoon ground cumin
- ¼ teaspoon cayenne pepper
- 2 teaspoons sugar
- 1 teaspoon kosher salt
- 2 scallions (white and green parts), finely chopped
- Grated Cheddar cheese, for serving
- Sour cream, for serving

1 Heat the olive oil in a large pot over medium-high heat. Add the onion and cook until soft, 3 to 4 minutes, stirring often. Add the bell pepper and continue to cook over medium heat until it softens, about 3 minutes longer. Stir in the garlic and cook until it's fragrant, 1 to 2 minutes.

2 Pour in the tomatoes, tomato sauce, broth, beans, chili powder, cumin, cayenne, sugar, and salt and bring to a simmer. Reduce the heat to medium-low and cook until the chili is thick, 25 to 30 minutes, stirring occasionally. Serve sprinkled with scallions, grated Cheddar, and a dollop of sour cream.

Clam Chowder with Crispy Bacon

I got a taste for New England clam chowder while I was in college in Vermont. On a tight student budget, I taught myself how to make an inexpensive version using canned clams instead of fresh, and a quick bécha-mel from butter, flour, and milk instead of pricey cream. I still make my chowder the same way. Stock up on clams when they're on sale or buy a huge can at a warehouse store for a few bucks more and have enough chowder to feed a small army (freeze it in gallon-sized resealable bags—a quick meal for winter nights!). My husband, Philippe, insists that a squeeze of fresh lemon juice is the perfect finishing touch.

● ● ● ○ ○ ○

serves 4

preparation time:
15 minutes

cooking time:
35 minutes

- 3 red potatoes, cut into bite-sized cubes
- ½ teaspoon kosher salt, plus 1 tablespoon for boiling the potatoes
- 2 bacon strips, finely chopped
- 2½ cups whole milk
- 2 tablespoons unsalted butter
- 1 yellow onion, finely chopped
- 2 carrots, peeled and finely chopped
- 2 celery stalks, finely chopped
- ¼ teaspoon ground black pepper
- ½ teaspoon dried thyme
- 3 tablespoons all-purpose flour
- ½ cup chicken broth
- 2 6½-ounce cans of clams with liquid
- Lemon wedges, for serving (optional)

1 Bring a large pot of water to a boil. Add the potatoes and 1 tablespoon of the salt and cook until the potatoes are tender, about 10 minutes. Drain and set aside.

2 While the potatoes cook, make the chowder. Place the bacon in a soup pot over medium heat and cook until the bacon is crisp and browned, stirring often, 6 to 8 minutes. Use a slotted spoon to transfer the bacon to a paper towel–lined plate and set aside. Pour the milk into a microwave-safe measuring cup and heat, about 1½ minutes. Set aside.

3 Add the butter to the bacon fat and, once melted, add the onion, carrots, celery, the remaining ½ teaspoon salt, and the pepper to the pot. Cook, stirring occasionally, until the vegetables are tender, 6 to 8 minutes. Stir in the thyme and flour and cook, while stirring, for 2 minutes. Pour in the broth, being sure to scrape up any bits from the bottom of the pot, and then pour in the milk. Bring to a simmer over medium-high heat; add the boiled potatoes and the clams with their liquid, and cook until the potatoes and clams are warmed through, 2 to 3 minutes. Turn off the heat and serve sprinkled with the crisp bacon and with a lemon wedge on the side (if using).

French Onion Soup

The secret to unforgettable French onion soup is its intensely rich, sweet, and oniony broth. Letting the onions slowly caramelize gets the job done while using both beef and chicken broth, plus a hearty splash of red wine adds a backdrop of flavor. A sizzling cheesy crust is a must, but traditional Gruyère cheese can be pricey, so I go with a blend of Swiss and Parmesan that adds just the right hit of decadence. In France, onion soup is traditionally served late at night or in the wee hours of the morning as a reviving treat after a night out.

● ● ●

serves 4

preparation time:
15 minutes

cooking time:
1 hour, 50 minutes

2 tablespoons unsalted butter

4 yellow onions (about 1¾ pounds), halved and thinly sliced crosswise

1 teaspoon kosher salt

1 teaspoon all-purpose flour

½ cup dry red wine

1½ cups beef broth

1½ cups chicken broth

1 cup water

1 teaspoon fresh lemon juice

1 tablespoon chopped fresh thyme

1 dried bay leaf

½ teaspoon ground black pepper

½ cup grated Swiss cheese

1 tablespoon grated Parmesan cheese

⅓ baguette (about 4 inches), sliced on a bias into four 1-inch-thick pieces

1 Melt the butter in a heavy-bottomed soup pot over medium-low heat. Add the onions and salt, cover, reduce the heat to low, and cook until deeply caramelized, 1 to 1½ hours, stirring occasionally. Increase the heat to medium and sprinkle the onions with the flour. Cook for 2 minutes, stirring constantly, then pour in the wine, stirring and scraping any browned bits up from the bottom of the pot. Add the beef and chicken broths, water, lemon juice, thyme, bay leaf, and pepper and simmer for 10 minutes. Taste and adjust salt and pepper if needed.

2 Adjust an oven rack to the upper-middle position and preheat the broiler to high. Mix the Swiss and Parmesan cheeses together in a small bowl. Remove the bay leaf and divide the soup among 4 oven-safe bowls; top each with a baguette slice followed by some cheese. Place the bowls on a rimmed baking sheet and put in the oven. Broil until the cheese is browned and bubbly, about 1 minute. Serve hot.

deals, dollars & sense: freezing soup

To save freezer space, freeze soups in gallon-sized resealable freezer bags (or use quart-sized bags for individual servings). Try to get as much air out of the bag as possible and then seal (remember to label the bag). Freeze flat on a baking sheet or plate, and then, once they are completely frozen, stack one on top of another. If a recipe calls for finishing touches of cream or fresh herbs, hold off on adding them until after the soup is thawed and reheated.

A well-made salad excites your palate with every bite: the brightness of vinegar or citrus (or both), the crunch of crispy vegetables, the delicacy of tender greens.

Add pungent cheese, savory meat, cooked beans, or toasted nuts and you have everything you need to create a fantastic salad. There are two ways to categorize salad: as a "side salad" that you eat *with* other things, like my Parisian Café Salad (page 90), or as a "meal salad," which, by combining greens with protein-rich add-ins such as meat or beans, turns simple greens and veggies into a hearty main-dish-worthy plate. Whether served on the side or as the main meal, quick-to-make salads are also a fantastic opportunity to explore flavor and textural combinations in creative ways. For example, roast root vegetables until they're tender and sweet and then lay them on a bed of fresh arugula. The contrast of the warm and caramelized vegetables to fresh and peppery greens is delicious. A salad can also be a way to turn ordinary and cheap ingredients—such as bread and lettuce—into fancy fare, whether by grilling them for a new toasty flavor profile or by adding hearty ingredients like tuna or lentils.

Parisian Café Salad with Classic Dijon Vinaigrette

This is my go-to everyday salad that I turn to when I need some green on the side. In Parisian cafés, green salads are served alongside steaks, omelets, or a piece of cheese or offered as a palate cleanser after the main course. While I lived in Paris, I learned a great secret for adding a deep savory flavor (called umami*) to vinaigrettes: a splash of soy sauce! The trick is adding just a tiny bit, not enough to detect the added soy sauce flavor, but just enough to make your dressing special.*

serves 4

preparation time:
10 minutes

cooking time:
none

for the vinaigrette

- 1 garlic clove, halved
- 1 teaspoon Dijon mustard
- 1 tablespoon red wine vinegar
- ¼ teaspoon soy sauce
  Pinch of kosher salt
- ¼ teaspoon ground black pepper
- 3 tablespoons olive oil

for the salad

- 3 cups mixed greens, such as arugula, frisée, and romaine

1 **To make the vinaigrette:** Rub the inside of a large salad bowl (preferably made of wood) with each half of the garlic clove. Add the mustard to the bowl and whisk in the balsamic vinegar and soy sauce until creamy, about 10 seconds. Whisk in the salt and pepper and then drizzle in the olive oil very slowly to make a creamy emulsion.

2 **To make the salad:** Add the salad greens on top of the dressing. Toss just before serving.

deals, dollars & sense: salad greens

Being flexible is the best way to go when it comes to saving money on salad. Mother Nature dictates which leafy greens will be plentiful, and thereby inexpensive, at the market. In the wintertime, hearty greens like kale and spinach are better deals than tender butter lettuce or baby arugula. Making a swap can breathe new life into your favorite salad recipe, changing the flavor and texture of the salad. Even pricey prewashed bags of greens can be a good buy if there is a two-for-one sale or manager's special.

Spinach Salad with Blue Cheese and Apples

When using blue cheese in a recipe like this salad, I buy the cheapest blue cheese crumbles I can find (often the store's brand). It still provides the pungent edge of blue cheese flavor but at a fraction of the price of an expensive wedge. To soften the sometimes harsh bite of red onions, give them a short soak in ice water before adding them to the salad. It's a great trick to have in your hip pocket for when you use raw onions, whether in a salad, on a burger, or chopped for tacos. If you have a ripe pear, use it instead of the apple.

● ● ● ○ ○ ○

serves **4**

preparation time:
15 minutes

cooking time:
7 minutes

⅓ cup pecan halves

2 pinches of kosher salt

½ small red onion, thinly sliced into rounds

1 Granny Smith apple, cored and thinly sliced

1 teaspoon fresh lemon juice

3 cups baby spinach

¼ cup crumbled blue cheese

1 tablespoon white wine vinegar

⅛ teaspoon ground black pepper

2 tablespoons olive oil

deals, dollars & sense: pecans

When buying pecans, the baking aisle of your market is perhaps the priciest place to go, even when pecans are on sale. Instead, stock up on pecan halves in the bulk aisle. When you get home, transfer your pecans to a large resealable plastic freezer bag and freeze for up to six months. If you need pecan pieces, just chop the pecan halves—halves are a more versatile ingredient than pieces, and they don't cost more when you buy in bulk.

1 Preheat the oven to 375°F. Place the pecans on a rimmed baking sheet and roast in the oven until fragrant and toasted, 5 to 7 minutes. Transfer to a large plate, sprinkle with a pinch of salt, and set aside.

2 Prepare an ice-water bath in a small bowl. Submerge the onion slices and set aside for 10 minutes. Drain, place the onions on a paper towel, and set aside.

3 Place the apple in a large salad bowl and gently toss with the lemon juice. Add the spinach, blue cheese, and onion. Whisk the vinegar, a pinch of salt, and the pepper together in a small bowl. Whisk in the olive oil and then pour over the spinach. Toss together, sprinkle the pecans over the top, and serve.

Salade Niçoise with Lemon-Thyme Vinaigrette

When tuna is the star of a dish, as in this salad, oil-packed light tuna is the way to go. It tastes richer than water-packed tuna. This is a composed salad, so instead of tossing it all together, you will arrange it on a large platter. It's a thoughtful presentation that makes this inexpensive and abundant-looking main-dish-worthy salad ideal for company.

● ● ●

serves **4**

preparation time:
25 minutes

cooking time:
12 minutes

for the salad

- 4 large eggs
- ½ pound green beans
- ½ teaspoon kosher salt, plus 2 teaspoons for boiling potatoes
- 2 large red potatoes, cut into bite-sized cubes
- 1 head romaine lettuce, sliced crosswise
- 2 5-ounce cans oil-packed light tuna, drained
- 2 scallions (white and green parts), trimmed and finely chopped
- 1 tomato, halved, seeded, and chopped
- ¼ teaspoon ground black pepper

1 **To cook the eggs:** Place the eggs in a large pot of water and bring to a boil. Cover, turn off the heat, and let sit for 15 minutes. Drain and run under cold water to cool, then peel and slice them lengthwise into quarters. Set aside.

2 **To make the vinaigrette:** Whisk together the mustard, lemon juice, and vinegar in a small bowl. While whisking, slowly drizzle in the olive oil until it makes a creamy emulsion. Whisk in the thyme, olives, salt, and pepper and set aside for 10 minutes.

3 **To make the salad:** Make an ice-water bath and set it on the counter. In a microwave steamer, cook the green beans until they're al dente, about 4 minutes (or bring a large pot of water to a boil with 2 teaspoons salt and cook the green beans until al dente, about 6 minutes). Transfer the green beans to a sieve and plunge into the ice-water bath to stop the cooking. Once the green beans are cool, remove them from the ice water, tap the bottom of the sieve on a kitchen towel to remove the excess water, and transfer to a medium bowl.

4 Bring a large pot of water to a boil. Add 2 teaspoons of the salt and the potatoes and cook until a paring knife easily slips into the center of a potato, 6 to 8 minutes. Drain in a sieve and plunge the sieve into a large ice-water bath to stop

recipe continues

the cooking. Once the potatoes are cool, remove from the ice water and set aside on a kitchen towel.

5 Arrange the lettuce on a large platter and top with the eggs, green beans, potatoes, tuna, scallions, and tomato. Sprinkle with the remaining ½ teaspoon salt and the pepper, drizzle with the vinaigrette, and serve.

for the vinaigrette

- 1 teaspoon Dijon mustard
- Juice of ½ lemon
- ½ teaspoon white wine vinegar
- ¼ cup olive oil
- 1 tablespoon finely chopped fresh thyme leaves
- ½ cup pitted and chopped black olives, such as niçoise
- ¼ teaspoon kosher salt
- ⅛ teaspoon ground black pepper

Toasted Sesame and Two-Bean Salad with Lime Vinaigrette

Edamame beans are delicious but can vary wildly in price, from inexpensive to downright pricey. Frozen lima beans are roughly half the average price of edamame—add some black beans, sesame oil, scallions, and lime juice, and this salad becomes wonderfully fresh and different from your classic bean salad. The toasted sesame seeds add a terrific crunch to each bite. It's nice as a salad before a meal or as a side dish.

● ●

serves 4

preparation time:
5 minutes

cooking time:
12 minutes

for the salad

1½ cups frozen lima beans

1½ cups cooked black beans

3 scallions (white and green parts), trimmed and thinly sliced on a bias

for the vinaigrette

Juice of 1 lime (about 1½ tablespoons)

2 teaspoons rice vinegar

2 teaspoons soy sauce

1 tablespoon sesame seeds

1 tablespoon sesame oil

1 **To make the salad:** Bring a small saucepan of water to a boil over high heat. Add the lima beans, reduce the heat to medium, and simmer until tender, 8 to 10 minutes. Drain in a sieve or colander and place under cold running water to stop the cooking. Set aside.

2 **To make the vinaigrette:** Whisk the lime juice, vinegar, and soy sauce together in a large bowl and set aside. Toast the sesame seeds in a small skillet over medium heat, stirring often, until fragrant and browned, about 2 minutes. Transfer the hot sesame seeds to the soy sauce mixture and then whisk in the sesame oil. Stir in the black beans, scallions, and cooled lima beans. Toss to coat and serve.

Lentil and Celery Salad with Provençal Vinaigrette

If you want to make a nutritious, hearty dish but didn't think ahead to soak dried beans, lentils are your answer. They're cheap and healthy and cook in about forty minutes. For perfectly tender lentils start checking them about ten minutes before they're supposed to be done cooking, since there is a small window between perfectly cooked and soft and mushy. This salad partners beautifully with a seared piece of salmon or even a simple grilled cheese sandwich.

● ● ○ ○ ○

serves 4

preparation time:
10 minutes

cooking time:
40 minutes (to boil the lentils)

for the salad

- 3 cups leafy greens, such as arugula, green or red leaf lettuce, romaine, or a blend
- 2 celery stalks, thinly sliced on a bias
- 2 tablespoons finely chopped celery leaves
- ¾ cup grape tomatoes, halved
- ½ cup cooked brown lentils

for the vinaigrette

- Juice of ½ lemon
- ½ teaspoon Dijon mustard
- ⅛ teaspoon herbes de Provence
- Pinch of kosher salt
- Pinch of ground black pepper
- 2½ tablespoons olive oil

1 **To make the salad:** Place the salad greens, celery, celery leaves, and tomatoes in a large salad bowl and toss to combine. Scatter the cooked lentils over the salad.

2 **To make the vinaigrette:** Whisk the lemon juice, mustard, herbes de Provence, salt, and pepper together in a small bowl. Whisk in the olive oil and pour the dressing over the salad. Gently toss and serve.

Tuna Panzanella Salad

Every Friday night is date night at the d'Arabian house. Most of the time it's dinner and a movie, but sometimes we change it up: dinner and a trip to the local home renovation store! On these occasions, we pack a to-go meal that we can eat picnic-style on the way. This satisfying, fresh, and nourishing tuna and bread salad is my husband Philippe's favorite on-the-run meal. I put the dressing in the bottom of the container and toss the salad in the container just before we eat it, so the bread doesn't get too soggy. Fresh basil adds a wonderful brightness but isn't a deal breaker; you can use half as much dried basil or herbes de Provence instead.

● ● ● ● ●

serves 4

preparation time:
20 minutes

cooking time:
none

- 1 cup halved cherry tomatoes
- ½ teaspoon kosher salt
- ¼ teaspoon ground black pepper
- 1 cup cooked Great Northern beans
- 5- to 6-ounce can oil-packed light tuna, drained and flaked with a fork
- ¼ cup pitted and sliced kalamata olives
- 1 shallot, halved and thinly sliced
- ½ baguette, sliced into ½- to ¾-inch cubes (day-old bread works fine)
- 1 tablespoon balsamic vinegar
- 2 teaspoons Dijon mustard
- 3 tablespoons olive oil
- 2 tablespoons roughly chopped fresh basil

1 Stir the tomatoes, ¼ teaspoon of the salt, and ⅛ teaspoon of the pepper together in a medium bowl and set aside for 10 minutes. Add the beans, tuna, olives, and shallot; stir to combine and then add the bread cubes, gently stirring to coat the bread.

2 Whisk the balsamic vinegar, the mustard, the remaining ¼ teaspoon of salt, and the remaining ⅛ teaspoon pepper together in a small bowl. Slowly drizzle in the olive oil while whisking to make a creamy emulsion. Pour the dressing over the salad, add the basil, and toss just before serving. Serve within 1 hour.

Chopped Salad with Chicken, Salami, and Mozzarella

In my post-MBA, pre-kids days, I worked in finance and strategy above a fabulous restaurant called La Scala. It's known for its chopped salad, and I became known for my lunchtime affinity for it! When I left L.A., I craved this salad and I started making my own. It's a great way to stretch a small amount of meat (in this case, chicken) among four people.

● ● ● ○ ○

serves 4

preparation time:
15 minutes

cooking time:
none

3 cups chopped lettuce, such as iceberg, green or red leaf lettuce, or romaine

1½ cups cooked chickpeas (one 15-ounce can), rinsed

3 scallions (white and green parts), trimmed and finely chopped

1 cup halved grape tomatoes

¾ cup shredded mozzarella cheese

⅔ cup chopped cooked chicken (about 1 breast)

½ cup chopped salami

1 tablespoon red wine vinegar

2 tablespoons roughly chopped fresh basil or oregano leaves

Pinch of kosher salt

Ground black pepper to taste

2 tablespoons olive oil

1 Place the lettuce, chickpeas, scallions, tomatoes, mozzarella, chicken, and salami in a large salad bowl.

2 Whisk the vinegar, basil, salt, and pepper together in a small bowl. Slowly whisk in the olive oil and then pour the vinaigrette over the salad. Toss gently to combine and serve.

Roasted Root Vegetable Salad with White Wine Vinaigrette

In about forty-five minutes, your oven can turn cheap and rustic root vegetables into deliciously sweet, tender, elegant ones. Scattered over a peppery arugula salad, this platter is simple and stunning, fancy enough for company but totally doable for the family on a Tuesday night. You can use sweet potatoes or russet potatoes as a substitute for one of the root vegetables.

● ● ● ○ ○

serves 4

preparation time:
20 minutes (plus 20 minutes to cool the vegetables)

cooking time:
40 minutes

deals, dollars & sense: beets

Beets are a buy-one-get-one-free vegetable—you buy the beets and get the leafy greens as a bonus! Slice the beet greens away from the beets when you get home from the market and use the greens within a few days, as they are more perishable than the beet itself. I like the greens sliced into thin ribbons and sautéed with olive oil and garlic. A perfect side dish.

for the salad

- 2 medium beets, peeled and halved, each half quartered into wedges (reserve the greens for another time)

- 2 medium carrots, peeled, quartered lengthwise, and sliced into 1½-inch pieces

- 1 large parsnip, peeled, quartered lengthwise, and sliced into 1½-inch pieces

- 1 tablespoon olive oil

- ¼ teaspoon kosher salt

- 3 cups arugula

1 **To make the salad:** Preheat the oven to 400°F. Line a rimmed baking sheet with aluminum foil. Place the beets on one third of the baking sheet; place the carrots and parsnip on the other side of the beets (the beets will stain the lighter-colored vegetables if they are too close together). Drizzle the vegetables with the olive oil and sprinkle with the salt. Gently rub the vegetables slightly with the olive oil and salt and roast until caramelized and tender, 35 to 40 minutes, turning midway through roasting. Remove from the oven and set aside to cool, 20 minutes to several hours at room temperature.

recipe continues

2 **To make the vinaigrette:** Pour the vinegar into a large bowl; add the sugar, onion, salt, and pepper, and stir to combine. Set aside for 10 minutes and then whisk in the olive oil. Add the arugula, toss to combine, and transfer to a large platter. Arrange the vegetables on top of the greens and serve.

for the vinaigrette

- 1½ tablespoons white wine vinegar
- Pinch of sugar
- 1 tablespoon finely chopped red onion or shallot
- Pinch of kosher salt
- Pinch of ground black pepper
- 2 tablespoons olive oil

buying loose, by the pound, and per piece

Here are some tips to consider when comparing prices in the produce aisle:

- Often, buying them loose will save you money.
- If produce is priced per pound, go for the smallest size to save money.
- If priced by the piece or bunch, then go for the heaviest, biggest one you can find!
- Don't forget, you can open a bag of grapes, a bunch of bananas, or a bundle of asparagus and take only what you need.

Tomato Salad–Topped Grilled Pizza

Sometimes changing how you present a dish gives it new life, such as a simple tomato and arugula salad. Instead of serving the salad solo, I use it as an unexpected topping for a quickly grilled pizza, a combo that brings both elements to a new level of sophistication. The bright tomato salad contrasts beautifully with the melted mozzarella and the char of the crust.

● ● ● ○ ○

serves 4

preparation time:
15 minutes (plus 30 minutes to rest the dough)

cooking time:
5 minutes

1 tablespoon olive oil, plus extra for rolling dough

1 pound store-bought pizza dough

1 large and very ripe tomato, cored and chopped, or 1¼ cups halved cherry tomatoes

1 teaspoon fresh lemon juice

¼ teaspoon kosher salt

6 fresh basil leaves, roughly torn

4 ounces fresh mozzarella cheese, thinly sliced and quartered

2 cups arugula (or other baby greens or chopped lettuce)

deals, dollars & sense: fresh mozzarella

I absolutely love the way fresh mozzarella melts into creamy, cheesy pools of deliciousness on pizza. It often goes on manager's special—when it does, grab it, and plan a pizza that week.

1 Rub a little olive oil onto a cutting board to lightly grease the surface. Place the pizza dough on the cutting board and turn over so both sides are lightly oiled. Cover with a kitchen towel and set aside for 30 minutes.

2 Heat one side of a charcoal or gas grill to medium-high heat and the other side to medium-low heat (if using a charcoal grill, bank most of the coals to one side while leaving a few hot coals on the other side).

3 Place the tomato in a medium bowl. Add the lemon juice, salt, basil, and the 1 tablespoon olive oil. Toss to combine and set aside.

4 Use a rolling pin to roll the dough into a circle about ¹⁄₁₆ inch thick. Carry the cutting board and all of the remaining ingredients plus the tomato salad out to the grill and place the dough on the hot side of the grill. Grill until the underside is browned and has grill marks, 1 to 2 minutes (watch

recipe continues

closely—the crust can burn quickly). Use a grilling spatula to turn the dough over onto the cooler side of the grill. Place the mozzarella on top of the pizza, cover the grill (if using a charcoal grill make sure the vent holes in the cover are open), and cook until the mozzarella is melted, 2 to 3 minutes longer.

5   Transfer the pizza back to the cutting board and slice. Top with the arugula. Use a slotted spoon to transfer the tomato salad to the pizza and serve.

Kale and Crispy Bacon Salad

In the wintertime, when many salad greens can be expensive, hardy kale is usually at its cheapest. To soften kale's firm bite for a salad, I rub acidic lemon juice or vinegar into the leaves before adding the oil to make the vinaigrette. Even though the leaves become more tender this way, the kale still holds up superbly when prepared ahead of time, making this nutrient-rich salad fantastic for picnics, potlucks, and brown-bag lunches.

● ●

serves **4**

preparation time:
15 minutes

cooking time:
6 minutes

2 bacon strips

Bunch of kale, tough ribs removed

Juice of ½ lemon

Juice of ½ orange

½ teaspoon kosher salt

2 scallions (white and green parts), trimmed and finely chopped

1 tomato, cored, halved, and chopped

2 tablespoons olive oil

¼ teaspoon ground black pepper

1 Heat a small skillet over medium heat. Add the bacon and cook until crisp on both sides, about 6 minutes total. Transfer to a paper towel–lined plate and set aside to cool. Once cooled, chop the bacon into small bits and set aside.

2 Stack 5 or 6 kale leaves on top of one another and slice crosswise into thin strips. Transfer to a large bowl and repeat with the remaining leaves. Add the lemon juice, orange juice, and salt and use your hands to rub the citrus and salt into the leaves. Let the kale sit for 5 minutes before adding the scallions and tomato. Drizzle with the olive oil, add the pepper and bacon, and toss to combine.

four ways to try kale Kale can be less than a buck a bunch during the winter, an incredible value for this vitamin-packed cabbage-related leafy green. It's fantastically versatile and can be served raw or cooked. These are some of my favorite ways to use it:

- To make kale chips, toss with olive oil, season with salt, then cook on a baking sheet at 275°F. for 20 minutes, turning midway through. (See Crispy Kale Chips, page 46.)

- Use in a Green Morning Smoothie (page 326): Remove the tough stalks, slice the leaves into ribbons, freeze them, and add them to the smoothie.

- Substitute kale for collard greens, spinach, or Swiss chard in braises, soups, and stews.

- Wilt the leaves in a small amount of chicken or vegetable soup to create a side dish for dinner.

Grilled Romaine Salad over Grilled Garlic-Rosemary Bread

When I fire up the grill, I try to get my whole meal on the grill, and this salad is no exception. Usually crisp and leafy romaine becomes more like pricey Swiss chard when grilled. The outer leaves get lightly charred while the inner ones become almost juicy-tender. I love grilled romaine simply piled over garlic bread that has the slightest hint of rosemary. It's a great way to take two inexpensive ingredients—lettuce and bread—and make them truly special.

● ●

serves 4

preparation time:
10 minutes

cooking time:
5 minutes

- 1 head romaine lettuce, halved lengthwise
- 3 tablespoons olive oil
- ½ teaspoon kosher salt, plus extra for seasoning
- ½ baguette, halved lengthwise
- 1 garlic clove, halved lengthwise
- 2 sprigs fresh rosemary
- ½ lemon

1 Heat a charcoal or gas grill to high. Place the halved head of lettuce on a plate and brush 1 teaspoon of the olive oil over each side. Sprinkle each cut side with ¼ teaspoon of the salt and grill, cut side down, until charred, 30 seconds to 1 minute. Use tongs to turn over the lettuce and char the other side, 30 to 45 seconds more. Remove from the grill and set aside.

2 Brush 1 teaspoon of the olive oil over the cut side of each baguette half. Season the bread with a pinch of salt and grill on both sides until lightly browned and warmed, 1 to 2 minutes total. Take a half garlic clove and rub it all over the cut side of the bread; repeat with the remaining garlic and the other piece of bread. Rub the rosemary into the bread and then slice each baguette half into quarters (so you have 8 pieces total). Place the bread on a platter.

3 Place the lettuce on a cutting board and, using a knife or a pair of scissors, cut the lettuce crosswise roughly into ribbons. Pile the grilled lettuce strips on top of the bread, drizzle the remaining 1 tablespoon olive oil over the lettuce, squeeze the lemon over the lettuce, season with salt, and serve.

// 4 //

fish & seafood

Strategies for Pricey Proteins

Fish and seafood are traditionally pricey proteins, but with some creative strategies, it's possible to include them in your weekly mealtime lineup.

One trick I like to use to stretch my fish dollar is to bulk up seafood with inexpensive ingredients like beans, pasta, and rice. A small amount of shrimp easily feeds four when you mix it with beans like I do with my Garlicky Shrimp and White Bean Gratin (page 135), or with noodles for Shrimp Pad Thai (page 118). Spiced Tilapia Tacos (page 130) call for only a small square of tilapia in each soft corn taco—it might seem skimpy until you pile a heap of spicy fresh cabbage slaw on top. Spending an extra few minutes on presentation goes a long way. A modest portion of cod or sole is surprisingly satisfying when plated and served with style. Even canned fish can be a great option for saving money, like the salmon in my Salmon Cakes (page 127). When buying fish, it's best to cook it within one to two days of purchasing.

Thyme and Lemon–Infused Fish en Papillote

If you are new to cooking fish, you should begin with this recipe, because you are nearly guaranteed moist and flavorful results. This is my go-to dish when I want a lean protein with veggies and very little fat. The fish, seasoned with white wine, lemon, and fresh thyme, is oven-steamed (so healthy!) with a colorful zucchini-and-carrot medley. Twelve minutes in the oven is all it takes. If you don't have parchment, aluminum foil works fine, too.

● ● ● ● ○

serves 4

preparation time:
20 minutes

cooking time:
12 minutes

- ½ red onion, thinly sliced lengthwise
- 1 zucchini, trimmed and thinly sliced into matchsticks
- 1 large carrot, peeled and thinly sliced into matchsticks
- 1 garlic clove, finely minced or pressed through a garlic press
- 1 tablespoon olive oil
- ½ teaspoon kosher salt
- ¼ teaspoon ground black pepper
- 4 4-ounce mild white fish fillets, such as flounder, hake, or sole
- 1 lemon, thinly sliced into 8 rounds, seeds removed
- 8 sprigs fresh thyme
- 1 tablespoon unsalted butter, cut into 4 pieces
- ¼ cup dry white wine

1 Preheat the oven to 375°F. Gently toss the onion, zucchini, carrot, and garlic together in a medium bowl. Add the oil, ¼ teaspoon of the salt, and ⅛ teaspoon of the pepper and toss to combine.

2 Set four 8 × 16-inch-wide pieces of parchment paper on the counter. Place a fish fillet in the center of each piece and season them with the remaining ¼ teaspoon salt and ⅛ teaspoon pepper. Place some vegetables on top of each fillet and then top each with 2 lemon slices, 2 sprigs thyme, and a piece of butter, then finish with 1 tablespoon white wine.

3 Fold the parchment over the fish to meet the other side and pinch together in tight ¼-inch folds to create a seam. Make sure to press firmly as you crimp and fold so the steam doesn't escape. Transfer the packets to a rimmed baking sheet and cook for about 12 minutes (a thinner fillet will need only 10 to 11 minutes to cook through, while a thicker fillet may need up to 14 minutes). Serve one parchment packet on each plate and tear the center of the parchment open just before serving. To serve without the parchment, use a spatula to lift the fish and vegetables out of the packet and onto a plate; top with the juices from the parchment.

Shrimp Pad Thai

I'm often hunting for ways to make a small amount of protein go a long distance without sacrificing flavor. Shrimp pad Thai hits all the marks. Its extra-lively taste comes from Asian pantry basics such as tart limes, spicy Sriracha sauce, sweet rice vinegar, and the sweet-salty taste of fish sauce. Add some linguine (Thai rice noodles are traditional, but linguine is often what I have on hand!) and you've just made it possible to feed your family on a half pound of shrimp. I often make this with other proteins since it's a great vehicle for using small amounts of leftovers such as grilled chicken, sautéed pork cutlets, or ground beef.

● ● ● ●

serves 4

preparation time:
20 minutes

cooking time:
25 minutes

for the sauce

- ¼ cup boiling water
- ¼ cup (packed) light brown sugar
  Juice of 1 lime
- ¼ cup fish sauce
- 2 tablespoons rice vinegar
- 1 tablespoon Sriracha hot sauce
- ½ pound medium shrimp (26–30 per pound), peeled and deveined

deals, dollars & sense: ethnic ingredients

If you have a little leftover cash in your weekly grocery budget, invest in a few ethnic ingredients that can really breathe new life and excitement into your dinnertime routine. Items such as rice vinegar, fish sauce, curry powder, coconut milk, harissa, and chipotle chiles in adobo (just to name a few) can carry the recipe in a whole new direction. International markets, ethnic specialty stores, and even the dollar store are all great sources for finding inexpensive global ingredients.

1 **To make the sauce:** Combine the boiling water and the sugar in a medium bowl. Add the lime juice, fish sauce, vinegar, and Sriracha sauce and stir to combine and dissolve the sugar. Add the shrimp and set aside.

2 **To make the pad Thai:** Bring a large pot of water to a boil. Add the linguine and the salt and cook until the pasta is barely al dente, about 1 minute less than the package instructions advise. Drain and set aside.

3 Heat the oil in a large skillet over high heat until very hot and almost smoking, 2 to 3 minutes. Add the onion and stir-fry until it begins to color, about 1 minute. Stir in the garlic and then add the eggs, cooking while stirring constantly, for 30 seconds. Add the cooked linguine and scallions and cook while stirring until the pasta is heated through, 1 to

2 minutes. Pour in the shrimp and sauce and cook until the shrimp are cooked through, about 1 minute. Stir in the carrot, peanuts, and cilantro and turn off the heat. Add the bean sprouts and use tongs to combine. Serve with lime wedges (if using).

for the pad thai

½ pound linguine, broken in half

1 tablespoon kosher salt

2 tablespoons vegetable oil

½ yellow onion, thinly sliced lengthwise

3 garlic cloves, finely minced or pressed through a garlic press

3 large eggs, lightly beaten

3 scallions (white and green parts), trimmed and sliced into ¾-inch segments

1 carrot, peeled and grated

½ cup chopped roasted peanuts

½ cup roughly chopped fresh cilantro

2 cups fresh bean sprouts

1 lime sliced into wedges for serving (optional)

Sautéed Flounder with Lemon-Butter Sauce

Elegant and fast, pan-seared flounder is an easy weeknight meal to pull together without a hassle. What sells this dish to my family is its extra-tasty crisp, browned crust. The key to crisp perfection is to make sure the fillets are extra dry by patting them with paper towels and dusting the fillets with just a tiny bit of flour. You may be tempted to pull out your nonstick skillet, but to get that crisp crust you're better off with a heavy-bottomed stainless steel pan. Any white fish fillet works in this recipe, so go with what looks good and is priced best.

● ● ● ● ● ●

serves 4

preparation time:
15 minutes

cooking time:
8 minutes

4   4-ounce ½-inch-thick flounder fillets

½   teaspoon kosher salt

¼   teaspoon ground black pepper

2   tablespoons vegetable oil

1   teaspoon all-purpose flour

3   tablespoons unsalted butter, cut into 4 slices

    Juice of 1 lemon (about ¼ cup)

2   tablespoons finely chopped fresh herbs, such as basil, chives, or flat-leaf parsley

1 Pat dry both sides of the fish with paper towels and then sprinkle both sides with salt and pepper. Heat the oil in a medium skillet (don't use nonstick) over medium-high heat until it ripples but isn't smoking, 1½ to 2 minutes. While the oil is heating, use a fresh paper towel to pat dry both sides of the fillets a second time.

2 Sprinkle a little flour over both sides of the fillets and then use your fingers or a silicone brush to evenly coat both sides. Add the fillets to the hot oil and cook, without moving, for 2 minutes. Slide a thin spatula underneath the fillets (making sure to use firm pressure to scrape up any of the golden crust that may be sticking to the bottom) and carefully flip them.

3 Place a slice of butter on top of each fillet. It will melt and drip into the saucepan. Cook until the fillets spring back to light pressure, about 2 minutes. Use a spatula to transfer the fish to a platter or to 4 plates. Pour the lemon juice into the pan and scrape up any browned bits stuck to the bottom of the pan. Stir in the fresh herbs and serve the sauce over the fish.

Cod in Garlic-Ginger Broth with Shiitake Mushrooms

Onion, ginger, garlic, and soy sauce combine to create a rich poaching liquid for cod that also doubles as the broth for serving. Shiitakes are expensive, but my recipe calls for only a handful, so buy them loose (by the pound) and only what you need. For extra texture, add chopped fresh spinach, bok choy, or bean sprouts.

● ● ● ● ● ○

serves **4**

preparation time:
15 minutes

cooking time:
20 minutes

½ yellow onion (leave the root end on), sliced into eighths lengthwise

2-inch piece fresh ginger, peeled and sliced into 4 rounds

4 garlic cloves, smashed

½ cup low-sodium soy sauce

3 cups water

1 12-ounce piece cod, skin removed

1 lime, juiced

8 shiitake mushrooms, stems removed, caps thinly sliced

1 carrot, peeled and sliced into thin matchsticks

3 scallions (white and green parts), finely chopped

2 tablespoons roughly chopped fresh cilantro

1 Place the onion, ginger, garlic, ¼ cup plus 1 tablespoon of the soy sauce, and 3 cups water in a medium saucepan and bring to a boil. Reduce the heat to a very gentle simmer and cook until very fragrant and the broth tastes medium-bodied, 10 to 12 minutes.

2 Place the cod on a cutting board and slice into 4 even pieces. Pour the remaining 3 tablespoons soy sauce and the lime juice into a shallow baking dish, add the cod fillets, and turn to coat both sides. Set aside for 5 to 10 minutes.

3 Strain the broth through a fine-mesh sieve and add to a large, deep skillet. Bring the broth back to a simmer, reduce the heat to very low, and add the fish. Cook until the fish is firm and cooked through, 5 to 8 minutes for 1- to 1½-inch-thick fillets. Using a spatula, carefully transfer each fillet to a bowl. Add the shiitakes and carrot to the broth and simmer for 1 minute over medium heat. Turn off the heat and divide the vegetables among the bowls. Pour the broth over the top and serve with the scallions and cilantro.

deals, dollars & sense: fresh ginger

Ginger isn't expensive, but it is perishable—that's why I keep mine in the freezer. Just use a teaspoon to scrape off the papery skin from the root, and then place the peeled ginger in a resealable freezer bag in the freezer, where it will keep for months. Grate it frozen for your recipes.

Sole Napoleon with Tomato-Caper Crudo

Ten Dollar Dinners is about saving money, feeling good, and eating well. This beautiful tower of sole, zucchini, and tomatoes is a perfect example of how you can take simple ingredients and plate them with grace to elevate an inexpensive piece of fish. Pretty plating doesn't cost a penny more, yet manages to make a meal seem that much more special. The warm fish paired with the room-temperature vegetables adds to its elegance. To get an extra-polished presentation, gently place a biscuit cutter on top of the sole and lightly pack the tomato-caper crudo in the ring, then carefully remove (or see the tip on page 127).

● ● ●

serves 4

preparation time:
20 minutes

cooking time:
8 minutes

deals, dollars & sense: fresh fish

Unlike beef and chicken, where sale items are usually prepackaged, the place to find the best deal on fish and seafood is at your supermarket's fresh fish counter, where on any given day there will be a major special. See what looks best and is marked down the most to help you decide what to make for dinner. Remember that the fish should be glistening and taut and smell like a fresh ocean, not fishy.

for the napoleon

- 1 large zucchini, trimmed and very thinly sliced
- ¾ teaspoon kosher salt
- 2 4- to 6-ounce sole fillets, halved crosswise (so you have four 2-inch-wide pieces)
- ¼ teaspoon ground black pepper
- 2 tablespoons finely chopped fresh basil
  Good-quality olive oil

1 **To make the napoleon:** Place the thinly sliced zucchini rounds in a colander. Sprinkle with ¼ teaspoon of the salt and toss to evenly coat, then place in the sink to drain while you prepare the crudo and broil the fish.

2 **To make the crudo:** Slice the cored tomatoes into ⅛-inch-thick rounds. Set the 4 nicest slices aside for the napoleon and chop the remaining slices into small cubes. Place the chopped tomatoes in a medium bowl and add the shallot, capers, balsamic vinegar, and salt. Stir and set aside.

3 Adjust an oven rack to the upper-middle position and preheat the broiler to high. Line a rimmed baking sheet with aluminum foil and place the sole fillets on top. Season

recipe continues

with ¼ teaspoon of the salt and the pepper and broil until the fillets spring back to light pressure, 6 to 8 minutes. Remove from the oven and set aside to cool slightly.

4 Place 1 tomato slice on each plate and sprinkle with a little of the remaining ¼ teaspoon salt. Arrange the zucchini slices in an overlapping circle on top of the tomatoes. Set a piece of sole on top of each tomato-zucchini stack. Use a slotted spoon to top each serving with the tomato-caper crudo. Sprinkle with basil, drizzle with olive oil, and serve.

for the crudo

- 2 large ripe tomatoes, cored
- 1 small or ½ large shallot, finely chopped
- 2 tablespoons capers, rinsed
- 1½ tablespoons balsamic vinegar
- ½ teaspoon kosher salt

Salmon Cakes

Discovering a new place to save money on groceries makes my day—so I was thrilled to find affordable canned salmon at the drugstore. Use it to create these incredible salmon cakes. The bacon gives them a hint of smoky flavor while the Parmesan adds a salty, nutty finish. The trick to the lightest, freshest-tasting cakes is to pan-sear them quickly and not to overcook them. These salmon cakes are delicious served plain or with a seasoned-mayonnaise dipping sauce (page 129).

● ● ● ○ ○ ○

serves 4

preparation time:
25 minutes

cooking time:
35 minutes

1 large russet potato

2 bacon strips

½ small yellow onion, finely chopped

1 large egg, lightly beaten

½ cup mayonnaise

2 teaspoons Dijon mustard

½ teaspoon sugar

Zest of ½ lemon

14-ounce can wild salmon

¼ cup dried bread crumbs

2 tablespoons grated Parmesan cheese

¼ teaspoon ground black pepper

½ cup vegetable oil

deals, dollars & sense: pretty plates

Reuse that can! Use a can opener to remove the bottom from an empty can of salmon (or tuna) and then wash the remaining ring really well in hot, soapy water (or run it through the dishwasher). Place it in the center of a plate and then add rice, lentils, pasta, or even a salad to shape it into a perfect cylinder.

1 Bring a medium saucepan of water to a boil. Add the potato and cook until a paring knife easily slips into the center of the potato, 10 to 15 minutes. Drain and, once the potato is cool enough to handle, peel it and place it in a bowl. Use a fork to break up and fluff the potato. Set aside.

2 Heat a medium skillet over medium heat and cook the bacon on both sides until browned and crisp, 3 to 5 minutes. Transfer to a paper towel–lined plate (save the fat in a small bowl), cool, and then crumble. Place the bacon in a medium bowl and set aside.

3 Heat 1 tablespoon of the reserved bacon fat in a small skillet over low heat. Add the onion and cook until translucent and soft, about 5 minutes. Turn off the heat and let the onion cool, then add to the bacon along with the egg, mayonnaise, mustard, sugar, and lemon zest, stirring to combine. Add the salmon and then the potato, mixing gently after each addition. Then form into 12 small patties.

recipe continues

4 In a small, shallow baking dish, mix the bread crumbs, Parmesan, and pepper. Press both sides of the salmon patties firmly into the bread-crumb mixture to evenly coat both sides.

5 Heat ¼ cup of the oil in a large skillet over medium heat. Cook the salmon cakes in 2 batches until they're golden on both sides, 6 to 8 minutes total, adding more oil when necessary. Serve warm.

fast homemade dipping sauces

A dipping sauce served alongside salmon cakes, french fries, or a pan-seared piece of fish adds an extra layer of flavor and deliciousness. So simple to make, you probably already have the ingredients in your cupboard and fridge. Here are a few of my favorite combinations. By the way, these are also great smeared on a burger bun, grilled chicken wraps, or a roast beef sandwich! Each sauce makes a generous ¼ cup.

- **Thousand Island:** 3 tablespoons mayonnaise + 1 tablespoon ketchup + a squeeze of lemon + 1½ teaspoons chopped capers

- **Spicy Chipotle:** 3 tablespoons mayonnaise + ¼ chipotle chile in adobo sauce, finely chopped + ½ teaspoon adobo sauce

- **Honey Dijon:** 3 tablespoons mayonnaise + 1 teaspoon Dijon mustard (smooth or seedy) + 1 teaspoon honey

- **Pickled Tartar:** 3 tablespoons mayonnaise + 1 tablespoon finely chopped red onion or shallot + 1 tablespoon chopped pickles + ½ teaspoon pickle juice

- **Asian Soy:** 3 tablespoons mayonnaise + 1 teaspoon soy sauce + 1 teaspoon grated fresh ginger + 2 teaspoons chopped fresh cilantro

- **Creamy Barbecue:** 3 tablespoons mayonnaise + 1 tablespoon ketchup + ½ teaspoon chili powder + ¼ teaspoon ground cumin + ¼ teaspoon ground paprika + drizzle of molasses

Spiced Tilapia Tacos with Red Cabbage–Jalapeño Slaw

I grew up in Tucson and probably ate my first fish taco before I could even talk! Serving fish tacos is a superb tactic for taking a relatively small portion of fish and making it seem abundant and fun. Red cabbage quick-pickled with some white vinegar turns the most breathtaking shade of fuchsia and is a cheap and tasty thrill. If kids are joining you at the dinner table, consider omitting the jalapeños or removing the seeds for a less intense heat. The slaw keeps up to three days, during which time it will continue to be spicier and taste more pickled.

● ● ●

serves 4

preparation time:
20 minutes

cooking time:
15 minutes

for the slaw

½ small red cabbage, halved and sliced crosswise into thin strips (about 3 cups sliced cabbage)

¼ red onion, thinly sliced lengthwise

1 small jalapeño pepper, thinly sliced crosswise

2 tablespoons roughly chopped fresh cilantro

1 lime

½ cup white vinegar

1 teaspoon sugar

1½ teaspoons kosher salt

1 **To make the slaw:** Place the cabbage, onion, jalapeño, and cilantro in a medium bowl. Slice the lime in half lengthwise and then cut one half into 4 wedges; set aside for serving. Juice the remaining lime half into a small bowl. Add the vinegar, sugar, and salt and whisk to dissolve, then pour the vinegar mixture over the cabbage mixture. Toss and squeeze with your hands to combine and set aside. Stir and squeeze the slaw every 5 to 10 minutes while you prepare the fish.

2 **To make the tacos:** Divide each tilapia fillet in half along its center seam (so you have 4 long pieces) and then halve crosswise so you have 8 pieces. Set the tilapia on a plate and blot dry with paper towels. Sprinkle both sides of the 8 pieces with the salt. Mix the coriander, cumin, and paprika together in a small bowl and sprinkle the spices over both sides of the fish, patting them on gently. Place the flour on a plate and lightly coat both sides of the fish in flour.

3 Heat the oil in a large skillet over medium-high heat. Add the fish and cook until golden and crisp on both sides, 4 to 6 minutes total. Use a spatula to transfer the fish to a plate and set aside.

4 Heat a medium skillet over medium-high heat and place a tortilla in the pan. Cook the tortilla until it's warmed through and pliable, 30 seconds to 1 minute, turning it over midway through. Place the tortilla on a kitchen towel–lined plate and wrap loosely, folding the edges of the towel over the tortilla to keep it warm. Repeat with the remaining tortillas, stacking and covering them as you go. Place 1 piece of fish inside each tortilla, top with cabbage slaw, and serve with a lime wedge.

for the tacos

2 6-ounce tilapia fillets

1 teaspoon kosher salt

1 teaspoon ground coriander

1 teaspoon ground cumin

¼ teaspoon sweet paprika

2 tablespoons all-purpose flour

2 tablespoons vegetable oil

8 6-inch fresh corn tortillas

Poor Man's Paella

My father-in-law cooks classic paella in the traditional style: in a massive pan over a live fire in the back-yard. Made with rice, seafood, saffron, sausage, and chicken, paella is expensive. I use less-pricey mussels or clams with chicken drumsticks and Italian sausage. A blend of turmeric and paprika can stand in for saffron, or use inexpensive dried safflower, a.k.a. "Mexican saffron," readily available on the West Coast.

● ● ● ● ◐

serves 4

preparation time:
15 minutes

cooking time:
45 minutes

1 large plum tomato, cored and quartered

1 small yellow onion, chopped

1 large red bell pepper, halved, seeded, and roughly chopped

2 garlic cloves, roughly chopped

4 chicken drumsticks

1½ teaspoons kosher salt

¼ teaspoon ground black pepper

1 tablespoon vegetable oil

¼ pound spicy Italian sausage, sliced into ½-inch pieces

¼ pound medium shrimp (26–30 per pound), peeled and deveined

Zest and juice of 1 lemon

½ teaspoon sweet paprika

¼ teaspoon ground turmeric

2 cups short-grain white rice

2 cups chicken broth

2 cups water

½ pound fresh clams or mussels

1 Place the tomato, onion, bell pepper, and garlic in a food processor and purée until semismooth.

2 Set the chicken on a cutting board, pat dry with paper towels, and season with ½ teaspoon of the salt and the pepper. Heat the oil in a large skillet over low heat. Place the chicken and sausage in the pan and cook on both sides until browned, 8 to 10 minutes. Use a slotted spoon to transfer the chicken and sausage to a plate and set aside. Add the shrimp to the pan and cook just until they begin to curl and color on the bottom, 1 to 1½ minutes. Quickly transfer them to the plate with the meat.

3 Pour the vegetable purée into the pan and cook, stirring often, until the purée turns into a dark red-orange semi-thick saucy paste, 5 to 8 minutes. Stir in the lemon zest, paprika, turmeric, and the remaining 1 teaspoon salt and then mix in the rice. Cook for 2 minutes and then pour in the broth and water, stirring and scraping any bits from the bottom of the pan. Raise the heat to medium and bring the liquid to a simmer, then reduce to medium-low. Gently simmer for 10 minutes, then remove the cover and place the chicken legs on top of the rice. Replace the cover and continue to simmer until all the liquid is absorbed, about 10 minutes more or until a crust forms under the rice.

recipe continues

4 Turn off the heat, uncover the pan, and add the sausage, shrimp, and shellfish. Pour the lemon juice over the top and cover. Let the pan sit until the shrimp have finished cooking through and the shellfish have opened, about 5 minutes. Serve.

deals, dollars & sense: buying seafood

If you're a fan of fish and seafood, make the seafood counter one of your first stops in the supermarket. Check out what perishable delicacies are on major sale and then work them into your dinner plans for that night or the next.

Garlicky Shrimp and White Bean Gratin

Shrimp and grits were my inspiration for this creamy, cheesy white bean and shrimp gratin. White beans are one of my favorite proteins—they're so healthy, nutritious, and cheap that they can easily become the most-used pantry item in your cupboard. In this gratin, I toss the beans with rosemary butter and Cheddar cheese before baking and topping with garlicky shrimp and fresh scallions. This is best served piping hot from the oven. I like it with steamed rice on the side.

● ● ●

serves 4

preparation time:
15 minutes

cooking time:
30 minutes •

4 tablespoons unsalted butter

2 teaspoons chopped fresh rosemary

3 cups cooked cannellini beans

¾ cup chicken broth

½ teaspoon kosher salt

½ cup grated Cheddar cheese

¾ pound medium shrimp (26–30 per pound), peeled and deveined

2 scallions (white and green parts), trimmed and finely chopped

1 garlic clove, finely minced or pressed through a garlic press

1 lemon, sliced into wedges for serving

1 Preheat the oven to 400°F. Adjust one oven rack to the lower-middle position and another to the upper-middle position. Melt 2 tablespoons of the butter in a large oven-safe skillet (cast iron is perfect) over medium heat. Add the rosemary and cook until fragrant, 30 seconds to 1 minute, then add the beans. Cook, stirring once or twice, until the beans are warmed through, about 3 minutes. Pour in the broth and then stir in ¼ teaspoon of the salt and the Cheddar cheese. Place the pan in the oven on the lower rack and bake the beans until they're bubbling around the edges, 15 to 20 minutes.

2 Meanwhile, microwave the remaining 2 tablespoons butter in a microwave-safe bowl until melted. Place the shrimp in a medium bowl. Pour the melted butter over the shrimp and add the scallions, garlic, and the remaining ¼ teaspoon salt. Toss to combine. Turn the shrimp out on top of the beans and place on the upper rack. Turn the broiler to high and broil the shrimp until they're sizzling and golden, about 4 minutes. Serve in bowls with a lemon wedge on the side.

// 5 //

chicken

The Irreplaceable Chicken Dinner

Chicken has long been considered the budget protein, and with good reason—it is often the least expensive meat at the market.

Since it freezes so well, I stock up on whatever happens to be a good value at the time, be it quick-cooking boneless and skinless chicken breasts, full-flavored thighs and drumsticks, or juicy bone-in breasts, buying enough to last until another sale. The challenge with chicken, however, is to keep it exciting (haven't we all fallen into a chicken rut at one time or another?). In this chapter, I provide plenty of interesting recipes for every occasion, whether you're looking for a dressed-up chicken dinner (check out Herb-Roasted Chicken with Potatoes on page 144), a family-friendly meal (like Chicken Meatballs on page 161), or something comforting, homey, and just right (Easy Coq au Vin, page 142).

Crispy Chicken a l'Orange

A boneless, skinless chicken breast is handy for dinner in a pinch, but sometimes I crave the juiciness and crispy-skin combo that can only happen when you're cooking a skin-on, bone-in chicken breast. Removing the bone after cooking is surprisingly simple—just take the tip of a sharp knife and, starting at the rounded top end of the cooked chicken breast, insert the tip where the meat meets the bone, gently separate the meat from the bone, and then thinly slice. Three breasts can easily feed four people. Orange juice concentrate is the secret to giving this sauce its sticky glaze.

serves 4

preparation time:
10 minutes (plus 10 minutes to rest)

cooking time:
25 minutes

- 3 skin-on, bone-in chicken breast halves, rinsed and patted dry
- 1½ teaspoons kosher salt
- ½ teaspoon ground black pepper
- 1 tablespoon vegetable oil
- ½ cup thawed orange juice concentrate
- ¼ cup honey

**deals, dollars & sense:
orange juice concentrate**

Keep a can of orange juice concentrate in the freezer and take out a scoop whenever you need it to wake up a pan sauce, make a smoothie, freshen up a salad dressing, or add a hint of citrus to cake and muffin batters.

1 Preheat the oven to 375°F. Place the chicken on a cutting board and season with ¾ teaspoon of the salt and ¼ teaspoon of the pepper. Heat the oil in a large skillet over medium-high heat and sear the chicken, skin side down, until brown and beginning to crisp, about 5 minutes.

2 Meanwhile, to make the orange glaze, in a small saucepan, bring the orange juice concentrate, honey, the remaining ¾ teaspoon salt, and the remaining ¼ teaspoon pepper to a boil over medium heat. Cook until syrupy, about 3 minutes, and then remove from the heat.

3 Transfer the chicken, skin side up, to a baking dish and drizzle half the glaze over the top. Bake until the internal temperature reads between 160°F. and 170°F. on an instant-read thermometer, about 15 minutes, then drizzle with the remaining glaze halfway through cooking. Remove the chicken from the oven and set aside for 10 minutes before moving it to a cutting board. Using tongs and a sharp knife, remove the meat from the bone (see note above) and thinly slice it diagonally on a bias. Transfer to a serving platter and serve.

Easy Coq au Vin

In France, long ago, coq au vin was a way to give new life to an old rooster and make it palatable for diners, but I see it as a great way to use a few cups of leftover red wine (or an excuse to open a bottle for dinner!). Cloves add complexity, a hint of warmth and spice, and a lot of flavor from one small ingredient.

● ● ● ● ○ ○

serves 4

preparation time:
15 minutes (plus 8 hours to marinate)

cooking time:
1 hour, 45 minutes

- 1½ pounds chicken drumsticks and thighs, rinsed and patted dry
- 1 large onion, finely chopped
- 3 whole cloves
- 1 tablespoon dried thyme plus a squeeze of lemon juice
- 1 dried bay leaf
- 1½ teaspoons kosher salt
- ½ teaspoon ground black pepper
- 2 cups inexpensive red wine, such as Merlot
- 1 tablespoon vegetable oil
- 4 bacon strips, finely chopped
- ½ pound button mushrooms, trimmed and quartered
- 2 tablespoons unsalted butter, at room temperature
- 1 tablespoon finely chopped fresh flat-leaf parsley (optional)

deals, dollars & sense: double batches

If you have a supersized Dutch oven or pot, make double batches of chili, soup, or any braised dish (such as coq au vin). Eat half tonight, and freeze the other half for another night. Not only are you using your time wisely by freezing a delicious, home-cooked meal to enjoy later, but you're also saving money by not opting for takeout pizza or a frozen store-bought entrée when you find yourself in need of a fast dinner.

1 Place the chicken on a cutting board and remove and discard the skin. Add the chicken to a gallon-sized resealable bag along with half of the onion, the cloves, thyme, bay leaf, 1 teaspoon of the salt, and the pepper. Pour the wine into the bag, seal, and refrigerate 8 hours or overnight.

2 Line a plate with paper towels and place the marinated chicken on it (save the marinade). Dab the top of the chicken with another paper towel and set aside. Heat 1 teaspoon of oil in a heavy-bottomed pot over medium heat, add the bacon, and cook until crisp, about 4 minutes, stirring often. Use a slotted spoon to transfer the bacon to a paper towel–lined plate and set aside. Place the chicken in the pot and cook until browned on all sides, about 8 minutes. Use tongs to transfer the chicken to a large bowl; set aside to cool slightly.

3 Add the remaining 2 teaspoons of oil and the mushrooms, the remaining chopped onion, and the remaining ½ teaspoon salt to the pan. Reduce the heat to medium-low and cook, stirring occasionally, until the onion is browned, the

mushrooms have released their liquid, and the pan is some-what dry, 10 to 15 minutes. Return the chicken to the pot and pour the marinade over the chicken. Raise the heat to high, bring to a boil, reduce the heat to medium-low, place the cover half on the pan, and gently simmer the chicken until it is very tender, about 1¼ hours. Divide the chicken among 4 plates. Remove the bay leaf from the pot and discard.

4 Stir the butter into the sauce and cook until melted. Turn off the heat and stir in the crispy bacon. Pour the sauce over the chicken and serve sprinkled with parsley (if using).

Herb-Roasted Chicken with Potatoes

My cooking, and especially my roast chicken, is very influenced by French flavors and techniques. In the 17th arrondissement of Paris, where I lived, I frequented a great old-fashioned butcher shop. So many years later, I can still smell the incredible aroma of their rotisserie chickens and the fat-basted potatoes beneath them. I worked for years to re-create that juicy, herby, and robust flavor. Fresh herbs are what make the chicken sing—they are a splurge-worthy must.

serves 4

preparation time:
15 minutes (plus 40 minutes to rest)

cooking time:
1 hour, 15 minutes

3- to 4-pound roasting chicken, rinsed and patted dry

4 tablespoons unsalted butter, at room temperature

2 tablespoons minced fresh rosemary

2 tablespoons minced fresh thyme

1 garlic clove, finely minced or pressed through a garlic press

1 teaspoon kosher salt

¾ teaspoon ground black pepper

½ cup dry white wine

1½ pounds red potatoes, quartered

2 tablespoons extra-virgin olive oil

Juice of ½ lemon

1   Place the chicken on a cutting board and let it rest at room temperature for 30 to 60 minutes (this will help it cook evenly). Preheat the oven to 425°F.

2   In a small bowl, mix together the butter, rosemary, thyme, garlic, ½ teaspoon of the salt, and ½ teaspoon of the pepper. Rub 3 tablespoons of herbed butter over the chicken skin and then use your fingers to slide about 1 tablespoon of herbed butter underneath the skin of the breast. Tuck the wings behind the chicken's back and, using kitchen twine, tie together the ends of the drumsticks.

3   Pour the wine into a small roasting pan or flame-safe baking dish, such as a ceramic baking dish. Place the chicken in the pan, breast side down, and roast for 15 minutes.

4   Remove the roasting pan from the oven and transfer the chicken, breast side up, to a plate. Add the potatoes to the bottom of the pan and toss them with the remaining ½ teaspoon salt, the remaining ¼ teaspoon pepper, and the olive oil. Slide the chicken on top of the potatoes and use a silicone brush or a knife to spread the remaining herbed butter over the chicken.

recipe continues

5 Lower the oven temperature to 325°F. and return the chicken to the oven to finish roasting until an instant-read thermometer inserted in the thickest part of the inner thigh (not touching the bone) reads 160°F., about 1 hour more. Take the pan out of the oven, transfer the chicken to a cutting board, and let it rest for 10 minutes before carving and arranging on a platter. Place the potatoes around the chicken on the serving platter.

6 While the chicken rests, make the sauce. Place the roasting pan on the stovetop over medium-high heat. Pour in the lemon juice and use a wooden spoon to stir and scrape up any bits stuck to the bottom (add up to ¼ cup water if the pan seems dry). Continue to cook the sauce, stirring often, until it comes to a boil. Turn off the heat and drizzle the sauce over the chicken and potatoes.

five tips for roasting the best chicken

1. Let the chicken temper on your counter for 30 minutes before cooking. You'll get a juicier bird.

2. Use fresh herbs. This is a case where dried herbs just don't make the cut.

3. Roast the chicken breast side down to initially protect it from the oven heat.

4. Start the chicken in a hot oven to render the fat and then lower the oven temperature to cook the chicken to juicy, tender perfection.

5. Let the chicken rest before carving it. Otherwise the juices will moisten your carving board instead of the chicken!

food for thought   **Why I Don't Freeze Whole Chickens**   Even when whole chickens are on sale, they're often not much cheaper than a full-price chicken. A whole chicken takes up a lot of space in the freezer and takes a full two days to thaw, so you have to remember that it's in the fridge. So my strategy is to buy a whole chicken today and use it by tomorrow.

Four-Step Chicken Piccata

This is my go-to recipe for an unplanned weeknight meal. It's super easy—in just four steps you get a family-friendly and company-worthy chicken dinner in minutes. To get extra mileage out of my chicken breast dollar, I like to slice a thick breast into two or three thinner cutlets. I find that three chicken breasts wisely prepped is plenty for serving a family of four. Plus, thin pieces of chicken cook more quickly than thicker ones, meaning dinner gets on the table that much faster. I love the bright citrus flavor and tanginess of the lemons and capers in piccata, but feel free to adjust the ingredients as you like. Be sure to check out the ideas on page 149 for ten ways to switch up this fail-safe recipe. Tip: Cutting chicken breasts into cutlets is easiest when the chicken is slightly frozen.

● ● ● ● ○ ○

serves 4

preparation time:
15 minutes

cooking time:
10 minutes

---

3 boneless, skinless chicken breasts, rinsed and patted dry

½ teaspoon kosher salt

¼ teaspoon ground black pepper

¼ cup all-purpose flour

2 tablespoons olive oil

¼ pound white button mushrooms, trimmed and thinly sliced

¼ cup dry white wine

Juice of 2 lemons

2 tablespoons capers, rinsed

2 tablespoons unsalted butter

1 Place a chicken breast on a cutting board and set your palm on top of it. Use a sharp knife to slice the chicken into 2 or 3 cutlets. Repeat with the other 2 breasts. Blot dry with paper towels and season with the salt and pepper. Place the flour in a shallow dish and dredge the chicken through it, evenly coating the chicken on both sides. Place on a plate and set aside. Heat the olive oil in a large skillet over medium-high heat. Set the chicken in the pan and cook on each side until browned, 6 to 8 minutes total. Transfer the chicken to a platter.

2 Add the mushrooms to the pan and cook, stirring often, until they are browned, about 5 minutes.

3 Pour the wine and lemon juice into the pan, using a wooden spoon to stir and scrape up any browned bits from the pan bottom.

4 Add the capers and then stir in the butter until it is melted and the sauce comes together. Turn off the heat and pour over the chicken before serving.

Four-Step Chicken in a Nutshell

Master this four-step method for making chicken and you'll never be in a chicken rut again. The recipe is infinitely adjustable to suit your tastes or to work with whatever you happen to have in the fridge (see the following recipe variations).

1. Dredge and brown the chicken.
2. Brown the veggies and aromatics.
3. Deglaze the pan to make a quick sauce.
4. Add some final flavorings and finishing touches.

four steps, many ways

While the steps remain the same, here are some ideas for switching up flavor. Try other combinations to create your own four-step recipe. You can also make four-step chicken using bone-in breasts—after browning, just transfer them to a 375°F. oven until cooked through.

VEGGIES AND AROMATICS	DEGLAZING LIQUIDS (USE ABOUT ¾ CUP)	FINAL TOUCHES (PLUS 2 TABLESPOONS BUTTER)
Yellow onions	Chicken broth and lemon juice	Chopped fresh basil
Red onions	Orange juice concentrate or fresh orange juice	Chopped fresh cilantro and lime
Leeks and garlic	Vermouth and chicken broth	Heavy cream (or sour cream with the burner turned off), about 2 tablespoons
Fennel	White wine	Spoonful of pesto
Mushrooms	Red wine	Crumbled blue cheese
Bacon and yellow onions	Cider vinegar and water	Chopped scallions
Yellow onions and garlic	Chicken broth	Grated Parmesan cheese
Red onions and oregano	White wine	Black olives and feta cheese
Yellow onions and green or red bell peppers	Water	Barbecue sauce
Shallots and dried thyme	Red wine vinegar and water	Parsley and grainy mustard

Preserved Lemon and Olive Chicken Tagine

I'm a fan of buying a few bold ingredients and stretching them out in different ways to spice up my cooking. This tagine calls for a few of them: preserved lemons (see page 153 for how to do this yourself, or in a pinch use fresh lemon zest), olives (search your grocery store's olive bar for variety and bargains on small quantities), and turmeric (an earthy and yellow-orange-hued spice used in many Eastern cuisines). Turmeric can be expensive, but if your supermarket has a bulk spice section, buy a tablespoon or two at a time. Sweet paprika instead of the turmeric is also delicious.

● ● ● ● ●

serves 4

preparation time:
15 minutes

cooking time:
1 hour, 10 minutes

1½ pounds chicken drumsticks and thighs, rinsed and patted dry

1 teaspoon kosher salt

½ teaspoon ground black pepper

1 tablespoon unsalted butter

2 tablespoons olive oil

1 onion, finely chopped

1-inch piece fresh ginger, peeled and minced or grated

½ teaspoon ground turmeric

½ teaspoon ground cinnamon

3 garlic cloves, finely minced or pressed through a garlic press

¼ cup fresh flat-leaf parsley, finely chopped

deals, dollars & sense: slow cooker version

On a busy day, toss all of the ingredients in a slow cooker and cook slow and low for 8 to 10 hours.

1 Place the chicken on a cutting board and, with dry hands, remove the skin from the chicken and discard. Season with ½ teaspoon of the salt and ¼ teaspoon of the pepper. Melt the butter with the olive oil over medium-high heat in a heavy-bottomed large pot or Dutch oven. Add the chicken, rounded side down, and cook until browned, 4 to 5 minutes. Turn the chicken and brown the other side, 3 to 4 minutes more. Transfer the chicken to a large plate and set aside.

2 Add the onion, ginger, turmeric, cinnamon, and the remaining ½ teaspoon salt and ¼ teaspoon pepper to the pan. Cook until the onion is translucent, stirring occasionally,

recipe continues

for about 3 minutes. Stir in the garlic, parsley, and cilantro and cook until the garlic is fragrant, about 1 minute. Raise the heat to high, pour in the wine, then add the broth and bring to a boil. Return the chicken to the pan, reduce the heat to medium-low, cover, and gently simmer until the chicken is tender, about 45 minutes. Transfer the chicken to a plate and set aside. Simmer the sauce over high heat until slightly reduced, about 5 minutes. Add the lemon wedges and olives and return the chicken to the pot. Cook to bring the flavors together, about 5 minutes, and serve.

3 tablespoons fresh cilantro, finely chopped

¼ cup dry white wine

¼ cup chicken broth

2 store-bought or homemade (see recipe opposite) preserved lemons, sliced into wedges

½ cup pitted briny black or green olives, gently smashed with the flat side of a knife

10 ideas for leftover cooked chicken

1. Shred and add to a chopped salad.

2. Mix with salsa and serve with fried eggs.

3. Stir with cheese, three beaten eggs, and ¾ cup heavy cream to make a crustless quiche.

4. Mix with tomatoes and croutons and toss with dressing for panzanella salad.

5. Use as a topping for beans and rice.

6. Tuck into a cheese quesadilla.

7. Simmer with chicken broth, beans, vegetables, and pasta for chicken minestrone.

8. Stir into chopped apples, raisins, and mayonnaise for chicken Waldorf salad.

9. Stir into whole-wheat spaghetti and finish with an Asian-style peanut sauce and thinly sliced fresh veggies.

10. Toss with tomatillo salsa and use as a filling for tacos or a burrito.

Homemade Preserved Lemons

When you buy preserved lemons at a gourmet store, a small jar at its cheapest can cost you ten bucks! For around $1.50 you can make your own. True, you do have to think ahead a few weeks, but the good news is that once you have them in your fridge, preserved lemons will last for months and they are a great item to have on hand. Just make sure that they stay submerged in the brine. Packed into nice jam jars with a cute label tied onto the neck with kitchen twine, these make a fantastic holiday, hostess, or housewarming gift.

making preserved lemons

Place 3 scrubbed lemons in a glass quart-sized jar. Add 3 tablespoons kosher salt and 4 whole black peppercorns, then completely cover with cold water. Place the lid on the jar, shake to combine, and refrigerate for 3 weeks to a few months.

10 ways to use preserved lemons

1. Chop and add to dough along with dried herbs to make savory scones.
2. Slice a few thin strips as garnish for grilled or broiled fish.
3. Mince and stir into orange marmalade for biscuits or toast.
4. Chop a few slices with fresh parsley, garlic, and lemon juice for a delicious condiment.
5. Purée into a walnut or parsley pesto.
6. Dice and toss with spaghetti, butter, and Parmesan cheese.
7. Finely chop and add to an oil-and-vinegar salad dressing.
8. Chop and mix into softened butter with chopped scallions for a compound butter (page 195).
9. Lightly warm with garlic, herbs, and whole olives in olive oil for spiced olives.
10. Chop and toss with couscous or orzo and parsley for a lemony side dish.

Grilled Chicken Breasts with Chimichurri Sauce

Chimichurri is a South American fresh herb sauce that gets a little tang from lemon juice and vinegar, depth from garlic and onions, and a touch of heat from red pepper flakes. It's amazing with nearly anything that comes off the grill, and once the uncooked sauce hits hot meat, the herbs and flavors in the sauce blossom and come into their own. It's a simple and inexpensive way to dress up a plain grilled chicken breast, a thrifty-priced steak, or even baked fish. Play with the flavors in the chimichurri—if you have basil or mint, swap it out for the cilantro. Or if limes are on sale, use them instead of lemons.

● ● ● ○ ○ ○

serves 4

preparation time:
25 minutes (plus 5 minutes to rest)

cooking time:
7 minutes

for the chimichurri

½ cup fresh cilantro leaves, roughly chopped

½ cup fresh flat-leaf parsley leaves, roughly chopped

1 tablespoon finely chopped onion

Juice of ½ lemon

2 teaspoons white wine vinegar

1 garlic clove, finely minced or pressed through a garlic press

Pinch of crushed red pepper flakes

1 teaspoon kosher salt

¼ teaspoon ground black pepper

⅓ cup olive oil

1 **To make the chimichurri:** Place the cilantro, parsley, onion, lemon juice, vinegar, garlic, red pepper flakes, salt, and pepper in the bowl of a food processor and pulse until roughly chopped. Slowly pour in the olive oil and process until the chimichurri is semismooth, about four seconds. Transfer to a small bowl, cover with plastic wrap, and set aside at room temperature or refrigerate for up to 1 day.

2 **To make the chicken:** Place the breasts on a cutting board rounded side down. Find the ridge along the side of the chicken breast and carefully slice off the tender, trim away any jagged edges, and set aside. Place a piece of plastic wrap or wax paper on a cutting board and set a chicken breast on top. Cover with another sheet of plastic wrap or wax paper. Using a meat mallet or a flat, heavy-bottomed cast-iron skillet, pound the breast until it is somewhat even, about ½ inch thick (one end will probably be thicker than the other). Repeat with the other breasts (if there is a thin little triangular tip at the bottom of the breast, slice it off and discard). Sprinkle the chicken tenders and cutlets with the salt and pepper and set aside at room temperature for 15 to 30 minutes.

recipe continues

3 Heat a charcoal or gas grill. When the grill is hot, brush the chicken with olive oil and place the cutlets pieces on the grill, with the thicker portion facing the hotter part of your grill (usually the back). Cook the chicken without moving it for 4 minutes; once the chicken has grill marks, use a spatula to turn it over, keeping the thicker side over the hotter part of the grill. Then, place the chicken tenders on the grill and cook for 3 minutes, turning halfway through. Once the chicken tenders are cooked through, the chicken breasts should be done, too (the chicken breasts cook for about 7 minutes total, while the tenders need only about 3 minutes to cook). Transfer the chicken to a platter, tent loosely with aluminum foil, and set aside for 5 minutes. Give the chimichurri a good stir and then spoon it over the warm chicken and serve.

for the chicken

- 4 boneless, skinless chicken breast halves, rinsed and patted dry
- ½ teaspoon kosher salt
- ¼ teaspoon ground black pepper
- ¼ cup olive oil

five secrets to juicy grilled boneless chicken breasts

1. Pound them until they're about ½ inch thick. It's okay if one side is thicker than the other.
2. Temper the chicken, letting it sit at room temperature for 15 to 30 minutes.
3. Season with salt and pepper and brush with oil before grilling.
4. Grill the chicken breast so the thicker end is always over the hotter part of the grill.
5. Don't overcook and take the time to rest the meat before slicing or serving.

Chicken Marengo

There is a story that after Napoleon was victorious over Austrian forces in Italy, he requested a celebratory meal from his chef—and without much food on hand or time to spare, this is what his chef created: Chicken Marengo. My recipe takes a few creative liberties, such as adding mushrooms and leaving out crayfish (some people add sardines). I think of it as my Ten Dollar Dinners wink to Napoleon.

● ● ● ● ● ● ●

serves 4

preparation time:
20 minutes

cooking time:
50 minutes

1½ pounds chicken thighs (about 8), skin removed, rinsed and patted dry

¾ teaspoon kosher salt

½ teaspoon ground black pepper

¼ cup all-purpose flour

1 tablespoon herbes de Provence

¼ cup olive oil

1 green or red bell pepper, halved, seeded, and thinly sliced

1 onion, halved and thinly sliced

8 ounces white button mushrooms, thinly sliced

3 garlic cloves, finely minced or pressed through a garlic press

¾ cup dry white wine

2 tablespoons tomato paste

½ cup beef broth

14-ounce can whole peeled tomatoes, chopped, liquid reserved

1 Place the chicken on a cutting board and season with ½ teaspoon of the salt and ¼ teaspoon of the pepper. Shake the flour and herbes de Provence together in a gallon-sized resealable bag, then add the chicken, seal, and shake to coat.

2 Heat 3 tablespoons of the olive oil in a heavy-bottomed Dutch oven or large pot over medium-high heat. Add the chicken, working in batches if you have to, and brown on all sides, about 8 minutes. Transfer the chicken to a large plate and set aside.

3 Pour the remaining 1 tablespoon olive oil into the pan, reduce the heat to medium, and add the bell pepper, onion, mushrooms, and the remaining ¼ teaspoon salt and ¼ teaspoon pepper and cook until soft, stirring occasionally, about 7 minutes. Stir in the garlic and cook until fragrant, 1 to 2 minutes longer. Raise the heat to high and pour in the wine, stirring and scraping any bits off the bottom of the pan, and letting the wine simmer for about 1½ minutes. Stir in the tomato paste and pour in the broth. Mix in the tomatoes and reduce the heat to medium-low. Return the chicken to the pan, place a lid on slightly askew, and simmer gently for 30 minutes to 2 hours for incredibly tender chicken, stirring occasionally (if cooking for longer than 30 minutes, do so over the lowest heat setting possible). Taste and season with more salt and pepper if needed.

Mustard Chicken

Using Dijon mustard is very common in classic French cooking. It's a flavorful way to build an elegant and interesting sauce for very little expense. Bold Dijon mustard gives the sauce for braised chicken depth and character and a surprising creaminess. If you don't already have Dijon mustard in your pantry, it's a worthy addition to your shopping list.

● ● ● ● ○ ○

serves 4

preparation time:
15 minutes

cooking time:
1 hour, 15 minutes

1½ pounds chicken thighs (about 8), rinsed and patted dry

½ teaspoon kosher salt

¼ teaspoon ground black pepper

2 tablespoons olive oil

1 onion, finely chopped

¼ pound white button mushrooms, quartered

3 garlic cloves, finely minced or pressed through a garlic press

1 tomato, cored, halved, and chopped, or ¾ cup canned chopped tomatoes

1 tablespoon all-purpose flour

1 teaspoon dried tarragon

½ cup dry white wine

1 cup chicken broth, plus extra if needed

¼ cup Dijon mustard

2 tablespoons sour cream (optional)

> **deals, dollars & sense: sour cream**
> I buy sour cream in small tubs because once opened, it should be used quickly. It's great in so many dishes and can even be used as a substitute for buttermilk, heavy cream, or plain yogurt in many recipes.

1 Preheat the oven to 350°F. Place the chicken on a cutting board and remove and discard the skin. Season the meat with the salt and pepper. Heat 1 tablespoon of the olive oil in a heavy-bottomed pot or Dutch oven over medium-high heat. Add the thighs, smooth side down, and cook until browned, about 4 minutes. Turn over the thighs and brown the other side, about 3 minutes more. Transfer the chicken to a plate and set aside.

2 Add the remaining 1 tablespoon olive oil along with the onion and cook until soft, stirring occasionally, for about 5 minutes. Stir in the mushrooms and continue to cook until the mushrooms are soft, 3 to 5 minutes. Add the garlic and cook until fragrant, 1 to 2 minutes, and then add the tomato and flour and cook, stirring, until the tomato begins to break down, about 3 minutes. Stir in the tarragon. Raise the heat and pour in the wine, letting it simmer for 1 minute before returning the chicken to the pot. Pour in enough broth to reach halfway up the sides of the chicken, then cover the pot and place it in the oven to braise, until the chicken pulls

recipe continues

away from the bone easily, about 45 minutes, removing the lid halfway through cooking.

3 Remove the pot from the oven, use tongs to transfer the chicken to a plate, and set aside. Add the mustard and sour cream (if using) to the sauce and stir to combine. Then return the chicken to the pot and back into the oven to cook for about 5 minutes to bring the flavors together before serving.

deals, dollars & sense: buying what you need

When trying out a new recipe, if you find yourself making a long shopping list full of items you never use, stop! Instead, think about what can be replaced (or even cut). If a recipe calls for smoked paprika, maybe you could add a dash of liquid smoke or bacon instead?

I'm all for trying new ingredients, especially ones like smoked paprika that can be used in so many ways (so even if that smoked paprika is $5, it'll last a long time and perk up everything from a Sunday pasta sauce to burgers and pan-fried potatoes). But, limiting the number of those ingredients on your list will cushion you against sticker shock. When you do buy something totally new, make a point to search out recipes that call for your new ingredient, so it doesn't sit there untouched on the shelf.

Chicken Meatballs

These meatballs are a great use for chicken breasts that you might not have considered before. Just grind up the meat (it's so easy) in the food processor with some big-flavor ingredients such as bacon for a smoky-salty richness and chili powder and cayenne pepper for a bit of kick, and you have the foundation for amazing meatballs. You'll be surprised how easy it is, plus, you can introduce new flavors to your family in a familiar package. Turn the chicken mixture into patties for nutritious and delicious burgers with a fun twist.

● ●

serves 4

preparation time:
25 minutes (plus 45 minutes to chill)

cooking time:
20 minutes

- 2 large boneless, skinless chicken breasts (about ¾ pound), rinsed and patted dry, sliced into 1-inch cubes
- 1 bacon strip
- 3 slices sandwich bread, roughly torn into small pieces
- 2 teaspoons chili powder
- ½ teaspoon cayenne pepper
- ½ teaspoon kosher salt
- ¼ cup whole milk
- 1 large egg, lightly beaten
- ½ small onion, finely chopped
- 2 garlic cloves, finely minced or pressed through a garlic press
- ⅓ cup grated Parmesan cheese, plus extra for sprinkling over the meatballs
- ¼ cup vegetable oil
- Fresh flat-leaf parsley, finely chopped (optional)

1 Place the chicken and the bacon on a plate and freeze to chill for 20 to 30 minutes.

2 Meanwhile, place the bread, chili powder, cayenne, and salt in the bowl of a food processor and pulse until you have fine bread crumbs. Divide the bread crumbs between two medium bowls. Set one bowl aside and stir the milk into the bread crumbs in the other bowl.

3 Add half the chilled chicken and all of the bacon to the food processor and pulse to combine into a rough mixture. Add the milk-and-bread-crumb mixture to the food processor along with the egg, onion, garlic, and Parmesan and process until very well combined (the mixture will be almost creamy). Add the remaining chilled chicken cubes to the food processor and pulse just to combine. The mixture will be semismooth with small chunks of chicken. Using a 1-inch small scoop, divide the mixture into about 30 small meatballs. Place the meatballs on a parchment paper–lined rimmed baking sheet and freeze for 15 minutes. Remove the pan from the freezer and roll the meatballs through the reserved bread crumbs to lightly and evenly coat the surface. Return the meatballs to the parchment-lined baking sheet.

recipe continues

4 Adjust an oven rack to the upper-middle position and preheat the broiler to high. Drizzle the meatballs with the oil and broil until they're cooked through, 5 to 6 minutes. Remove from the oven, sprinkle with Parmesan and the parsley (if using), rest for 5 minutes, and serve.

deals, dollars & sense: bacon

I am totally crazy about using bacon as an ingredient in my recipes. I love what it does to food—how it gives it that salty, smoky, fantastic hit. The downside is that once the package is open, bacon can spoil quickly. My solution is to keep it in the freezer. Whenever I want to include the equivalent of one strip of chopped bacon in a recipe, I just pull the package out of the freezer and cut off about ½ inch of bacon lengthwise, and I have perfect recipe-ready lardons. Fry them up to give pasta, stuffing, burgers, or salad dressing a bacony boost.

Chicken Taquitos

My mom was a master at stretching out every last scrap of food, and she used to make these cute little fried tacos whenever we had a few nuggets of leftover meat in the house. These taquitos are a fun way to use up extra roasted chicken, Thanksgiving turkey, braised pork shoulder (page 178), uneaten burgers (page 193), or a roasted chicken (page 144). If you have spare roasted, boiled, or mashed potatoes in the fridge, add them to the meat mixture to bulk it up and make even more taquitos.

● ● ●

serves **6**

preparation time:
25 minutes

cooking time:
30 minutes

1½ to 2 cups plus 1 tablespoon vegetable oil

1 small white onion, finely chopped

1 jalapeño pepper, stemmed, halved, and minced (seeded for less heat)

1 garlic clove, finely minced or pressed through a garlic press

1½ cups shredded cooked chicken

1½ cups shredded Monterey Jack cheese

½ cup canned tomatoes (preferably ones flavored with Mexican herbs and spices), drained and finely chopped

Kosher salt

¼ teaspoon ground black pepper

18 5- to 6-inch white or yellow corn tortillas

Jarred salsa, for serving

Sour cream or plain yogurt, for serving (optional)

1 Heat 1 tablespoon of oil in a medium skillet over medium-high heat. Add the onion, jalapeño, and garlic and cook, stirring occasionally, until soft, about 3 minutes. Turn off the heat and transfer to a large bowl. Once cool, stir in the chicken, cheese, tomatoes, ½ teaspoon salt, and pepper. Set aside.

2 Stack the tortillas on a microwave-safe plate, cover with a damp paper towel, and microwave in 30-second increments until they're warm and pliable, about 1 minute. (This will keep them from breaking when rolling.)

3 Set a tortilla on a cutting board and place 1 tablespoon of the chicken filling in the middle. Roll into a thin cylinder and seal it shut using a toothpick or trimmed wood skewer. Repeat with the remaining tortillas and filling.

4 Line a large plate with paper towels. Pour 1½ cups of the oil into a large skillet (if the oil isn't at least ½ inch deep, add another ½ cup) and warm it over medium heat until an instant-read thermometer inserted into the oil reads between 350°F. and 375°F. (Drop in a small piece of tortilla and if bubbles surround it the oil is ready.) Add 2 to 3 taquitos to the pan and fry, using a frying spider or slotted spoon to turn the taquito often, until it's crisp and brown on all sides, about 3 minutes. Transfer the taquitos to the paper towel–lined plate, sprinkle with a little salt, remove the toothpick, and set aside to cool. Repeat with the remaining taquitos. Serve with salsa and sour cream (if using) on the side.

Spinach and Cheese–Stuffed Chicken with Lemon Butter

Fancy-looking stuffed chicken is actually a last-minute pantry supper at my house. I'm a huge fan of frozen spinach and consider it a must-have freezer item because it's so easy to add to a soup or pasta dish, to make into a side dish with garlic and lemon, or to turn into creamed spinach. The idea for this dish came from a few string cheese nubs in the fridge and a package of frozen spinach. To add a nice creaminess, I use cream cheese, another must-have ingredient in the fridge.

● ● ● ●

serves 4

preparation time:
20 minutes

cooking time:
23 minutes

- 8 ounces thawed frozen chopped spinach (about half a 1-pound bag)
- ¼ pound (4 ounces) sliced, shredded, or chunks of cheese, such as Cheddar, mozzarella, provolone, or Swiss
- 2 tablespoons cream cheese
- Zest and juice of 1 lemon
- 1 garlic clove, roughly chopped
- 1 teaspoon kosher salt
- ¼ cup all-purpose flour
- 4 6- to 8-ounce boneless, skinless chicken breasts, rinsed and patted dry
- 2 tablespoons canola or olive oil
- 2 tablespoons unsalted butter, cut into small pieces

deals, dollars & sense: cream cheese

Cream cheese goes on sale fairly frequently, and since it has a long shelf life, you can stock up when it's a bargain. It has both savory and sweet uses, so it gives you a lot of mileage for one ingredient.

1 Preheat the oven to 375°F. Place the thawed spinach in a paper towel, squeeze out the excess liquid, and transfer the spinach to the bowl of a food processor. Add the cheese, cream cheese, lemon zest, garlic, and ½ teaspoon of the salt. Pulse until the cheese is broken up into small pieces and everything is nicely mixed, about five 3-second pulses. Set aside.

2 Place the flour in a shallow baking dish and set aside. Place your palm flat on top of a chicken breast and, using a sharp paring knife and starting about ½ inch from the tip, make a long slit in the side of the chicken, working the knife about three quarters of the way through to the other side, but not cutting through the breast completely, to make a good-sized pocket. Repeat with the remaining 3 breasts and then stuff each with a few tablespoons of the spinach stuffing. Thread 2 or 3 toothpicks (or shortened wood skewers) from top to bottom through the edge of the pocket to fasten it shut. Season with the remaining ½ teaspoon salt and then roll the breasts through the flour, lifting out and gently tapping each one to knock off extra flour.

3 Heat the oil in a large oven-safe skillet over medium-high heat. Add the chicken breasts, smooth side down, and cook until browned, 4 to 5 minutes. Use tongs to turn over the breasts and brown on the other side, about 3 minutes more. Drizzle the lemon juice over the chicken and sprinkle the butter pieces over the chicken. Place the chicken in the oven until cooked through and firm to the touch, about 15 minutes. Serve drizzled with the sauce from the pan.

// 6 //

pork & beef

Here's to Meat on a Budget!

Everyone thinks of chicken as the go-to inexpensive cut of meat, but really, pork and beef can also be affordable, especially when it's a loss leader (page 172).

There are definitely inexpensive cuts to know about, and if you treat these cuts right, you can coax out their incredible flavor and tenderness. Pork goes on sale almost as often as chicken; just be strategic about how you deal with the different types of meat. Cheap pork shoulders are fantastic braised (pages 178 and 182) because they become succulent cooked low and slow, and because they can generously feed a crowd (or a family with bonus leftovers). I also love boneless pork loin roasts, which go on sale often and give you loads of options, such as boneless pork chops, cubes for kebabs (page 184), or a roast (page 172).

When it comes to beef, cost-conscious cooks know that ground beef can be a go-to meat because it's so versatile and family-friendly, whether turned into meatballs (page 190), a comfort meat loaf (page 189), or a dressy burger (page 193). That said, if you shop smart, cook it right, and plate it in a clever way, you *can* serve steak to your family without breaking the bank. With bigger cuts of meat, such as classic roast beef, the key is to cook it right to turn its toughness into tenderness for a super decadent meal that tastes expensive without costing you an arm and a leg.

Pork Loin Marsala

When you go to the grocery store, keep your eye on the pork loin (not tenderloin—that's a different, smaller, and much pricier cut) and wait for it to go on sale about once a month when it's a loss leader and marked down by 50 percent, and then pounce! I call on some of my favorite dried herbs to give this pork a great crust and full flavor, then deglaze the roasting pan with sherry-like Marsala wine. The secret to a juicy pork loin is simple—don't overcook it and let it rest before slicing.

● ● ● ● ● ●

serves 6

preparation time:
15 minutes (plus 10 minutes to rest)

cooking time:
1 hour, 15 minutes

1 teaspoon dried rosemary

1 teaspoon dried sage

1 teaspoon dried thyme plus a squeeze of lemon juice

1 teaspoon kosher salt

½ teaspoon ground black pepper

2-pound pork loin, fat trimmed, tied into a roast

2 teaspoons Dijon mustard

2 tablespoons vegetable oil

1 onion, halved and sliced into medium-thick wedges

2 tablespoons unsalted butter

2 teaspoons all-purpose flour, at room temperature

½ cup Marsala wine

> ### deals, dollars & sense: marsala wine
> Marsala wine is a fortified wine similar to port and sherry. Even a splash adds tons of body and richness to a pan sauce, elevating its flavor profile tremendously. A decent Marsala shouldn't set you back more than $6 (of course you can buy a bottle for more money, but it's not necessary). The Marsala from the cooking wine aisle doesn't have as much flavor as real Marsala and has added salt. You can use it in a pinch; just remember to then decrease the salt in a recipe.

1 Preheat the oven to 425°F. Stir the rosemary, sage, thyme, salt, and pepper together in a small bowl. Place the pork roast on a cutting board and rub the mustard all over its surface, including the ends. Sprinkle and pat the herbs over the entire roast.

2 Heat the oil in an oven-safe skillet (cast iron is ideal). Brown the pork on all sides, about 15 minutes total. Remove the roast from the pan and set aside. Add the onion to the pan and toss to coat. Turn off the heat, nestle the roast in the middle of the pan, and place the roast in the oven for 15 minutes. Mash the butter and flour together to make a paste and set aside.

3 Reduce the oven temperature to 350°F. and roast until the internal temperature of the pork reads about 150°F., an additional 20 to 25 minutes. Remove the pan from the oven and place the pork on a cutting board, cover loosely with foil, and let it rest for 10 minutes.

4 Set the skillet on the stovetop over medium heat. Add the wine and stir to incorporate, then scrape in the butter-flour paste. Cook, stirring often for 2 minutes, to cook out the raw taste in the flour. Turn off the heat. Thinly slice the pork roast and serve with the sauce.

buy big now, save big later

I'm a huge fan of buying large value packs of meats on sale. Whatever you do, don't toss that five-pound value pack straight into the freezer. When you are stuck on a harried Tuesday night and don't know what to cook, you want to open the freezer and see a recipe waiting to happen—not a giant block of frozen meat. So take five minutes to prep it out and divide it into manageable bundles. It's a small investment to make that can pay off big-time later.

PORK LOIN
- Cut off a roast (or two).
- Slice meat into cubes for kebabs or smaller ones for stir-fry.
- Cut into boneless pork loin chops.

GROUND BEEF
- Brown a pound or two and freeze.
- Preform burgers.
- Make and shape meatballs. (See page 191 for meatball varieties.)
- Divide into one-pound portions for recipes.

BONELESS, SKINLESS CHICKEN BREASTS
- Divide into freezer bags with 2 breasts per bag.
- *If you have time:* Half an hour after they go into the freezer, cube some up to use later (they're easier to cut once they're semifrozen!).

Pork Loin Milanese with Arugula Salad

Milanese makes my girls happy because it reminds them of chicken fingers. And the thin and crisp-breaded cutlets remind me and my husband of a bistro meal, especially because I serve them alongside a simple yet sophisticated salad of peppery arugula (a little pricier than other greens, but what better place to splurge than the produce aisle?). I also love that they're fast and easy for a weeknight meal.

● ● ● ●

serves 4

preparation time:
25 minutes (plus 15 minutes to marinate)

cooking time:
8 minutes

1½ cups panko bread crumbs

1 pound pork loin, sliced into 4 pieces (or four 4-ounce boneless pork loin chops)

¼ cup olive oil

2 garlic cloves, finely minced or pressed through a garlic press

½ teaspoon plus a pinch of kosher salt

1 large egg

½ cup vegetable oil

1 lemon, half juiced, other half sliced into 4 wedges

¼ teaspoon ground black pepper

3 cups arugula or other baby greens

Parmesan curls (made by shaving a wedge of Parmesan cheese with a vegetable peeler) or freshly grated Parmesan for serving

1 Place the bread crumbs in a shallow dish and set aside. Set a piece of pork on top of a sheet of wax paper or plastic wrap, cover with another sheet, and using a meat mallet, pound the pork until it is about ¼ inch thick. Set aside and repeat with the remaining pieces.

2 Pour 2 tablespoons of the olive oil into a gallon-sized resealable bag. Add the garlic and ½ teaspoon of the salt, then seal and shake to combine. Add the pounded pork cutlets, seal the bag, and massage to coat. Refrigerate for 15 minutes.

3 Whisk the egg in a medium bowl. Remove the pork from the refrigerator, take a piece out of the bag, and dip both sides in the egg. Place the pork in the bread crumbs, lightly press down on the pork, and then turn it over to coat the other side. Set the breaded cutlet on a plate and repeat with the remaining pieces of pork.

4 Heat the vegetable oil in a large skillet over medium-high heat. Add the pork cutlets to the pan and brown on each side, about 6 minutes total. Use a spatula to transfer the pork to a paper towel–lined plate and set aside.

5 Whisk the remaining 2 tablespoons olive oil with the lemon juice, a pinch of salt, and the pepper in a salad bowl. Add the arugula and toss to combine. Divide the salad and pork between 4 plates and serve with Parmesan and a lemon wedge.

Kielbasa and Black-Eyed Peas

I give franks and beans an adult spin with smoky, garlicky kielbasa and black-eyed peas. I almost always go for dried beans, but already cooked beans (canned or frozen) are a good option when you're cooking with beans you don't use often. You can make this dish with other kinds of beans and sausage—just be sure to thoroughly cook the sausage if it's raw. Kielbasa is precooked, so it needs only a quick sear.

● ● ● ●

serves 4

preparation time:
15 minutes

cooking time:
25 minutes

1 tablespoon vegetable oil

½ pound kielbasa, cut into ¼-inch-thick pieces

1 onion, finely chopped

½ teaspoon kosher salt

¼ teaspoon ground black pepper

2 garlic cloves, finely minced

½ teaspoon dried thyme plus a squeeze of lemon juice

2 tablespoons tomato paste

2 tablespoons red wine vinegar

1 tablespoon (packed) light brown sugar

2 teaspoons Dijon mustard

1 dried bay leaf

2 cups cooked black-eyed peas (about 1½ 15.5-ounce cans)

1½ cups fresh or frozen chopped spinach (optional)

Corn bread or steamed white rice, for serving

Hot sauce, for serving (optional)

1 Heat the oil in a large skillet over medium-high heat. Add the kielbasa and brown on both sides, about 6 minutes total. Transfer to a paper towel–lined plate and set aside. Add the onion, salt, and pepper and cook, stirring often, until the onion is soft and starting to brown, about 4 minutes. Stir in the garlic and thyme and cook until the garlic is fragrant, about 1 minute. Mix in the tomato paste, cooking until it starts browning on the bottom of the pot, about 2 minutes, stirring constantly.

2 Pour in 1 cup water and the vinegar, stirring it into the onion, then add the sugar, mustard, bay leaf, and black-eyed peas. Return the kielbasa to the pan, reduce the heat to medium-low, cover, and cook until the sauce is rich-colored and slightly thick, about 10 minutes. Stir in the spinach (if using), until wilted. Remove and discard the bay leaf. Serve in big bowls with corn bread or over rice, with hot sauce on the side (if using).

deals, dollars & sense: fresh spinach

I like to add a handful of fresh spinach to dishes. It adds brightness, texture, and a dose of nutrients to stir-fries, a pot of beans, or soup. Also try it instead of lettuce on a sandwich or in a wrap or a green veggie smoothie (page 326).

Slow Cooker All-Purpose Pork Shoulder

When pork shoulder goes on sale, it's often as little as a buck a pound—such a value for a comforting, big-flavored cut of meat. I like to make this when I have a crazy week ahead of me. I pop the roast in the slow cooker in the morning and let it go all day long for a sublime, tender, and tasty foundation on which to make all kinds of dishes, from a quick barbecue pulled-pork sandwich to a rich pork ragù for pasta. See page 181 for more of my favorite ways to serve pork shoulder. If you don't have a slow cooker, you can braise the pork shoulder in a 325°F. oven for 2½ to 3 hours or until tender.

serves **8**

preparation time:
10 minutes

cooking time:
4 to 8 hours (depending on whether you set the slow cooker to high or low heat)

3- to 4-pound boneless pork shoulder (or 4½-pound bone-in pork shoulder)

1 tablespoon kosher salt

2 teaspoons ground black pepper

1 onion, roughly chopped

4 garlic cloves, finely minced or pressed through a garlic press

½ cup dry white wine

1 Rinse the pork, place on a cutting board, pat dry with paper towels, and rub in the salt and pepper. Set the pork into the bowl of a slow cooker, scatter the onion over the pork, sprinkle in the garlic, and add the wine. Cook until the meat easily pulls apart with a fork, about 8 hours on low or 4 hours on high.

2 Turn off the slow cooker and transfer the pork to a platter. Use a fork to shred the meat and use in one of the ways that follow.

10 Ways to Use
Slow-Cooked Pork Shoulder

On page 178, I share the most basic way to make a pork shoulder—with very few ingredients and in the slow cooker. The good news is that pork shoulder is incredibly versatile and a great flavor base for a lot of dinner options. A great strategy is to set aside half of the braised meat for dinner tonight and freeze the rest for dinner another night. It's like getting two meals for the effort of one! Here are ten of my favorite ways to turn a simply cooked pork shoulder into other meals.

1. **Carnitas-style pork tacos:** Fry chopped jalapeños in some oil, add the pork, season with salt, and brown until it's crispy around the edges (you can brown both sides if you like). Pile into warmed corn tortillas and finish with a squeeze of lime.

2. **Barbecued pork sandwich:** Mix together three parts barbecue sauce with one part white vinegar and toss with the pork. Pile on a toasted bun and top with crunchy coleslaw.

3. **Pasta and shredded pork:** Toss the pork with steaming hot pasta, a little pasta water, some halved grape tomatoes, and a spoonful of prepared pesto. Finish with grated Parmesan cheese.

4. **Pork tamale pie:** Place the leftover pork in a baking dish, toss with salsa, and top with your favorite corn bread batter. Bake at the oven temperature as instructed in the corn bread recipe until the corn bread is cooked through.

5. **Pork chili:** Sauté onions and peppers until soft, add chili powder and some chopped canned tomatoes, stir in some pork and canned or cooked dried beans, and heat through.

6. **Pork sloppy joes:** Sauté onions and peppers until soft, add equal parts ketchup to the barbecue sauce and pork, and heap on a warmed bun.

7. **Pork shepherd's pie:** Place leftover pork in a baking dish and top with cooked peas and then a layer of garlic mashed potatoes. Sprinkle with grated cheese and bake until warmed through.

8. **Pork burritos:** Wrap leftover rice in a tortilla with smashed beans, pork, chopped tomatoes, shredded lettuce, grated cheese, salsa, and sour cream.

9. **Pork hash:** Sauté onions and peppers until soft, add diced potatoes, and cook until tender. Stir in the pork and serve with eggs.

10. **Pork turnovers:** Cut 6-inch circles out of puff pastry, add a spoonful of pork, salsa, and some grated cheese, fold, crimp, and bake according to the puff pastry package instructions until golden.

Succulent Pot Roast–Style Pork Shoulder

As much as I love making pork shoulder in the slow cooker (page 178), something special happens when you braise it in the oven. The depth of flavor and level of succulence get cranked up and make for a great pot roast. I love making this when I have people over for a homey, comforting meal (filling the house with a welcoming, delicious fragrance). Satisfying and so flavorful, this kind of cooking hits all the right spots. It works well with a bone-in shoulder, too (3 to 3½-pounds instead).

● ● ● ● ○ ○

serves 4

preparation time:
15 minutes

cooking time:
3 hours, 30 minutes

2-pound boneless pork shoulder cut into 6 pieces

1½ teaspoons kosher salt, plus extra if needed

1 teaspoon ground black pepper, plus extra if needed

2 tablespoons olive oil

2 celery stalks, finely chopped

1 carrot, peeled and finely chopped

1 onion, finely chopped

1 garlic clove, roughly chopped

2 tablespoons tomato paste

2 tablespoons all-purpose flour

1 cup dry red wine

1½ cups beef broth

Bunch of flat-leaf parsley stems, tied with kitchen twine

2 dried bay leaves

1 Preheat the oven to 325°F. Place the pork on a cutting board, pat dry with paper towels, and season with the salt and pepper. In a large heavy-bottomed pot or Dutch oven, heat the olive oil over medium-high heat, and, working in two batches, brown the meat on all sides, about 10 minutes total per batch. Transfer the browned meat to a plate and set aside.

2 Add the celery, carrot, and onion to the pan and cook, stirring often, until soft, 5 to 7 minutes. Stir in the garlic and cook until fragrant, about 2 minutes. Stir in the tomato paste and cook until it starts to turn a little darker, about 3 minutes. Sprinkle with the flour and cook another 2 minutes, stirring constantly. Whisk in the wine, beating out any flour lumps. Simmer the wine until it is reduced by half, 2 to 4 minutes. Return the pork to the pot and stir in the broth. Add the parsley stems and bay leaves (if the liquid in the pot doesn't cover the pork, add enough water to just rise above the top of the pork).

3 Bring the liquid to a simmer, turn off the heat, cover the pot, and place the pot in the oven to braise until the meat shreds easily when pulled by a fork, about 3 hours. Transfer the pork to a platter, taste, and season with more salt and pepper if needed. Remove and discard the bay leaves and serve the sauce on the side.

Grilled Tandoori Pork Kebabs

Plain yogurt is one of my favorite pantry ingredients. It goes on sale often, making it a great item to buy now for using later (keep yogurts with upcoming "best by" dates in the front so they are used first). In this recipe, I use plain yogurt to tenderize the pork cubes before they hit the grill to char up. I love the kebabs with grilled naan or pita bread, but they're great wrapped inside a flour tortilla, too. If using wood skewers instead of metal ones, be sure to soak them in water for 20 minutes before threading. These work great under the broiler, too.

● ● ● ● ○ ○

serves 4

preparation time:
15 minutes (plus 2 hours to marinate)

cooking time:
20 minutes

2 teaspoons sweet paprika

1 teaspoon ground turmeric (optional)

1 teaspoon ground coriander

1 teaspoon ground cumin

¼ teaspoon cayenne pepper

½ teaspoon kosher salt

1-inch piece fresh ginger, peeled and grated (about 1 tablespoon)

1 garlic clove, finely minced or pressed through a garlic press

1½ pounds pork loin, cut into six 1-inch-thick slices and then cut into 1-inch cubes

6-ounce container plain yogurt

Juice of ½ lemon

Naan or pita bread, for serving

1 lemon or lime sliced into wedges, for serving

1 Whisk the paprika, turmeric (if using), coriander, cumin, cayenne, and salt together in a large bowl. Add the ginger, garlic, and pork and toss and rub with the spices. Transfer the pork to a gallon-sized resealable bag and add the yogurt and lemon juice. Seal and massage to combine so all of the pork cubes are evenly coated. Refrigerate for at least 2 hours or overnight.

2 Heat a charcoal or gas grill to high heat. Thread the pork pieces on 4 skewers and grill until charred and browned on all sides, about 10 minutes. Remove from the grill and place the naan or pita bread on the grill to warm. Serve the kebabs over the bread with the lemon wedges on the side.

Pot Roast Carbonnade

Beef, bacon, onions, and beer make the stew rich and decadent. This is my take on a classic Belgian carbonnade. I use beef chuck meat for its fantastic flavor that also happens to hit just the right price point. When slowly simmered, it becomes silky and beyond comforting. The prunes kind of melt into the sauce, giving it a slightly sweet depth and wonderful texture. Inexpensive egg noodles are an ideal side.

● ● ● ●

serves 4

preparation time:
20 minutes

cooking time:
3 hours

½ pound thick-cut bacon (about 8 strips), cut into ¼-inch pieces

2 onions, halved and thinly sliced

1¾ teaspoons kosher salt

¾ teaspoon ground black pepper

1 tablespoon vegetable oil

1½ pounds beef chuck, cut into 1½-inch cubes

5 carrots, peeled and cut into thirds

1½ tablespoons all-purpose flour

12-ounce bottle of beer (any kind is fine)

1 cup beef broth

6 pitted prunes

1 tablespoon dried thyme plus a squeeze of lemon juice

1 Preheat the oven to 325°F. Place the bacon in a large heavy-bottomed pot or Dutch oven and slowly render the fat over medium-low heat, cooking until it just starts to crisp around the edges, 8 to 10 minutes. Use a slotted spoon to transfer it to a large plate and set aside. Add the onions, ¾ teaspoon of the salt, and ¼ teaspoon of the pepper; reduce the heat to low and slowly cook until the onions are deep brown and caramelized, about 30 minutes.

2 Use tongs or a slotted spoon to transfer the onions to the plate with the bacon, leaving behind as much fat as possible. Add the oil to the pot, raise the heat to high, season the beef with the remaining 1 teaspoon salt and ½ teaspoon pepper, and sear in two batches until the meat is browned on all sides, about 10 minutes per batch.

3 Return all of the bacon and beef to the pot and add the carrots and onions. Sprinkle the flour over the meat and vegetables and stir it in, cooking while stirring constantly for 1 minute. Pour the beer into the pot and use a wooden spoon to stir it into the other ingredients, scraping any browned bits off the bottom of the pot and into the liquid. Pour in the broth and add the prunes and thyme. Bring the mixture to a simmer, cover the pot, and turn off the heat. Place the pot in the oven to braise until the meat is pull-apart tender, about 2 hours. Serve hot.

Everyday Roast Beef

Why reserve a classic roast beef just for holidays and special occasions when it's such a great family meal? I live down the street from my sister and most weeks we have at least one big family dinner. No small feat considering that she has five kids and I have four! I go for top round (bottom round is my second choice)— not the fanciest or most tender cut, but when cooked gently it becomes wonderfully tasty. I cook it slowly at a low temperature and then give it a final blast of heat for a gorgeous browned crust.

serves **6**

preparation time:
15 minutes (plus 1 hour, 15 minutes to rest)

cooking time:
1 hour, 50 minutes

3-pound top round beef roast

1 tablespoon kosher salt, plus extra if needed

2 teaspoons ground black pepper, plus extra if needed

4 garlic cloves, sliced into thick slivers

2 tablespoons vegetable oil, plus extra for the rack

½ cup dry red wine

1 teaspoon all-purpose flour (optional)

1 Place the roast on a cutting board and use paper towels to pat dry. Rub in the salt and pepper and then, using a sharp paring knife, poke deep slits all over the top and sides of the roast. Fill each slit with a garlic sliver. Set the roast aside at room temperature for 1 hour. Preheat the oven to 250°F. Set a roasting rack in a roasting pan, grease with a little oil, and set aside.

2 Heat the 2 tablespoons oil in a large heavy-bottomed skillet and brown the roast on all sides, 8 to 12 minutes total. Transfer the roast to the rack in the roasting pan and set aside. Pour ½ cup water into the skillet and stir and scrape any browned bits off the bottom of the pan. Turn off the heat and pour the liquid from the pan, along with the wine, into the roasting pan.

3 Roast the meat until its internal temperature reaches 120°F., 1 hour to 1 hour and 20 minutes. Remove the roasting pan from the oven and raise the oven temperature to 475°F. Return the roasting pan to the oven and cook the roast until a nice crust forms, 8 to 10 minutes. Remove the roasting pan from the oven, transfer the roast to a carving board, tent with foil, and set aside for 15 minutes.

4 Meanwhile, place the roasting pan over medium heat and bring the juices to a simmer to make the sauce. Cook until the pan juices are reduced by one third, 2 to 3 minutes (if you like a thicker sauce, whisk 1 teaspoon flour into the sauce to thicken). Taste the sauce and season with more salt and pepper if needed. Carve the roast and serve with the sauce.

rescue my tough roast!

It's happened to all of us. You get caught up on a phone call or you get distracted by the kids and before you know it, your roast is overcooked. You may think that your roast is beyond repair, but it's not! It can be rescued—here's how.

IF YOUR ROAST IS JUST A BIT OVERCOOKED AND DRY

Slice it as thinly as possible (an electric knife is absolutely your best friend in this scenario), lay the slices on a platter, and pour lots of pan juices right over the meat (don't thicken the juices with flour). If you don't have enough pan juices, supplement with hot store-bought beef broth.

IF YOU REALLY MESS UP YOUR ROAST

Don't throw it away—it will still be great for tomorrow's dinner (there's no shame in ordering a pizza for tonight!). Stick the whole thing in a slow cooker along with a chopped onion, the pan juices (or water or store-bought beef broth if you don't have any pan juices), and ¼ cup barbecue sauce. Cook the roast until you can insert a fork and easily pull it out, about 4 hours on low. Toast up some buns and you have delicious barbecue beef sandwiches.

five tips for a perfect roast

1. Let the roast sit out at room temperature for 1 hour before cooking so it roasts evenly and stays juicy.
2. Brown the roast in a pan before roasting; this is key for developing a nice crust.
3. Cook low and slow and give the meat a blast of high heat at the end for a gorgeous crust.
4. For the juiciest meat, let the roast rest for 15 minutes after cooking.
5. Thinly slice the meat against the grain (an electric knife is great for thin pieces).

Moroccan Meat Loaf

I take inspiration from North Africa to give this all-American dish an exotic twist. This is as delicious served with classic mashed potatoes as it is with couscous. To get a perfect meat loaf shape and yummy glazed sides, I use a loaf pan to shape the meatloaf and then invert it out of the pan and onto a baking sheet to cook it.

serves 6

preparation time:
30 minutes (plus 10 minutes to rest)

cooking time:
1 hour, 5 minutes

for the glaze

- ¼ cup ketchup
- Zest and juice of 1 lemon
- 1 garlic clove, finely minced
- 1 tablespoon (packed) light brown sugar
- ¼ teaspoon crushed red pepper flakes
- ¼ teaspoon ground cinnamon

for the meat loaf

- 2 large eggs
- ¼ cup ketchup
- ⅓ cup finely chopped fresh cilantro leaves
- 2-inch piece fresh ginger, peeled and minced
- 2 teaspoons ground cumin
- ¼ teaspoon ground cinnamon
- 1 teaspoon kosher salt
- ½ teaspoon ground black pepper
- ⅔ cup finely ground rolled oats or bread crumbs
- 1½ pounds 80% lean ground beef

1 **To make the glaze:** Whisk together the ketchup, lemon zest and juice, garlic, sugar, red pepper flakes, and cinnamon in a small bowl. Set aside.

2 Preheat the oven to 350°F. Line a rimmed baking sheet with aluminum foil and set aside.

3 **To make the meat loaf:** In a large bowl, whisk together the eggs, ketchup, cilantro, ginger, cumin, cinnamon, salt, and pepper. Add the oats and stir to combine, then add the ground beef, breaking it up into small pieces as you add it to the bowl, and stir with a wooden spoon (or your hands) until well combined.

4 Line a 9 × 5-inch loaf pan with two long sheets of plastic wrap so the whole pan is covered and you have long plastic handles (this makes it easier to get the loaf out of the pan). Pat the meat mixture into the prepared loaf pan and then flip it upside down onto the prepared baking sheet. Pull off the loaf pan and remove the plastic wrap. Brush some glaze over the meat loaf (be sure to get the ends and sides). Bake in the oven until the internal temperature reads 160°F. and the meat loaf is cooked through (it will be pinkish from the ketchup), 45 minutes to 1 hour, brushing with more glaze halfway through. Turn the broiler to high and brown the top until sizzling, 1 to 2 minutes. Let the meat loaf rest for 10 minutes before slicing and serving.

Lemon-Thyme Meatballs

When I was a kid my mom used to make a marinated flank steak dinner for special occasions. I borrowed the flavors of that dinner—lemon, thyme, scallions, and soy sauce—and put them into an everyday package, 30-minute meatballs. These deeply flavored meatballs are just as delicious with a loaded baked potato as they are on the go sandwiched into a baguette.

● ● ○ ○ ○

makes **24** meatballs

preparation time:
30 minutes

cooking time:
20 minutes

1 large egg

2 scallions (green parts only), finely chopped

2 garlic cloves, finely minced or pressed through a garlic press

Zest and juice of ½ lemon

¼ cup soy sauce

2 teaspoons dried thyme

½ teaspoon ground black pepper

⅔ cup bread crumbs

1 pound 80% lean ground beef

1 Preheat the oven to 375°F. Lightly coat a rimmed baking sheet with nonstick pan spray and set aside.

2 In a large bowl, whisk together the egg, scallions, garlic, lemon zest and juice, soy sauce, thyme, and pepper. Stir in the bread crumbs, then add the ground beef, breaking it up into small knobs as you add it to the bowl.

3 Use a spoon or your hands to gently mix together and then form the mixture into twenty-four 1-inch balls. Place the balls on the prepared baking sheet and bake until they are browned and slightly resistant to pressure when pressed, about 20 minutes. Serve hot.

Five-Pound Value Pack Meatball Variations

When I buy a five-pound value pack of ground beef (see page 173) I turn some of it into quick meatballs. After mixing the ground beef with herbs and seasonings and shaping them into balls, set them in the freezer on a baking sheet; once they're semifrozen, transfer them to a gallon-sized resealable freezer bag (let them sit out at room temperature for 20 minutes and then bake 5 minutes longer than the recipe instructs). Or, shape, cook, and *then* freeze. Then all you need to do is defrost in the microwave and pan-fry to heat through before serving. With a five-pound package of ground beef, you can make five different varieties and ten dozen meatballs!

To 1 pound of ground beef add 1 large egg, ⅔ cup bread crumbs, 2 minced garlic cloves, ½ teaspoon kosher salt, and ½ teaspoon ground black pepper. Then add any of the following mix-ins:

BARBECUE MEATBALLS
Add ¼ cup barbecue sauce.

SWEET TERIYAKI MEATBALLS
Add ¼ cup teriyaki sauce and 3 tablespoons canned crushed pineapple or applesauce.

BASIC ITALIAN MEATBALLS
Add ¼ cup Italian salad dressing, ¼ cup grated Parmesan cheese, and 1 teaspoon Worcestershire sauce.

GINGER-SOY MEATBALLS
Add 3 tablespoons soy sauce, 3 tablespoons rice wine vinegar, 2 chopped scallions, and 2 teaspoons finely minced peeled fresh ginger.

Grilled Two-Cheese Burgers with Garlic Dressing

This recipe is my way of dressing up a burger without sacrificing what we all love: its juicy beefiness. My perfect burger keeps the patty simple and then gets to the bells and whistles—the sauces, fresh herbs, two cheeses, and extra stuff—on top. The herby taste of this creamy garlic sauce is pure magic! Of course you can also grill the burgers on a stovetop grill pan with fantastic results.

● ● ●

serves 4

preparation time:
35 minutes

cooking time:
10 minutes

deals, dollars & sense: best burger meat

Don't assume that leaner ground beef is better just because it is more expensive. For burgers, 80 percent lean ground beef is my top choice for juicy, flavorful results. I love it when my first-choice ingredient is also one of the cheapest!

for the sauce

- ½ cup mayonnaise
- 3 tablespoons sour cream
- 3 tablespoons roughly chopped fresh basil (or chives, parsley, or mint)
- 1 scallion (white and green parts), trimmed and roughly chopped
- 1 garlic clove, quartered
- ½ teaspoon Worcestershire sauce
- ¼ teaspoon kosher salt
- ¼ teaspoon ground black pepper

for the burgers

- 1¼ pounds 80% lean ground beef
- 1 tablespoon vegetable oil
- ¾ teaspoon kosher salt
- ½ teaspoon ground black pepper
- ¼ cup shredded mozzarella cheese

1 **To make the sauce:** Place the mayonnaise, sour cream, basil, scallion, garlic, Worcestershire sauce, salt, and pepper in the bowl of a food processor and purée until creamy and pale green. Transfer to a small bowl, cover with plastic wrap, and refrigerate until you are ready to use it.

2 **To make the burgers:** Heat a charcoal or gas grill to medium-high. Divide the ground beef into 4 equal pieces and gently form into patties. Use your thumb to make a small indentation in the middle of each burger (this is so the burger grills flat and doesn't contract and puff up on the grill). Brush both sides of the burgers with the oil and then season with salt and pepper.

recipe continues

3 Place the burgers on the grill and cook until they have grill marks, about 4 minutes. Flip the burgers, cook 2 minutes longer, and then top each with about 1 tablespoon of the mozzarella. Cook the burgers 2 more minutes for medium-rare doneness and remove from the grill. Place the buns on the grill, cut side down, and lightly toast, 30 seconds to 1 minute.

4 Set a burger on each bottom bun half. Top with a salted tomato slice. Spread 1 tablespoon of the garlic-herb sauce on the top bun half, sprinkle with Parmesan, cover the burger, and serve with more sauce on the side for dipping.

4 hamburger buns

1 tomato, cored, thinly sliced, and lightly salted

2 tablespoons grated Parmesan cheese

Simple Sirloin Steak with Shallot Butter

This recipe proves that you can eat an honest steak dinner even if you are a budget-driven food shopper. Sirloin is affordable even when not on sale and downright cheap when on sale. It's flavorful on its own, but adding shallot butter elevates it to a high-end flavor profile. You can also slice the steak, fan it on a plate, and drizzle with chimichurri sauce (page 154) for an equally delicious yet quite different take on sirloin.

● ● ●

serves 4

preparation time:
20 minutes (plus 1 hour, 10 minutes to chill and rest)

cooking time:
6 minutes

for the butter

8 tablespoons unsalted butter, at room temperature

1 small shallot, finely chopped, or 2 garlic cloves, finely minced or pressed through a garlic press

1½ tablespoons finely chopped fresh herbs (basil, chives, cilantro, flat-leaf parsley, tarragon, or thyme)

for the steak

2 10- to 12-ounce sirloin steaks

1 teaspoon kosher salt

½ teaspoon ground black pepper

2 tablespoons vegetable oil

**deals, dollars & sense:
getting the most out of your steak**

For a great steak, let it sit at room temperature before cooking, don't overcook it, and let it rest after cooking. Don't be tempted to skip this final step; the impact of resting is huge.

1 **To make the shallot butter:** Place the butter in a medium bowl and stir in the shallot and herbs. Transfer the butter to the center of a piece of plastic wrap and tightly fold it around the butter. Roll the plastic-wrapped butter into a log and refrigerate for 1 hour to 2 days (or freeze for up to 1 month).

2 **To make the steak:** Set the steaks on a cutting board and slice them in half crosswise so you have 4 steaks. Using your knife, round out the clean-cut edges so the sides look softer. Use paper towels to pat dry both sides of the steaks, then season all over with the salt and pepper. Set the steaks aside for 15 to 30 minutes to come to room temperature.

3 Heat a grill pan over medium-high heat. Brush both sides of each steak with vegetable oil and place it in the pan, letting it cook without moving it for 3 minutes. Flip the

recipe continues

steaks over and for medium-rare cook until the steaks are 125°F. (the steaks will continue to cook as they rest). Transfer the steaks to 4 plates.

4 Unwrap the butter log and slice off 2 to 3 thin pieces. Place them on top of each steak and let the steaks rest for 5 to 10 minutes (the butter will melt over the steaks) before serving.

dry-aging at home

Dry-aging meat is a great technique to concentrate the beefy flavor of a steak or roast. Doing it yourself won't cost you a pretty penny, though dry-aged meat will if you buy it from a butcher shop. Here's how to dry-age:

1. Place the steaks or roast on a rack (so air can circulate around the meat) set over a rimmed sheet pan.

2. Leave in the refrigerator at least 3 to 4 days.

3. Slice off any hard, dried bits on the surface before cooking.

working the plate

You know the saying "you eat with your eyes"? I like to think that you save with your eyes, too—if you're smart about how you plate your food. For visual volume and psychological satisfaction, I thinly slice meat—steak, chicken breast, boneless pork roast—then fan it out on the plate. It covers more of the plate's surface area while allowing you to stretch out less meat.

Since the plate is visually abundant, the portion seems incredibly satisfying and you get more mileage, ounce per ounce. Of course this way of presenting meat is healthier, too, since you're not eating as much meat as you would if you were sitting down to a giant portion.

Another way I achieve visual bulk is to fill the plate with a sauce or side made using cheaper ingredients—creamy white beans (page 246) or a simple side dish of sautéed spinach (page 235) gives more heft to the presentation. I don't want to look at a plate and feel deprived—instead I feel like I'm treating myself and my family to a great and indulgent meal.

French-Cut Steak with Caramelized Onions

I love creating meals inspired by Parisian bistros, and this is a play off one of my favorite steak dishes, bavette aux eschallotes. I substitute a moderately priced yet flavorful skirt steak and go for buttery and deeply caramelized onions instead of the pricey shallots. It's one of my favorite ways to eat steak without breaking the bank.

serves 4

preparation time:
10 minutes (plus 15 minutes to marinate)

cooking time:
35 minutes

1 teaspoon sweet paprika

½ teaspoon onion powder

½ teaspoon garlic powder

1¼ teaspoons kosher salt

½ teaspoon plus a pinch of ground black pepper

1 pound skirt steak, halved crosswise

4 tablespoons unsalted butter

2 tablespoons vegetable oil

2 sweet onions, such as Maui or Vidalia, halved and thinly sliced

⅓ cup dry white wine

2 tablespoons red wine vinegar

⅓ cup beef broth

1 Mix the paprika, onion powder, garlic powder, 1 teaspoon of the salt, and ½ teaspoon of the pepper together in a small bowl. Sprinkle the mixture over both sides of the steak, then place the steak on a large plate and set aside for 15 minutes.

2 Meanwhile, melt 1 tablespoon of the butter with 1 tablespoon of the oil in a large skillet over low heat. Once the butter is melted, add the onions and cook, stirring occasionally, until soft, caramelized, and golden brown, about 20 minutes. Transfer the onions to a bowl and set aside.

3 Wipe the pan with a paper towel and melt 1 more tablespoon of the butter with the remaining 1 tablespoon oil over high heat. Add the steaks and sear until nicely browned, about 3 minutes on each side for medium-rare doneness. Transfer the steaks to a cutting board and loosely tent with aluminum foil.

4 Pour the wine and vinegar into the pan and simmer until reduced by half, about 2 minutes. Return the onions to the pan with the broth and simmer until reduced by half, about 4 minutes. Add the remaining ¼ teaspoon salt and pinch of pepper, turn off the heat, and whisk in the remaining 2 tablespoons butter. Slice the steak into thin pieces, divide among 4 plates, and serve with the onions and sauce.

vegetables

As a Main or a Side

I like to start my meal planning in the produce aisle because that's where many of the best bargains in the supermarket are.

A lot of people think if you want to save money, you have to skip the fresh vegetables, but it's not true. If you avoid the high-end purchases, like asparagus flown in from South America in January, you almost can't break the bank in the produce aisle. My strategy is to load up with what's on sale in the supermarket weekly flyer (don't forget to check the organic section for deals) and then fill in the blanks with the rest of the produce.

In the produce aisle, the laws of supply and demand work in your favor. If there is factory overstock, the factory in this case being Mother Nature, the price goes down. Overstock happens on a seasonal basis—for instance, ten ears of sweet summer corn for $1—and of course vegetables taste their best when they're in season. It's one of the few times when cheaper is better. You've got to love that! In this chapter you'll find a ton of ways to take advantage of the produce department, whether you choose to feature veggies as an inexpensive main course or a side dish.

Bulgur-Stuffed Veggies

This recipe relies on a farmer's market mentality and is inspired by beautiful and bountiful vegetables that are available and in season. Just about any vegetable that can be made into a cup for holding the bulgur works, such as tomatoes, peppers, portobello mushroom caps, cabbage leaves, eggplant halves, onions, and summer squash. I stuff vegetables with nutty, toothsome bulgur because it stays fluffy and has a nice texture, even when compressed into a vegetable. That said, brown rice, millet, and quinoa can all stand in for the bulgur if you prefer.

● ● ● ● ○

**serves 4 as a main dish;
8 as a side dish**

preparation time:
35 minutes (plus 20 minutes to rest)

cooking time:
1 hour, 15 minutes

  1 cup bulgur

1¼ cups chicken broth

  2 bell peppers (preferably 1 red and 1 yellow)

  2 zucchini (or 1 zucchini and 1 yellow summer squash)

  2 large tomatoes

  2 tablespoons olive oil

  1 small onion, finely chopped

  ¼ pound white button mushrooms, finely chopped

  3 garlic cloves, finely minced or pressed through a garlic press

  1 teaspoon kosher salt

  ½ teaspoon ground black pepper

  2 teaspoons fresh tarragon, finely chopped

  ¼ cup grated Parmesan cheese

1 Preheat the oven to 350°F. Place the bulgur in a large heatproof bowl. Pour the broth into a medium saucepan, add 1½ cups water, bring to a boil, and then pour over the bulgur. Cover the bowl with plastic wrap and set aside until the bulgur is tender, about 20 minutes.

2 Meanwhile, prepare the vegetables. Slice off the top third of the bell peppers, cut out the stems, and then finely chop the flesh; set aside for later. Use your fingers or a paring knife to remove the ribs and seeds from the bottom of each pepper to make a cup that will hold the stuffing.

3 Halve the zucchini crosswise. Finely chop half of the zucchini and slice the other half lengthwise, then use a teaspoon to scoop out the seeds so you have a boat. Halve the tomatoes crosswise and use a spoon to remove the seeds from the bottom and top to make 4 cups.

recipe continues

4   Heat the olive oil in a large skillet over medium heat. Add the onion and cook until it softens and becomes translucent, 3 to 4 minutes. Add the reserved chopped bell peppers and zucchini, mushrooms, and garlic to the pan, season with ¾ teaspoon of the salt and ¼ teaspoon of the black pepper, and cook until the vegetables are tender, about 10 minutes. If there is a lot of liquid in the pan, drain the vegetables in a fine-mesh sieve before proceeding. If there is remaining liquid in the bowl with the bulgur, drain the bulgur in a fine-mesh sieve and return to the bowl along with the sautéed vegetables. Stir in the tarragon.

5   Place the pepper and tomato cups and zucchini boats on a cutting board. Season the inside of the vegetables with the remaining ¼ teaspoon salt and ¼ teaspoon black pepper and then stuff the vegetables with the bulgur mixture until filled to their rims. Carefully transfer the vegetables to a 13 × 9-inch baking dish, cover with aluminum foil, and bake for 45 minutes. Remove the foil, sprinkle with the Parmesan, and bake until the cheese is browned, about 10 minutes longer. Serve warm or at room temperature.

Easy Peasy Frozen Peas

Along with spinach, peas are one of my must-have freezer staples—I always have a bag on hand. They are so versatile. You can serve them as a side dish or use them as an ingredient in pasta, soup, or rice, or even use just a tablespoon or two as a garnish to finish a dish. Since they stay individually frozen, you can take out as much or as little as you need without thawing the whole bag at once. In this recipe, I combine peas with simple everyday pantry ingredients: olive oil, lemon, and black pepper for a side dish that takes ten minutes to make and is as comfy with meat loaf as it is with fresh fish.

serves 4

preparation time:
2 minutes

cooking time:
8 minutes

 1 tablespoon olive oil
    Zest and juice of ½ lemon
¼ teaspoon ground black pepper
10 ounces frozen peas
½ teaspoon kosher salt

1 Pour the olive oil into a large skillet and add the lemon zest and pepper. Turn the heat to medium-high and cook the lemon zest and pepper, stirring occasionally, until sizzling and fragrant, 2 to 3 minutes.

2 Add the peas and salt to the pan and stir to coat the peas. Cover the pan and cook until the peas are tender and warmed through, 4 to 5 minutes, stirring halfway through. Toss with the lemon juice and serve warm.

Fennel-Onion Quiche

Quiche should definitely be in the budget cook's mealtime rotation. Eggs are a fantastic source of protein and are so affordable. Even at their most expensive, eggs are still usually cheaper than any meat you'll find, even if the meat is on sale. Quiche is one of my hip-pocket recipes. It's easy, elegant, inexpensive, and so versatile. Be sure to check out ten variations for this quiche on page 209.

● ● ●

serves 4 as a main dish

preparation time:
20 minutes (plus 10 minutes to cool)

cooking time:
60 minutes

1 sheet thawed puff pastry, from a 17.3-ounce box

4 tablespoons unsalted butter

1 fennel bulb, fronds reserved, cored, halved, and finely chopped

1 onion, halved and finely chopped

½ teaspoon kosher salt

¼ teaspoon ground black pepper

2 garlic cloves, finely minced or pressed through a garlic press

3 large eggs

1 cup whole milk

½ cup grated Swiss cheese (about 4 ounces)

deals, dollars & sense: puff pastry

A lot of people are intimidated by puff pastry, but I encourage you to think of it as one of the world's most wonderful convenience foods. True, it will cost you a couple bucks a sheet, but it's a quick way to turn inexpensive ingredients into something special. The money that you invest really elevates even the simplest pantry staples such as eggs, lunch meat, and vegetables into impressive turnovers, tarts, pot pies, and quiche.

1 Preheat the oven to 350°F. Place a 9-inch deep-dish pie plate on your work surface. Unfold the sheet of puff pastry and place it floured side down on a cutting board. Use a rolling pin to lightly roll it until it is just under ¼ inch thick and big enough to easily fit into the pie plate. Fit the pastry into the corners, trimming any edges that hang over the sides of the plate. Crimp the edges and set aside.

2 Melt 2 tablespoons of the butter in a large skillet over medium-low heat. Add the fennel, onion, salt, and pepper and cook, stirring occasionally, until very soft and barely golden, about 10 minutes. Stir in the garlic and cook until fragrant, about 1 minute. Turn off the heat and set aside.

3 Whisk the eggs and milk together in a large bowl. Scrape the fennel mixture into the eggs, add the cheese, and whisk to combine. Pour the egg mixture into the prepared pie plate and arrange the filling so the fennel and onions are evenly dispersed.

4 Set the pie plate on a rimmed sheet pan and bake the quiche until the edges of the quiche are firm, the center is set, and the crust is golden brown, 45 to 50 minutes. Cool for 10 minutes before slicing and serving. The quiche is great warm or at room temperature.

quiche, *10* ways

Quiche is one of my favorite go-to anytime pantry recipes because it can really be made on the fly with whatever you have in the fridge. Start with 3 eggs, 1 cup milk or cream, and add:

1. Chopped crispy bacon, sautéed zucchini, and Parmesan cheese

2. Leftover roasted cauliflower, chopped scallions, and Gouda cheese

3. Diced deli ham, sautéed mushrooms, and Swiss cheese

4. Sautéed red onions, halved grape tomatoes, and crumbled blue cheese

5. Crumbled cooked meat loaf or burgers tossed with salsa and Cheddar cheese

6. Chopped crispy bacon, chopped spinach, sautéed mushrooms, and Swiss cheese

7. Chopped roasted red peppers, sautéed onions with rosemary, and Fontina cheese

8. Diced deli ham, sautéed bell peppers, sautéed onions, and pepper Jack cheese

9. Chopped salami, sautéed onions, and mozzarella cheese

10. Tomatoes, basil, grated fresh mozzarella cheese, and Parmesan cheese

Veggie Moussaka

Between college and graduate school, I worked on a cruise ship in the Greek islands. The off-boat excursions were the best—there really is nothing quite like riding a donkey up the steep trails to the tip-top of the island of Santorini. Besides the stunning view, the big payoff was the moussaka I ate there. Moussaka is like a Greek lasagne that uses eggplant slices instead of noodles for layering. It is often made with ground beef or lamb but this version is vegetarian, so for a meaty texture I use mushrooms. In a pinch, you could use a jarred marinara instead of the mushroom sauce. This is a great make-ahead dish.

● ● ● ●

serves 4 (plus leftovers) as a main dish; 8 as a side dish

preparation time:
45 minutes (plus 10 minutes to cool)

cooking time:
1 hour, 35 minutes

for the moussaka

- 2 tablespoons olive oil, plus extra for greasing the baking sheet and baking dish
- 2 red potatoes, thinly sliced
- 1 tablespoon plus ½ teaspoon kosher salt
- 1 small eggplant, trimmed and cut into ¼-inch-thick rounds
- ¼ teaspoon ground black pepper
- 1 cup finely grated Parmesan cheese

1 **To make the moussaka:** Preheat the oven to 400°F. Grease a rimmed baking sheet with a little olive oil and set aside.

2 Bring a large pot of water to a boil. Add the potatoes and 1 tablespoon of the salt and cook until the potatoes are parboiled, about 5 minutes. Drain and set aside.

3 Place the eggplant in a medium bowl and toss with 1 tablespoon of the olive oil, the remaining ½ teaspoon salt, and the pepper. Set the slices on the prepared baking sheet and roast until the underside is golden, 6 to 7 minutes. Turn over the slices and roast until the other side is golden, an additional 6 to 7 minutes. Remove the eggplant from the oven, reduce the temperature to 350°F., and set the eggplant aside.

4 **To make the mushroom sauce:** Heat the olive oil in a large skillet over medium heat. Add the onion and salt and cook, stirring often, until soft, about 5 minutes. Stir in the mushrooms and cook, stirring occasionally, until they start to brown, 6 to 7 minutes. Mix in the garlic, oregano, cinnamon, and nutmeg and cook until the garlic is fragrant, about 1 minute. Raise the heat to high and pour in the wine, stirring and scraping any browned bits off the bottom of the pan. Let the wine reduce for 1 minute and then stir in the tomato sauce. Reduce the heat and gently simmer, stirring occasionally, until the sauce thickens, about 5 minutes. Turn off the heat and set aside.

5 To make the béchamel: Heat the milk in the microwave or in a saucepan until warm and set aside. Melt the butter in a large saucepan over medium heat. Whisk in the flour to make a paste and cook, whisking constantly, until the paste bubbles and turns a light golden brown, about 2 minutes. Slowly whisk in about 1 cup of the warm milk a little at a time to avoid lumps. Once the mixture is thick and creamy, slowly whisk in the remaining 2 cups milk. Once the sauce begins to bubble, reduce the heat to low and cook, stirring often, until thick, about 10 minutes. Stir in the nutmeg, salt, and pepper, turn off the heat, and set aside.

6 To assemble and bake the moussaka: Grease a 13 × 9-inch baking dish with olive oil. Lightly grease the matte side of a long sheet of aluminum foil with oil and set aside.

7 Taste the vegetables, the mushroom sauce, and the béchamel and season with more salt and pepper if needed. Place the potato slices flat in the pan, lightly pressing them into the corners and sides. Sprinkle with ¼ cup of the Parmesan. Lay the eggplant slices on top of the potatoes and sprinkle with another ¼ cup of the Parmesan. Scrape the mushroom mixture over the vegetables and top with another ¼ cup of the Parmesan. Finish with the béchamel and the remaining ¼ cup Parmesan.

8 Place the greased aluminum foil over the baking dish, crimping the edges to seal. Place the baking dish on a sheet pan and bake the moussaka for 30 minutes. Then uncover and bake until bubbly and golden brown, about 30 minutes more. Cool for 10 minutes before slicing and serving.

for the mushroom sauce

- 1 tablespoon olive oil
- 1 onion, finely chopped
- ¼ teaspoon kosher salt
- ¾ pound mushrooms, trimmed and finely chopped
- 3 garlic cloves, finely minced or pressed through a garlic press
- 2 teaspoons dried oregano
- ½ teaspoon ground cinnamon
- ½ teaspoon ground nutmeg
- ½ cup dry red wine
- 8 ounces canned tomato sauce

for the béchamel

- 3 cups whole milk
- 5 tablespoons unsalted butter
- 5 tablespoons all-purpose flour
- ⅛ teaspoon ground nutmeg
- ¾ teaspoon kosher salt
- ¼ teaspoon ground black pepper

Black Bean "Nacho" Burgers

I'm lucky to have my sister and her family just a few doors down from me, and we love getting together for big meals. I'm always on the hunt for creative vegetarian main courses because my nephew doesn't eat meat. The trick is to find something that not only satisfies him but will keep the rest of our brood happy, too. These burgers are a hit—they're cheesy and toasty and have great texture thanks to tortilla chips, and they don't cost an arm and a leg to make. In fact, this recipe made with beef instead of beans would be twice the price.

● ● ○ ○ ○ ○

serves 4 as a main dish

preparation time:
25 minutes (plus 30 minutes to chill)

cooking time:
12 minutes

2 cups cooked black beans

1 cup finely crushed tortilla chips (preferably blue corn chips)

½ cup salsa, plus extra for serving

½ cup grated Cheddar cheese

1 large egg, lightly beaten

1 scallion (white and green parts), trimmed and finely chopped

¼ teaspoon kosher salt

¼ teaspoon ground black pepper

4 hamburger buns

3 tablespoons vegetable oil

Sour cream, for serving (optional)

1. Use a food processor or potato masher to smash the beans in a large bowl until you have a rough-textured and chunky mixture with a few semi-whole beans left. Stir in the tortilla chips, salsa, cheese, egg, scallion, salt, and pepper. Set the mixture aside for 10 minutes to allow the chips to absorb some of the liquid, then shape into 4 patties.

2. Place the patties on a plate, cover with plastic wrap, and refrigerate for at least 30 minutes or overnight.

3. Preheat the oven to 350°F. Place the buns on a baking sheet and place in the oven until warm to the touch, 4 to 6 minutes. While the buns warm, heat 2 tablespoons of the oil in a large nonstick skillet over medium heat. Set the burgers in the pan and cook until golden brown, 4 to 5 minutes. Flip the burgers, add the remaining 1 tablespoon oil, and cook until the other side is golden, 4 to 5 minutes. Turn off the heat and serve the burgers topped with salsa and sour cream (if using) on the warmed buns.

Roasted Eggplant, Onion, and Tomato Tian

This stunning vegetable side dish is all about celebrating the simple flavors of the Mediterranean. Rubbing the baking dish with garlic imparts the slightest hint of garlic (a trick I learned from my mother-in-law; it's a very south-of-France thing to do) to flavor the vegetables without having a strong garlic taste. It's a beautiful dish to serve company, and its ease of preparation gives it weekday night dinner potential, too. This is one of my favorite potluck dishes because it travels so nicely. If eggplant is pricey, swap it for thinly sliced zucchini instead (though there's no need to precook).

● ●

serves 4

preparation time:
15 minutes

cooking time:
35 minutes

- 2 tablespoons olive oil
- 1 small eggplant, trimmed and sliced ¼ inch thick
- ¾ teaspoon kosher salt
- 2 small onions, sliced into ¼-inch-thick rounds
- 1 garlic clove, smashed
- 2 small plum tomatoes, sliced into ¼-inch-thick rounds
- ¼ cup grated Parmesan cheese

1 Preheat the oven to 375°F. Heat 1 tablespoon olive oil in a large skillet over medium-high heat. Add the eggplant, sprinkle with ¼ teaspoon salt, and cook until golden brown on both sides, 4 to 5 minutes total. Transfer the eggplant to a plate and set aside.

2 Pour 2 teaspoons of olive oil into the skillet and add the onions. Season with ¼ teaspoon salt and cook until soft and just starting to brown, about 2 minutes. Slide a spatula under the onions and turn them over to brown the other side, about 2 minutes. Transfer to a plate and set aside.

3 Rub the smashed garlic clove all over the interior of a 9½-inch deep-dish pie plate. Alternate adding an onion round, then an eggplant slice, then a tomato slice. Repeat, working your way around the edge of the pan first and then repeat with a smaller circle in the middle of the pan to create two concentric circles. Sprinkle with the remaining ¼ teaspoon salt and drizzle with the remaining 1 teaspoon olive oil.

4 Cover the baking dish with aluminum foil and bake until the vegetables are heated through and the tomatoes are soft but still hold their shape, about 20 minutes. Remove the baking dish and turn the broiler to high. Sprinkle the tomatoes with the Parmesan and broil to melt and brown the cheese, about 2 minutes. Remove from the oven and serve warm or at room temperature.

Fennel and Cabbage Slaw

For this slaw, I use this strategy: stretch a somewhat expensive ingredient, such as fennel, with a less expensive ingredient, cabbage. The fennel's feathery fronds are great used like an herb, whether in this slaw or in any dish to which you might add chives or dill. For the sweetest cabbage flavor, use a freshly bought head. To boost the fennel flavor even more, add 1 teaspoon smashed fennel seeds to the dressing.

● ●

serves 4 (plus leftovers)

preparation time:
10 minutes

cooking time:
8 minutes

- 2 bacon strips, chopped
- 1 fennel bulb, fronds removed and reserved, bulb cored, quartered, and thinly sliced
- 1 cup thinly sliced red cabbage
- 2 scallions (white and green parts), trimmed and finely chopped
- ¼ cup mayonnaise
- Zest of ½ orange
- 3 tablespoons red wine vinegar
- 1 teaspoon sugar
- ¼ teaspoon kosher salt
- ½ teaspoon ground black pepper

deals, dollars & sense: orange rind

Next time you grab an orange for a snack, peel the skin and freeze it in a resealable freezer bag. You can use it for zest another time; just use a little extra since the essential oils in the peel do lose a bit of their aromatic punch once frozen. I like to think of it as free flavor.

1 Place the bacon in a medium nonstick skillet over medium heat. Cook until browned and very crisp, while stirring often, 6 to 8 minutes total. Transfer the bacon to a paper towel–lined plate to cool and then transfer to a large bowl.

2 Add the fennel, cabbage, and scallions to the bacon and toss to combine. In a small bowl, whisk the mayonnaise, orange zest, vinegar, sugar, salt, and pepper together and pour over the vegetables. Toss to coat and serve.

Can Organic Produce Be a Good Value?

Ten Dollar Dinners is all about purposeful spending—getting the best price for what you want. Even organic produce can be a good value if you follow these tips:

- Check the organic section of the produce aisle for weekly specials; the on-sale organic produce will often be cheaper than regular-price conventional fruits and vegetables.

- Prioritize and buy the organic items that are most important to you (for example, banana peels and anything they may be sprayed with gets removed before eating, so organic bananas fall low on my list).

- Don't forget the freezer section where frozen organic fruits and vegetables often go on sale (coupon cutters: note that unlike fresh produce, organic frozen produce manufacturers often print coupons).

Roasted Broccoli with Parmesan Cheese

Roasting broccoli really brings out its sweetness. Add some grated Parmesan cheese and it becomes a crave-worthy side dish. People often throw away the stems of broccoli, but instead give them a two-second trim with the vegetable peeler and they become wonderfully tender and delicious. I keep them attached to the florets and trim the broccoli into long and lanky trees. The broccoli looks more elegant that way, plus my kids think it's fun to eat "trees" for dinner! Preheating the pan gives the broccoli a boost to help it caramelize right from the start and prevents the crowns from drying out.

● ● ● ● ●

serves 4

preparation time:
10 minutes

cooking time:
15 minutes

1 head broccoli

2 tablespoons olive oil

½ teaspoon kosher salt

¼ teaspoon ground black pepper

2 tablespoons grated Parmesan cheese

1 Place a rimmed baking dish on the oven's middle rack. Preheat the oven to 400°F.

2 Place the broccoli on a cutting board. Use a vegetable peeler to peel away the tough outer skin of the stalk, then halve the broccoli lengthwise. Slice each broccoli half into 3 or 4 long "trees," keeping the florets attached to the stalk.

3 Arrange the broccoli in a single layer, cut side down, in the prepared baking dish and drizzle with the olive oil. Season with the salt and pepper and place in the oven to roast until the sides start to brown, about 10 minutes. Remove the pan from the oven and turn over the broccoli. Sprinkle with the grated Parmesan and cook until the cheese melts, about 5 minutes. Transfer to a platter and serve hot.

deals, dollars & sense: hearty vegetables

When you shop for produce, it's a smart tactic to buy a few hearty vegetables along with the more fragile ones. Long-lasting veggies like broccoli and carrots keep well in the crisper, ensuring you always have a vegetable on hand even at the end of the week. Use up the more fragile veggies, such as salad greens and mushrooms, first.

Steamed Broccoli with Garlic Aïoli

When I feel like I've been overindulging, my go-to feel-good food is steamed broccoli with a small dish of mayonnaise on the side for dipping. For years my husband thought I was nuts! Then I started making homemade garlic mayonnaise, also known as aïoli, and now he's in my camp. The flavor of the broccoli and dipping it in the garlicky mayo reminds me of eating artichokes—but I'm spending a whole lot less and getting a lot more vegetable in every bite. This is a side dish, but feel free to serve it my way on a big plate for snacking.

serves 4

preparation time:
20 minutes

cooking time:
5 minutes

- 1 large egg yolk
- 1 teaspoon lemon zest plus 1 tablespoon fresh lemon juice
- 1 teaspoon Dijon mustard
- ¾ cup vegetable oil
- 1 garlic clove, finely minced or pressed through a garlic press
- ¼ teaspoon kosher salt, plus 1 tablespoon for the cooking water
- Pinch of ground black pepper
- 1 large head broccoli, ends trimmed, stalks peeled

1 In a mini food processor or blender, combine the egg yolk, lemon juice, and mustard until smooth (you can also whisk the ingredients together in a medium bowl). With the machine running, begin adding the oil a few drops at a time through the food chute. Once you have added about ¼ cup, you can add the remaining oil in a slow stream (if mixing by hand, add the oil just a few drops at a time, while whisking vigorously, until all of the oil is added and the mixture is creamy). When the mixture is thick and creamy, transfer it to a medium bowl and whisk in the garlic, lemon zest, ¼ teaspoon of the salt, and the pepper. Cover the bowl with plastic wrap and refrigerate.

2 Place the broccoli on a cutting board and slice it into long "trees." Fill a large skillet with 1 inch of water, add 1 tablespoon of the salt, and bring it to a simmer over high heat. Add the broccoli trees, cover, reduce the heat to medium-low, and cook until the broccoli is al dente, 3 to 4 minutes (if you prefer your broccoli more tender, cook for an extra 1 to 2 minutes).

3 Use tongs to remove the broccoli from the pan, gently shaking off any liquid. Serve hot or at room temperature with the chilled aïoli on the side for dipping.

Sweet Zucchini Sauté

This recipe comes from my mother-in-law, who used sweet sautéed zucchini to get my husband to eat his vegetables when he was a kid. It's simple and flexible—the zucchini can be cooked for longer or for less time and served warm or at room temperature. Whenever the rest of your meal is ready, this will be ready, too. The sweetness of the onion absolutely makes the dish. Try it and you'll understand why kids (of all ages) eat it up.

● ● ● ● ●

serves 4

preparation time:
10 minutes

cooking time:
35 minutes

- 3 tablespoons olive oil, plus extra if needed
- 2 medium onions, halved and thinly sliced
- 1 teaspoon kosher salt
- 3 large zucchini, trimmed and halved lengthwise, thinly sliced into half circles
- 1 teaspoon herbes de Provence or ½ teaspoon dried basil plus ½ teaspoon dried oregano or marjoram
- ½ teaspoon ground black pepper

Heat the oil in a large skillet over medium-high heat. Add the onions and ½ teaspoon of the salt and cook, stirring often to avoid browning, until they're just starting to soften, 2 to 3 minutes. Add the zucchini, herbes de Provence, the remaining ½ teaspoon salt, and the pepper and cook, stirring often, until it starts to brown, about 5 minutes. Reduce the heat to low, add a little oil if the pan looks dry, and cook, stirring occasionally, until very soft, 20 to 25 minutes. Turn off the heat and serve warm or at room temperature.

Provençal Tomatoes

Whenever I make this stunning and tasty side dish, it always brings me back to Coudoux, the tiny village near Aix-en-Provence, where my husband grew up. This simple and fast dish is a celebration of summer tomatoes. The best time to make it is when plum tomatoes are at their sweet peak, readily available, and also at their cheapest.

● ○ ○ ○ ○ ○

serves 4

preparation time:
10 minutes

cooking time:
10 minutes

4 plum tomatoes, halved lengthwise

½ teaspoon kosher salt

¼ teaspoon ground black pepper

3 tablespoons olive oil

2 garlic cloves, finely minced or pressed through a garlic press

1 teaspoon herbes de Provence or ½ teaspoon dried basil plus ½ teaspoon dried oregano or marjoram

¼ cup plain bread crumbs

1 Place the tomatoes on a cutting board, cut side up, and season with the salt and pepper. Heat 2 tablespoons of the olive oil in a medium skillet and add the tomatoes, skin side down, to the pan and cook until the bottoms start to soften, about 3 minutes. Flip the tomatoes and cook 2 more minutes, then gently slide a spatula under each one and transfer, cut side up, to an aluminum foil–lined baking sheet. Set aside.

2 Pour the remaining 1 tablespoon oil into the pan, add the garlic, and cook until fragrant, about 1 minute. Add the herbes de Provence and bread crumbs and cook, stirring constantly, until the bread crumbs are fragrant and well coated with the oil, about 2 minutes. Remove from the heat.

3 Adjust an oven rack to the upper-middle position and preheat the broiler to high. Divide the bread crumbs over the tomato halves and broil until golden, 30 seconds to 1 minute (watch your broiler closely; broiler intensity varies). Serve hot or at room temperature.

Roasted Radishes and Carrots

I roast a ton of vegetables. In the oven, the sharp crunch of radishes transforms into a mellow, tender, and earthy-sweet bite. An extra bonus is that they roast up pretty and pink, which my four daughters love! I like to leave a little of the green tops on the radish to give them a fresh-from-the-garden look. Paired with carrots, this is a very elegant and beautiful side dish. I often have baby-cut carrots in the crisper to eat as a fast snack—if you are more likely to have full-size carrots, peel and trim them into 2-inch lengths and use those instead.

● ○ ○ ○ ○ ○

serves 4

preparation time:
5 minutes

cooking time:
20 minutes

12 baby-cut carrots

Bunch of radishes (about 12), trimmed (halved if large)

1 tablespoon olive oil

2 teaspoons finely chopped fresh thyme or 1 teaspoon dried plus a squeeze of lemon juice

½ teaspoon kosher salt

¼ teaspoon ground black pepper

½ lemon

deals, dollars & sense: dried thyme

Dried thyme is grassier than fresh, so when using dried thyme, add a squeeze of citrus. When making the substitution, remember to reduce the amount of thyme by half—so for every teaspoon of fresh thyme called for, use half as much dried thyme.

Preheat the oven to 450°F. Place the carrots and radishes in a 9-inch baking dish and toss to coat with the olive oil, thyme, salt, and pepper. Roast until they're tender on the outside with a slightly firm core, about 20 minutes. Remove from the oven, squeeze the lemon over the top, and serve.

Braised Escarole with Olives and Parmesan Cheese

Braising greens is a habit I'd love everyone to enjoy. Greens are so inexpensive and you can get a lot of great varieties, such as kale and escarole, in the winter when other vegetables are more expensive. The olives add a briny saltiness that balances out the richness of the Parmesan, the hint of pepper, and the lemon—it's so delicious. This is a great starter greens recipe for anyone because escarole cooks up nice and tender and has a very mild flavor.

● ●

serves 4

preparation time:
10 minutes

cooking time:
20 minutes

½ cup pitted kalamata olives

2 tablespoons olive oil

3 garlic cloves, finely minced or pressed through a garlic press

⅛ teaspoon crushed red pepper flakes

1 head escarole, sliced crosswise into ½-inch strips

½ cup chicken broth or water

Zest and juice of 1 lemon, plus 1 lemon sliced into wedges for serving

3 tablespoons grated Parmesan cheese

1 Place the olives on a cutting board, smash with the side of a knife, and then roughly chop. Set aside. Heat the olive oil in a large, deep skillet over medium heat. Add the garlic and red pepper flakes and cook, stirring often, until the garlic is fragrant, about 1 minute. Add the olives and escarole and cook, stirring often, until the escarole starts to wilt, 2 to 3 minutes.

2 Stir in the broth and lemon zest and juice, and cover. Reduce the heat to low and cook until the escarole is tender, about 10 minutes. Remove the lid, raise the heat to high, and simmer the escarole until the liquid in the pan is reduced by one quarter, 1 to 2 minutes. Serve warm sprinkled with Parmesan and with a lemon wedge on the side.

Creamy Celery with Savory Pecan Granola Crumble

I'm always looking for ways to use up those few stalks of celery that seem to linger in the crisper drawer. This recipe is great because the celery isn't just an ingredient—it's the dish! I cook the celery until it's tender and then bake it in a wonderfully creamy béchamel sauce that gets a hint of nuttiness from Parmesan cheese. The crunchy and buttery pecan granola on top is like bread crumbs brought to a whole new level. It also works beautifully sprinkled over any kind of vegetable gratin or as a nice textural counterpoint to a pan-seared fish fillet.

● ● ● ● ● ●

serves 4

preparation time:
10 minutes (plus 5 minutes to cool)

cooking time:
35 minutes

for the pecan crumble

- 3 tablespoons plain bread crumbs
- 3 tablespoons old-fashioned rolled oats
- 3 tablespoons chopped pecans
- ½ teaspoon kosher salt
- ¼ teaspoon ground black pepper
- 2 tablespoons softened unsalted butter

deals, dollars & sense: savory granola

I like to make an unsweetened version of granola to add a nutty crunch to savory dishes. Here are some ways I like to use it:

- Sprinkled on top of fish before baking.
- Sprinkled over baked pasta during the last 10 minutes of cooking.
- Used in place of bread crumbs.
- Baked and tossed into a simple green salad.
- Mixed with herbs and sprinkled over steamed vegetables.

1 Preheat the oven to 375°F. Coat the bottom and edges of a small 1-quart baking dish with nonstick pan spray and set aside.

2 **To make the pecan crumble:** Stir the bread crumbs, oats, pecans, salt, and pepper together in a small bowl. Add the butter and use a fork to stir to combine until the mixture is crumbly. Set aside.

recipe continues

3 **To make the celery:** Bring a large pot of water to a boil, add 1½ teaspoons of the salt and the celery, and cook until almost tender and still just a little crunchy in the middle, 8 to 9 minutes. Drain the celery and set it aside. Meanwhile, warm the milk in the microwave or in a small saucepan and set aside.

4 Melt the butter in a small saucepan over medium heat. Whisk in the flour and cook while whisking for 1 minute. Whisk in a little of the warm milk until the paste is smooth, then whisk in the remaining milk. Reduce the heat to medium-low and cook, whisking occasionally, until the sauce thickens, about 7 minutes. Remove the pan from the heat and whisk in the Parmesan, the remaining ½ teaspoon salt, and the pepper.

5 Use a heatproof rubber spatula to mix the cooked celery into the sauce and then scrape the mixture into the prepared baking dish. Sprinkle the crumble over the celery and bake until the celery is bubbling around the edges and the crumble is golden brown, about 15 minutes. Remove from the oven and cool for 5 minutes before serving.

for the celery

- 2 teaspoons kosher salt
- 5 celery stalks, trimmed, roughly chopped
- 1 cup whole milk
- 1 tablespoon unsalted butter
- 1 tablespoon all-purpose flour
- 2 tablespoons grated Parmesan cheese
- ¼ teaspoon ground black pepper

Roasted Cauliflower with Mustard Vinaigrette

Roasting coaxes out the sweetness of cauliflower and brings on a completely different earthy tenderness when compared to steamed or boiled cauliflower. While it's delicious simply roasted with olive oil and salt, sometimes I like the brightness and extra tang of tossing it with a quick Dijon vinaigrette. Flexible side dishes like this one, which can be served warm, at room temperature, or cold, are a huge asset to home cooks because they offer a generous window of opportunity for getting them on the table.

serves 4

preparation time:
10 minutes

cooking time:
45 minutes

1 large head cauliflower, separated into medium-sized florets

3 tablespoons olive oil

1 teaspoon kosher salt

for the vinaigrette

Juice of ½ lemon

1 teaspoon Dijon mustard

1 scallion (white and green parts), trimmed and finely chopped, or 1 tablespoon chopped fresh chives

¼ teaspoon ground black pepper

1 Preheat the oven to 400°F. Place the cauliflower in a large baking dish and toss with 2 tablespoons of the olive oil and ¾ teaspoon of the salt. Roast until tender, about 45 minutes, stirring halfway through.

2 To make the vinaigrette: Meanwhile, make the vinaigrette. In a small bowl, whisk together the lemon juice, mustard, scallion, the remaining ¼ teaspoon salt, and the pepper. Slowly add the remaining 1 tablespoon olive oil, whisking until the vinaigrette is thick and creamy. Remove the cauliflower from the oven and toss with the vinaigrette. Serve warm, at room temperature, or chilled.

deals, dollars & sense: a flexible dinner

Here's a real saving grace for getting dinner on the table in a busy household: always plan at least one dish in your lineup to be very time flexible. For example, roasted cauliflower, quiche (page 209), or a vegetable tian (page 214) can be served hot, warm, or chilled, and will wait on you, rather than you waiting for it.

Sautéed Spinach with Garlic

This is my go-to super fast veggie side dish. I love it served as a side dish or underneath a protein such as a fish fillet, a piece of chicken, or a steak. Fresh spinach is really the way to go here, but in a pinch, frozen works fine, too.

● ● ○ ○ ○

serves 4

preparation time:
5 minutes

cooking time:
3 minutes

2 tablespoons olive oil

2 garlic cloves, peeled and thinly sliced

Pinch of crushed red pepper flakes

¾ pound baby spinach or roughly chopped large leaf spinach (tough ribs removed)

¼ teaspoon kosher salt

Lemon wedges, for serving

Heat the oil, garlic, and red pepper flakes in a large skillet over medium heat until the garlic is fragrant, about 1 minute. Add half of the spinach and all of the salt, gently tossing with tongs until the spinach starts to wilt, about 1 minute. Add the remaining spinach and continue to toss until only a few slightly raw leaves remain, about 1 minute. Turn the spinach out into a colander and drain, then transfer to a medium bowl or plate and serve.

check out your local CSA

Community Supported Agriculture, or CSA, is a great thing. For a lump sum you pay a farm or cooperative and in return you get a box of beautiful just-picked produce, meat, flowers, and even eggs on a weekly or biweekly basis. CSAs aren't necessarily the cheapest way to buy vegetables up front; you are likely to get more for your dollar at the supermarket.

What is true, though, is that buying a share of a CSA is a heck of a lot cheaper than counting on processed foods or takeout. Plus, there are so many ancillary benefits that make it a great family project: kids and grown-ups get more excited about eating the farm-fresh veggies, and eating more vegetables is healthy and also lowers your overall grocery bill. There are additional advantages, too, such as inspiring creativity in the kitchen and reducing your carbon footprint since the produce is grown locally. Even a small box delivered every other week is a low-cost way to cash in on these benefits.

// 8 //

starchy sides
Opportunities to Save Your Budget

A side dish is an opportunity for budget cooks to strategize and be smart about how to present a meal.

Say, for example, you spend a few extra bucks on your main dish. A super cheap side, such as a rice dish or roasted potatoes, can help round out the cost of the dinner. Another way to get sides to work for you is to let them stretch out pricey protein. Shrimp and steak are more affordable when served in smaller portions and accompanied by a protein-rich side dish such as beans or quinoa. You can even turn a side dish into a main dish by adding a green salad (page 90), topped with a little chopped leftover chicken, pork, or steak.

Creamiest Slow Cooker Polenta

I became slightly obsessed with making polenta after I tried Scott Conant's rich version at his New York City restaurant, Scarpetta. I made dozens of batches, but it was never the same as his. I finally asked him what his secret was and he said it came down to time and liquid. To get that amazing texture, polenta needs more liquid than you might think. Also, it needs to cook for two hours, and be stirred every few minutes. I came up with a fantastic home kitchen solution: make it in the slow cooker. The low, slow, gentle heat works like a charm, yielding a low-maintenance polenta that is satisfying and creamy.

● ●

serves 4

preparation time:
5 minutes

cooking time:
2 hours, 5 minutes

1 cup whole milk

1⅓ cups half-and-half

2 tablespoons unsalted butter

⅓ cup coarse polenta or corn grits

½ teaspoon kosher salt

Ground black pepper

½ cup grated Parmesan cheese

1. Spray the bowl of a slow cooker with nonstick pan spray. Turn on the slow cooker to high.

2. Bring the milk, 1 cup of the half-and-half, 1 tablespoon of the butter, the polenta, salt, and pepper to a boil in a medium saucepan over medium-high heat, whisking constantly to avoid lumps. Cook until the polenta begins to thicken, 2 to 3 minutes, and then transfer it to the slow cooker. Cover the bowl and cook on high until the polenta is very thick and creamy, about 2 hours, giving it a quick stir every 30 minutes.

3. Heat the remaining ⅓ cup half-and-half in the microwave until it's warm, about 15 seconds. Remove the cover from the polenta and whisk in the remaining 1 tablespoon butter, the warm half-and-half, and the Parmesan. Serve immediately.

Golden Pan-Fried Potatoes

There are three steps to cooking my perfect pan-fried potatoes. First, start them in a pan to caramelize the outside. Second, add water and cover the pan to give the potatoes a quick steam for the fluffiest interior texture. Third, finish the potatoes in the oven so the sides can continue to crisp up and brown without your having to worry about stirring or burning—transferring the potatoes to the oven offers more hands-off flexibility.

serves **4**

preparation time:
5 minutes

cooking time:
35 minutes

¼ cup vegetable oil

3 russet potatoes, peeled and cut into ½-inch cubes

1 teaspoon kosher salt

½ teaspoon ground black pepper

1 tablespoon unsalted butter

1 Preheat the oven to 375°F. Heat the oil in a large skillet over medium-high heat. Add the potatoes, salt, and pepper and cook, stirring often, until they start to turn golden, about 5 minutes.

2 Raise the heat to high and stir in 3 tablespoons water, then cover and steam until the water is gone, 3 to 4 minutes, stirring every minute so the potatoes don't stick. Reduce the heat to medium and cook uncovered until all traces of water are gone, 1 to 2 minutes longer.

3 Stir in the butter and, once it has melted, transfer the potatoes to a rimmed baking sheet and roast until crisp and browned, 15 to 25 minutes, depending on how dark you want them. Transfer the potatoes to a serving bowl and serve hot.

Spicy Buffalo-Style Potato Wedges

These wedged oven-baked spicy potatoes were inspired by one of my favorite tapas dishes, patatas bravas, *a tomato-y sautéed potato dish, as well as by buffalo chicken wings. I roast the potatoes until they're golden, then toss them with ketchup and hot sauce. The sauce gets absorbed just enough to flavor the potato while still giving it the slightest glaze. These are delicious and inexpensive, and a fun alternative to game-day chicken wings—just add some blue cheese dressing!*

● ● ● ● ●

serves 4

preparation time:
5 minutes

cooking time:
55 minutes

1½ tablespoons vegetable oil, plus extra for greasing the pan

3 russet potatoes

1 teaspoon kosher salt

1 tablespoon unsalted butter, melted

1 tablespoon hot sauce, such as Frank's

1 tablespoon ketchup

1 Preheat the oven to 425°F. Grease a rimmed baking sheet with a little oil and place it in the oven while you prepare the potatoes.

2 Place the potatoes on a cutting board and halve lengthwise. Slice each half into quarters so you get 4 long potato wedges per half (24 wedges total). Transfer the potatoes to a large bowl and toss with the oil and salt. Turn out onto the prepared baking sheet and roast until the underside is browned, about 35 minutes.

3 Slide a spatula under each potato and flip over. Continue to roast until the potatoes are cooked through and browned on both sides, 10 to 15 minutes longer. Remove the pan from the oven. Adjust an oven rack to the top position and preheat the broiler to high.

4 Whisk the butter, hot sauce, and ketchup together in a large bowl. Use a spatula to transfer the potatoes to the bowl and shake the bowl to toss and turn the hot potatoes in the sauce. Turn the potatoes back out onto the baking sheet and broil until sizzling and crisp at the edges, 1 to 2 minutes. Remove from the oven and serve hot.

Crispy Potato Cake

When grated and fried into a potato cake, super cheap potatoes take on an impressive and fancy look that every budget-minded cook can appreciate. A crispy, browned potato cake (often called a roësti potato cake) makes an excellent side dish to meat loaf or any saucy dish, and I especially love it paired with fried or poached eggs and a little salsa. Eggs and potatoes for dinner costs so little to make and tastes so comforting and indulgent at the end of a busy day.

serves 4

preparation time:
10 minutes

cooking time:
20 minutes

- 2 tablespoons vegetable oil
- 2 tablespoons unsalted butter
- 2 large russet potatoes, peeled and grated
- ¾ teaspoon kosher salt
- ¼ teaspoon ground black pepper
- 2 tablespoons finely chopped fresh flat-leaf parsley

1 Heat the oil and butter over medium heat in a nonstick 10-inch skillet. Once the butter is melted, sprinkle the grated potatoes into the pan in an even layer and, using a spatula, gently press them into the pan. Season with about half of the salt and pepper and let the potatoes cook without shaking or stirring the pan, until they're crisp and browned on the bottom, 8 to 10 minutes.

2 Slide the potato cake onto a large plate and invert it onto another plate. Slide the potato cake back into the pan, browned side up, and season the top with the remaining salt and pepper. Continue to cook until the underside is nicely browned and the potato cake is cooked through, 7 to 9 minutes longer.

3 Slide the potato cake onto a cutting board. Cut into wedges, sprinkle with parsley, and serve.

White Beans with Cumin, Oregano, and Garlic

Dried beans are one of the cheapest proteins that exist. Served alongside a meat, veggie, or grain dish, they can really round out a meal, and they add a nice hit of protein and fiber. This recipe is one of my favorite ways to use white beans as a side dish. The earthy cumin, grassy oregano, and pungent garlic give the beans a beautiful, hearty flavor that works just as well with a Mediterranean-flavored main as it does with a Mexican-spiced one. You can turn this into a main dish by adding some pasta and Parmesan cheese. For more about beans, see A Hill of Beans, page 77.

serves 4

preparation time:
5 minutes

cooking time:
15 to 20 minutes

2 tablespoons olive oil

½ white or yellow onion, finely chopped

½ teaspoon kosher salt

1 garlic clove, finely minced or pressed through a garlic press

1 teaspoon ground cumin

¼ cup dry white wine

1½ cups cooked navy beans

2 tablespoons finely chopped fresh oregano or 2 teaspoons dried

¼ teaspoon ground black pepper

1 Heat the olive oil in a medium skillet over medium heat. Add the onion and ¼ teaspoon of the salt and cook, stirring occasionally, until the onion is soft, about 5 minutes. Stir in the garlic and cumin and cook until fragrant, 1 to 2 minutes.

2 Raise the heat to high and pour in the wine. Cook until the wine is reduced by half, 1 to 2 minutes, and then stir in the beans, oregano, the remaining ¼ teaspoon salt, and the pepper. Reduce the heat to medium and cook, stirring occasionally, until the beans are warmed through and they absorb some of the liquid, 10 to 15 minutes. Serve warm.

Rice with Fresh Herbs

Ten Dollar Dinners viewers know how much I love my $5 rice cooker and the perfectly steamed rice it makes. Boiling rice is another easy way of making rice that yields a firmer and less starchy texture. You can even boil the rice ahead of time, refrigerate it for a few hours, and then finish it with the butter before serving warm or at room temperature. For the prettiest presentation, wait to stir in the herbs until just before serving.

serves **4**

preparation time:
5 minutes

cooking time:
20 minutes

1½ cups long-grain white rice

1 tablespoon plus ½ teaspoon kosher salt, plus extra if needed

2 tablespoons unsalted butter

¼ cup finely chopped fresh herbs, such as basil, chives, cilantro, mint, or tarragon, or a combination of many

1 Bring a large pot of water to a boil over high heat. Add the rice and 1 tablespoon of the salt and cook, stirring occasionally, until the rice is tender, 12 to 15 minutes. Drain through a fine-mesh sieve and rinse under cold water to stop the cooking. Shake the sieve to drain as much water as possible.

2 Melt the butter in a large nonstick skillet over medium heat. Add the rice and the remaining ½ teaspoon salt and stir with a heatproof rubber spatula to coat all the rice with the butter. Once the rice is warmed through, about 3 minutes, transfer the rice to a serving bowl and add the herbs plus additional salt, if needed. Stir with a fork to incorporate and fluff the rice and serve warm or at room temperature.

Savory Baked Rice

At eight to nine cents a serving, rice is about the cheapest thing you can put on your plate. I'm always looking for ways to keep rice easy and interesting. This recipe coaxes out a fluffy texture from long-grain white rice. Its savory flavor calls on a short list of pantry ingredients you probably have on hand most of the time.

serves 4

preparation time:
10 minutes

cooking time:
55 minutes

1 tablespoon unsalted butter

1 yellow onion, finely chopped

1 celery stalk, finely chopped (leaves chopped and reserved, optional)

¼ teaspoon dried thyme plus a squeeze of lemon juice

¼ teaspoon plus a pinch of kosher salt

1½ cups long-grain white rice

1 cup chicken broth

1 cup water

Finely chopped fresh flat-leaf parsley, for serving (optional)

1 Preheat the oven to 350°F. Melt the butter in an oven-safe heavy-bottomed pot over medium heat. Add the onion and celery and cook, stirring occasionally, until they start to get soft, 3 to 4 minutes. Stir in the thyme and ¼ teaspoon of the salt and cook until fragrant, about 1 minute more. Stir in the rice and cook, stirring occasionally, until it's opaque, about 2 minutes. Pour in the broth and water (add an extra ¼ cup if you like very soft rice), raise the heat to high, stir the rice, and bring to a boil (but don't stir the rice anymore).

2 Cover the pot, turn off the heat, and transfer the pot to the oven to bake until the rice is cooked through, 40 to 45 minutes. Remove from the oven, add the pinch of salt, fluff the rice with a fork, and serve sprinkled with the chopped parsley and celery leaves (if using).

Parmesan Breadsticks

There are a few spots in the grocery store that are must-visits, and the day-old bread rack (sometimes near the dairy department and not in the bakery) is one of them. This is where you'll find perfectly fine bread for 50 percent off. I take baguettes and slice them into long and thin batons to make these cheesy and dramatic Parmesan breadsticks.

● ● ◌ ◌ ◌ ◌

makes 12 breadsticks

preparation time:
10 minutes

cooking time:
7 minutes

1 baguette

3 tablespoons olive oil

1 teaspoon sweet paprika

½ teaspoon kosher salt

¼ teaspoon ground black pepper

3 tablespoons grated Parmesan cheese

deals, dollars & sense: parmesan cheese

I'm a big fan of keeping a wedge of good-quality Parmesan cheese on hand. It might seem a bit pricey, but you get a lot of flavor from a little bit of cheese—just a few tablespoons often does a dish right. I like to grate it myself because I think the flavor is nicer, but on a harried weekday night, it's really nice to have a container of already grated Parmesan ready for action.

1 Preheat the oven to 400°F. Place the baguette on a cutting board and slice off the ends. Slice the baguette in half crosswise and then lengthwise so you have 4 halves. Slice each quarter lengthwise into 3 long strips (you'll end up with 12 strips). Brush each strip with some olive oil and then place on an aluminum foil–lined rimmed baking sheet.

2 Sprinkle the bread strips with the paprika, salt, pepper, and Parmesan. Bake the breadsticks until they are golden, about 7 minutes. Serve warm or at room temperature.

Quick Sour Cream Biscuits

If you start right now, in twenty minutes you could be eating a deliciously tender, soft, and flaky homemade biscuit. There is nothing like homemade bread to round out a meal, and biscuits are an easy everyday option. I use sour cream in my recipe because I always have it in the fridge, so I never have to plan to make biscuits, they can just happen!

makes **6 biscuits**

preparation time:
10 minutes

cooking time:
12 minutes

- 3 tablespoons unsalted butter, cut into ½-inch cubes
- 1 cup all-purpose flour, plus extra for shaping
- 1 tablespoon baking powder
- 1 teaspoon sugar
- ¼ teaspoon baking soda
- ½ cup sour cream, plus 2 teaspoons for brushing

1 Place the butter on a plate and freeze while you gather the rest of the ingredients. Preheat the oven to 425°F. Line a baking sheet with parchment paper and set aside.

2 Place 1 cup of the flour and the baking powder, sugar, and baking soda in the bowl of a food processor and pulse to combine. Add the chilled butter and process until the mixture resembles wet sand, about eight 1-second pulses. Add ½ cup of the sour cream and pulse until it comes together into a rough dough ball.

3 Transfer the dough to a lightly floured work surface (I flour a sheet of wax paper for easy cleanup). Pat the dough into a 4-inch circle and then cut it in half down the middle. Divide each half into 3 wedges, so you get 6 dough wedges total. Transfer to the prepared baking sheet. Brush with the remaining 2 teaspoons sour cream and bake until golden and fluffy, 10 to 12 minutes. Remove from the oven and serve while warm.

Cheesy Popovers

Popovers are a fantastic quick bread to get into the habit of making. They're fast, easy, tasty, and inexpensive, and you don't need a special pan to make them (I use a muffin tin). For perfect popovers: first, preheat the muffin tin for a fast rise; second, make sure the batter is at room temperature so the popovers stay airy (that's why I call for warmed milk); and third, serve them straight from the oven for the absolute best flavor and texture. I add Swiss cheese to send them over the top, but you can make them without the cheese and they'll still be delicious.

makes **8** popovers

preparation time:
5 minutes

cooking time:
45 minutes

- 1 tablespoon unsalted butter, melted, plus 1 tablespoon cut into 8 small pieces
- 1 cup 2% milk
- 2 large eggs
- 1 cup all-purpose flour
- 1 teaspoon kosher salt
- ½ cup grated Swiss cheese

1 Preheat the oven to 400°F. Place 1 butter piece in each of 8 cups of a 12-cup muffin tin. Place the tin in the oven for 1½ to 2 minutes.

2 Heat the milk in the microwave until it is warm, about 30 seconds. In the bowl of a stand mixer (or a large bowl if using a hand mixer), beat the eggs on high speed until they're pale yellow, 1 to 2 minutes. Reduce the speed to medium and mix in the warmed milk. Add the flour, salt, and the remaining tablespoon melted butter and beat on medium speed until the batter is smooth, about 1 minute.

3 Remove the muffin tin from the oven and divide the batter among the 8 greased muffin cups. Spoon 1 tablespoon of the cheese on top of each cup. Return the tin to the oven and bake until the popovers are tall and golden, 30 to 35 minutes. Remove the tin from the oven and serve the popovers immediately.

Lemon-Thyme Orzo

Orzo is rice-shaped pasta, but instead of cooking it in a big pot of boiling water and draining it like pasta, I let it simmer more like a risotto, stirring it every now and then, until it becomes wonderfully creamy. While it's quick to make, note that it's not great made way ahead of time because it firms up as it cools. If you need to buy a little time (late guests or dillydallying kids) just stir in a splash of cream or milk to restore its luscious richness. This side dish hits that sweet spot of being easy to throw together and upscale enough for company.

● ● ○ ○ ○

serves **4**

preparation time:
5 minutes

cooking time:
15 minutes

1½ cups chicken broth

1 garlic clove, finely minced or pressed through a garlic press

Pinch of crushed red pepper flakes

2 cups water

¾ cup orzo

Zest of ½ lemon

2 tablespoons finely chopped fresh thyme

¼ teaspoon kosher salt

2 tablespoons grated Parmesan cheese

1 Bring the broth, garlic, red pepper flakes, and water to a boil in a medium saucepan over high heat. Stir in the orzo and reduce the heat to medium-low. Simmer until about two thirds of the liquid is absorbed and the orzo still looks creamy and loose, stirring occasionally, for about 10 minutes (the orzo will soak up more liquid as it cools).

2 Turn off the heat and stir in the lemon zest, thyme, salt, and Parmesan cheese. Serve warm.

deals, dollars & sense: mason jars

I buy most small pasta and loose grains in large quantities or in bulk and transfer them to mason jars when I get home. They look so great on a shelf, all filled with different shapes and colors of grains. Buy jars at the craft store (with a coupon from the Sunday paper) to use for iced tea, as a country-rustic vase for flowers, or to package homemade gourmet gifts.

Couscous with Dates

Couscous should be in every busy budget cook's cupboard. I count on it as a pasta-like side that bridges the gap between being kid-friendly, elegant, and fast. If you buy couscous in the bulk aisle of your supermarket, you'll save as much as 75 percent when compared to the per-ounce price of the couscous that comes in a small box or container. Chopped dates give my couscous an exotic sweetness while keeping the flavor versatile enough to pair with saucy braises and stews (dried apricots are also delicious). You can also stir in a spoonful of date or fig jam or orange marmalade for a hint of fruit flavor.

● ● ● ● ● ●

serves 4

preparation time:
5 minutes

cooking time:
10 minutes

1 cup chicken broth or water

1 cup water

1 tablespoon olive oil

¼ cup finely chopped pitted dates

1 cup couscous

½ teaspoon kosher salt

¼ teaspoon ground black pepper

deals, dollars & sense: dried fruit

Guess where you can find a great deal on dried fruit? The drugstore and dollar store! You can find dried apricots, dates, figs, or raisins for as little as a buck a box. The box is typically small, but the benefit is that you'll use up all of the dried fruit in a recipe or two while the dried fruit is still plump and hasn't had a chance to dry out from air exposure.

Pour the broth, water, and olive oil into a small saucepan and bring to a boil over medium heat. Stir in the dates and then add the couscous. Cover the pan, turn off the heat, and let the couscous plump in the liquid for 5 minutes. Uncover and fluff the couscous with a fork. Season with the salt and pepper and serve.

Quinoa Tabouli

Tabouli is a fresh herb salad usually made with bulgur wheat. Here I make it with quinoa, a protein-rich seed that "pops" when you bite into it. Quinoa gives this side dish a lot of nutritional bang for your buck. You can also add a few pieces of leftover chicken or pork to turn tabouli into a meal. It also works well as a vegetarian main dish. Tabouli is hearty enough to stand up to rich meats, but the herbs and lemon juice give it a freshness that pairs well with fish and poultry, too. Whether you make it for dinner, a picnic, or a brown-bag lunch, this make-ahead-friendly recipe hits a lot of notes.

serves **4**

preparation time:
15 minutes (plus 1 hour to marinate)

cooking time:
10 minutes

½ cup quinoa

1½ cups water

Bunch of flat-leaf parsley, finely chopped

½ bunch of cilantro, finely chopped

2 tablespoons finely chopped fresh mint

2 ripe tomatoes, halved, seeded, and finely chopped

3 scallions (white and green parts), trimmed and finely chopped

Zest and juice of 1 lemon

3 tablespoons olive oil

½ teaspoon kosher salt

¼ teaspoon ground black pepper

1 Rinse the quinoa under cold water in a fine-mesh sieve. Turn it out into a large microwave-safe bowl and add the water. Cover and microwave on high for 9 minutes. Set aside for 2 minutes and then carefully uncover and fluff with a fork. The quinoa should have a tender snap when you bite it—if it doesn't, cover and microwave for up to 1 minute longer.

2 Stir the parsley, cilantro, mint, tomatoes, and scallions into the quinoa. Whisk the lemon zest and juice with the olive oil, salt, and pepper in a small bowl to make a vinaigrette and pour it over the quinoa. Cover the bowl with plastic wrap and set aside at room temperature for 1 hour for the flavors to combine before serving.

// 9 //

pasta

A Budget Staple

Pasta is a long-standing favorite for budget cooking (remember cooking pasta on a hot plate in your college dorm?).

Whole-grain and protein-rich pasta costs only a bit more than regular pasta and is an excellent long-lasting pantry staple to have at the ready for a quick weeknight dinner.

Just because dried pasta is inexpensive doesn't mean that the meal itself can't be special. Since you're saving on the bulk of food on your plate, you can afford to splurge on the accessories—such as shrimp for scampi-style linguine, walnuts for a pesto-inspired meal, and good olive oil for a light and bright no-cook pasta sauce. In this chapter, I offer several tasty ways to dress up your pasta dollar. Delicious and quick, these are hip-pocket recipes that you can count on.

Crisper Drawer Pasta

The most expensive food is the one you have to throw away because you forgot to use it. Once a week, be sure to take a quick peek into your crisper drawer to take stock of veggies and herbs. My two favorite ways to use the odds and ends from the crisper drawer are to make either an anything-goes pasta or a "kitchen sink"–style soup (see page 75). This is a plug-and-play recipe, meaning you can use any of the vegetables you have in the house simply by following the parameters given.

● ● ● ● ○ ○

serves 4

preparation time:
10 minutes

cooking time:
20 minutes

2 tablespoons olive oil

1 small red or yellow onion, finely chopped

½ teaspoon dried herbs, such as basil, marjoram, oregano, thyme plus a squeeze of lemon juice, or herbes de Provence

2 garlic cloves, finely minced or pressed through a garlic press

1 to 2 cups soft vegetables or leafy greens (see opposite)

Kosher salt

14.5-ounce box pasta

1 to 2 cups cut-up hard vegetables (see opposite)

2 tablespoons sour cream

½ cup grated Parmesan cheese, plus extra for serving

1 tablespoon finely chopped aromatics or fresh herbs (see opposite)

1 Heat the olive oil in a large skillet over medium-high heat. Add the onion and cook, stirring occasionally, until soft, about 3 minutes. Stir in the dried herbs and the garlic and cook until fragrant, 30 seconds to 1 minute, and then stir in the soft vegetables or leafy greens and ½ teaspoon salt. Cook, stirring occasionally, until the vegetables are tender and the greens are wilted, 30 seconds to 4 minutes, stirring often. Turn off the heat and set aside.

2 Bring a large pot of water to a boil. Add the pasta and 1 tablespoon salt and cook for 3 minutes. Add the hard vegetables and continue to cook according to the package instructions until the pasta is al dente. Reserve ½ cup of the pasta water, then drain the pasta and vegetables and return them to the pot. Stir the sour cream and the remaining ½ teaspoon salt into the pasta, then add ½ cup of the Parmesan, the aromatics, and ¼ cup of the pasta water. Stir to combine, add the cooked soft vegetables or leafy greens, and add more pasta water if needed. Serve with more Parmesan on the side.

HARD VEGETABLES
- Beets (chopped)
- Broccoli (cut into small florets)
- Carrots (chopped)
- Cauliflower (cut into small florets)
- Celery (chopped)
- Green beans (chopped)
- Zucchini (chopped)

SOFT VEGETABLES
- Bell peppers (thinly sliced)
- Corn
- Eggplant (chopped and salted)
- Escarole (sliced crosswise)
- Fennel (thinly sliced)
- Mushrooms (thinly sliced)
- Peas
- Spinach (chopped if using large leaves)
- Swiss chard (stemmed and chopped)

AROMATICS
- Basil
- Chives
- Crushed red pepper flakes
- Dill
- Fennel fronds
- Flat-leaf parsley
- Lemon zest
- Scallions
- Tarragon

Fusilli with Chicken, Basil, and Walnuts

Saving money in the kitchen isn't just about spending wisely—it's about inventory management, too. Pasta is a fantastic way to stretch a small amount of uneaten protein from earlier in the week. Here I make a quick deconstructed pesto using walnuts instead of pricey pine nuts, Parmesan cheese, and basil, but feel free to switch up the cast with ingredients you have in the fridge.

serves 4

preparation time:
10 minutes

cooking time:
20 minutes

- ½ cup walnut halves, roughly chopped
- ¼ cup olive oil
- 2 garlic cloves, finely minced or pressed through a garlic press
- 14.5-ounce box fusilli pasta (rotini is great, too)
- 1 teaspoon kosher salt, plus 1 tablespoon for the pasta water
- 1 cup shredded cooked chicken at room temperature (about 1 small breast or ½ large breast)
- ⅓ cup grated Parmesan cheese, plus extra for serving
- ½ cup loosely packed fresh basil leaves, roughly chopped

1. Place the walnuts in a small skillet over medium heat and cook, shaking the pan often, until the walnuts are fragrant and toasted, 4 to 5 minutes. Turn off the heat and transfer to a small plate. Set aside.

2. Wipe out the pan with a damp paper towel, then dry. Heat the olive oil in the skillet over medium heat. Add the garlic and cook gently until fragrant, about 2 minutes (reduce the heat if the garlic starts to brown). Turn off the heat and set aside.

3. Bring a large pot of water to a boil. Add the pasta and 1 tablespoon of the salt and cook according to the package instructions until the pasta is al dente. Reserve ½ cup of the pasta water, then drain the pasta and return it to the pot. Add the chicken and then pour the garlic oil over the pasta and toss to combine. Add the walnuts, Parmesan, ¼ cup of the pasta water, and the remaining 1 teaspoon salt, then stir. If the pasta looks dry, add more of the pasta water. Sprinkle with the basil, stir, and serve with more Parmesan on the side.

Cheesy Corn and Zucchini Lasagna

Sweet and creamy Mexican festival corn—the kind served on a long wood stick and doused with lots of grated cheese, cilantro, and crema—was my inspiration for this fresh, summery lasagna. I use cottage cheese instead of pricey ricotta cheese and add lots of fresh cilantro, garlic, and vegetables that give the lasagne a bright flavor. Taking a familiar dish and using it to showcase unexpected ingredients such as zucchini and cilantro is a great way to introduce new flavors to the family table.

● ● ● ●

serves 4 (plus leftovers)

preparation time:
25 minutes (plus 10 minutes to cool)

cooking time:
1 hour, 20 minutes

9 lasagna noodles

1 teaspoon kosher salt, plus 1 tablespoon for the pasta water

2 tablespoons olive oil

2 zucchini, quartered lengthwise and chopped

1 small red onion, finely chopped

2 cups fresh or frozen corn

1½ cups cottage cheese

1 large egg

5 garlic cloves, roughly chopped

1 cup lightly packed fresh cilantro leaves

1½ cups shredded cheese, such as Mexican cheese blend, Cheddar, Monterey Jack, or mozzarella

1 Preheat the oven to 350°F. Bring a large pot of water to a boil. Add the lasagna noodles and 1 tablespoon of the salt and cook according to the package instructions until the noodles are al dente. Pour off most of the hot water, place the pot in the sink, and cover the noodles with cold water. Set aside.

2 Heat the olive oil in a large skillet over medium-high heat. Add the zucchini and onion and cook until soft but not browned, 4 to 5 minutes, stirring often. Stir in the corn and ½ teaspoon of the salt and cook until the corn is warmed through, 1½ to 2 minutes. Turn off the heat and set aside.

3 Place the cottage cheese in the bowl of a food processor. Add the egg, garlic, cilantro, and the remaining ½ teaspoon salt and combine for eight 1-second pulses. Add 1 cup of the cheese and combine for two 1-second pulses. Set aside.

4 Stack 3 paper towels on top of one another. Place 3 noodles on the paper towels and blot the top with another paper towel. Slightly overlap 3 noodles in the bottom of a 9-inch baking dish. Cover with a somewhat even layer of one third of the cottage cheese mixture followed by one third of the vegetables. Repeat twice, sprinkling the remaining ½ cup cheese over the top. Bake until the cheese is golden brown, about 45 minutes. Remove from the oven and cool for 10 minutes before slicing and serving.

Weeknight Spaghetti Bolognese

Pasta with meat sauce may be the most comforting food of all time. To make a really bold and rich sauce, though, you usually need to dedicate several hours and lots of stirring. In my version, I start with bacon to build that deep and meaty flavor so important to Bolognese, and then I add vegetables that have been puréed using a food processor to speed along their caramelization. I get a nice and deep meatiness that tastes like an all-day Sunday sauce but simmers in no time on a Tuesday night.

● ● ● ○ ○ ○

serves 4 (plus leftovers)

preparation time:
20 minutes

cooking time:
30 minutes

2 carrots, peeled and roughly chopped

2 celery stalks, trimmed and roughly chopped

1 yellow onion, halved and roughly chopped

2 garlic cloves, roughly chopped

1 bacon strip, chopped

2 tablespoons olive oil

1 pound 80% lean ground beef

1 teaspoon dried thyme plus a squeeze of lemon juice

Pinch of ground cinnamon

1 teaspoon kosher salt, plus 1 tablespoon for the pasta water

½ teaspoon ground black pepper

14-ounce box spaghetti

6-ounce can tomato paste

½ cup dry red wine

¼ cup grated Parmesan cheese

1 Bring a large pot of water to a boil. Meanwhile place the carrots, celery, onion, and garlic in the bowl of a food processor and purée to a paste. Set aside.

2 Heat a large skillet over medium-high heat. Add the bacon and cook until it's crisp, about 5 minutes, stirring occasionally. Scrape the vegetable purée into the pan and pour in 1 tablespoon of the olive oil. Raise the heat to high and cook until the steam dissipates, 1 to 2 minutes, stirring constantly. Add the ground beef, thyme, cinnamon, 1 teaspoon of the salt, and the pepper and use a wooden spoon to stir it into the mixture in the pan, breaking up the meat into small pieces. Cook until the meat stops letting off steam and starts browning, about 5 minutes. Drizzle the remaining 1 tablespoon olive oil over the meat and let it sizzle for 1 minute without stirring.

3 Add the spaghetti to the pot of boiling water along with the remaining 1 tablespoon salt. Cook according to the package instructions until the pasta is al dente. (The pasta should be done cooking around the same time that the Bolognese is finished.) While the pasta is cooking, finish the sauce.

4 Mix the tomato paste into the sauce and cook, stirring often, until it becomes a darker shade of red, 1 to 2 minutes. Pour in the wine and stir and scrape any browned bits from the bottom of the pan. Cook, stirring frequently, until the wine is reduced by half, about 2 minutes. Pour in ½ cup

water and cook, stirring often, until the sauce is thick and no longer runny, 2 to 3 minutes. Turn off the heat and stir the Parmesan into the sauce.

5 Once the pasta is al dente, turn off the heat. Use tongs to transfer the pasta straight from the hot water to the Bolognese sauce and serve.

Shrimp Scampi Linguine

If you think shrimp is out of your price range, it's true only if you don't take advantage of the mega sales at your supermarket's fish counter. Fresh medium unpeeled shrimp go on sale often because they are so perishable. Not only is buying shell-on shrimp cheaper, but the shells are a bonus ingredient because you can use them to make a wonderfully rich and flavorful shrimp broth that gives this scampi its edge. Two-for-one items like shrimp, beets (beet root and beet greens), and citrus (citrus juice and zest) maximize ingredients because you count on more than one way to get the most out of them.

serves **4**

preparation time:
15 minutes

cooking time:
30 minutes

6 garlic cloves, finely minced or pressed through a garlic press

5 tablespoons olive oil

Zest and juice of 2 lemons

1 teaspoon crushed red pepper flakes

½ teaspoon kosher salt, plus 1 tablespoon for the pasta water

¼ teaspoon ground black pepper

¾ pound medium shrimp (26–30 per pound), peeled (reserve shells), deveined, and butterflied

¼ onion

¾ pound thin linguine

2 tablespoons unsalted butter

Small bunch of fresh flat-leaf parsley, leaves finely chopped

1. Stir the garlic, olive oil, zest and juice of 1 lemon, red pepper flakes, ¼ teaspoon of the salt, and the black pepper together in a medium bowl. Add the shrimp, toss to coat, and set aside.

2. Meanwhile, make a quick shrimp stock using the shells. Place the shells and onion in a medium saucepan, cover with water, and bring to a boil over high heat. Reduce the heat to medium-low and simmer for 20 minutes. Strain through a fine-mesh sieve and into a medium bowl. Discard the shells and the onion.

3. While the shrimp stock simmers, cook the pasta. Bring a large pot of water to a boil over high heat. Add 1 tablespoon of the salt and the linguine and cook until it's barely tender, about 2 minutes less than the package instructions. Drain, reserving ½ cup of the pasta water.

4. Heat a large skillet over high heat. Use a slotted spoon to add the shrimp to the pan and cook until they turn pink and start to brown around the edges, 2 to 3 minutes. Transfer the shrimp to a plate and set aside. Pour the remaining marinade into the pan; cook until the garlic is fragrant, 1 to 2 minutes, and then pour in 1 cup of the shrimp stock and the reserved pasta water. Add the remaining lemon zest and juice, the butter, the remaining ¼ teaspoon salt, and the parsley and stir to combine. Add the shrimp and pasta and use tongs to toss with the sauce. Serve immediately.

Rigatoni with No-Cook Tomato Sauce

I love smelling a slow-cooking pasta sauce, but when I have ripe, in-season tomatoes, this no-cook sauce is what I make. It's fresh and fast and can be mixed together at the last minute or made in the morning to eat later in the day (the heat of the pasta warms it up). Of course it really sings when tomatoes are at their peak, but I've made it in the winter using canned whole tomatoes with delicious results.

● ● ● ● ● ●

serves 4

preparation time:
15 minutes (plus 30 minutes to rest)

cooking time:
12 minutes

- 3 ripe tomatoes, cored, halved, seeded, and chopped (or 5 whole canned tomatoes, chopped)
- 2 scallions (white and green parts), finely chopped
- ⅓ cup olive oil
- 2 teaspoons balsamic vinegar
- 1 teaspoon lemon zest
- 3 tablespoons chopped fresh basil
- 1 garlic clove, smashed
- ½ teaspoon crushed red pepper flakes
- 1 teaspoon kosher salt, plus 1 tablespoon for the pasta water
- ¼ teaspoon ground black pepper
- 16-ounce box rigatoni
- ¼ cup grated Parmesan cheese

deals, dollars & sense: canned tomatoes

Whole canned tomatoes are a versatile pantry staple because they can be adapted to fit any recipe: they can be chopped, pulsed in a food processor for crushed tomatoes, or puréed in the food processor for quick tomato sauce. Pre-diced canned tomatoes tend to be really firm, so if you buy whole canned tomatoes and chop them yourself, they'll be softer and more luscious.

1 Place the tomatoes, scallions, olive oil, balsamic vinegar, lemon zest, basil, garlic, red pepper flakes, 1 teaspoon of the salt, and the black pepper in a large bowl. Stir and then use the back of a wooden spoon to press the ingredients against the sides of the bowl. Set the bowl aside for 30 minutes (or refrigerate up to 8 hours).

2 Bring a large pot of water to a boil. Add the pasta and the remaining 1 tablespoon salt and cook following the package instructions until it's al dente. Drain the hot pasta and transfer it to the tomato sauce. Let the pasta sit on top of the sauce for 1 minute and then toss together. Serve sprinkled with Parmesan.

Roasted Vegetables and Whole-Grain Penne with Sausage

It makes me happy when I know that even a simple bowl of pasta is delivering lots of fiber and protein to my family. That's why I'll often spend $1 extra (yes, that's me telling you to spend more money!) to buy a whole-grain, legume, or flaxseed-enhanced pasta. The money I save by not making meat the primary protein of the meal more than makes up for the extra cost of the pasta.

● ● ● ● ○

serves 4

preparation time:
15 minutes

cooking time:
50 minutes

1 sweet onion, such as Maui or Vidalia, sliced into wedges

1 zucchini, halved lengthwise

1 red bell pepper

½ pound white button mushrooms, stemmed

2½ tablespoons olive oil

1 teaspoon kosher salt, plus 1 tablespoon for the pasta water

½ teaspoon ground black pepper

½ pint grape tomatoes

12 ounces whole-grain penne

2 sweet or hot Italian sausages, casings removed

¼ cup dry white wine

¼ cup grated Parmesan cheese

deals, dollars & sense: whole-grain pasta

Whole-grain pasta is fiber- and protein-rich, and a staple in my pantry. There is always at least one brand on sale. If you haven't tried a whole-grain pasta in a while, give it a go. You may be pleasantly surprised.

1 Preheat the oven to 400°F. Place the onion, zucchini, bell pepper, and mushrooms in a large bowl. Drizzle with 1½ tablespoons of the olive oil, ½ teaspoon of the salt, and ¼ teaspoon of the black pepper and toss to combine. Turn the vegetables out onto a rimmed baking sheet and roast for 15 minutes.

2 Put the tomatoes in a small bowl and toss with the remaining 1 tablespoon olive oil. Season with ¼ teaspoon of the salt and the remaining ¼ teaspoon black pepper and add to the baking sheet with the other vegetables. Roast until the onion is nicely caramelized, about 15 minutes longer. Remove the vegetables from the oven and set aside until cool enough to handle, transfer to a cutting board, and roughly chop. Set aside.

3 Bring a large pot of water to a boil over high heat. Add 1 tablespoon of the salt and the penne and cook according to the package instructions until the pasta is al dente. Drain, reserving ½ cup of the cooking water.

recipe continues

4 Crumble the sausage into a large skillet and cook over medium heat until it's cooked through, 5 to 7 minutes, stirring often. Raise the heat to high and pour in the wine, using a wooden spoon to stir and scrape up any browned bits from the bottom of the pan.

5 Add the vegetables and any juices to the skillet with the sausage. Stir in the penne and the reserved pasta water to moisten the pan (if needed). Taste, season with the remaining ¼ teaspoon salt (if needed), and serve sprinkled with the Parmesan.

deals, dollars & sense: grated cheese

When they are on sale, bags of grated cheese are often pound-for-pound the same price as blocks of cheese, making them a great bargain and a big time saver. I like to buy the big size and divvy them up into quart-sized resealable bags for freezing.

Mac and Cheese

Macaroni and cheese owns a prized corner in the hearts of children for good reason—it's creamy, cheesy, rich, and comforting and it tastes really homey, especially when made from scratch. My trick for a silky-smooth sauce is to add a little American cheese into the béchamel to stabilize it. To make my twins happy I add a dash of paprika to the cheesy sauce to give it that classic mac-and-cheese color, and to make my husband and me happy, I always try to have a few adult-friendly toppers on the side such as sautéed shallots or mushrooms. If serving macaroni and cheese as a side dish, it will easily feed eight people.

● ● ● ● ○

serves 4 (plus leftovers)

preparation time:
25 minutes

cooking time:
40 minutes

1 tablespoon unsalted butter, at room temperature, plus 3 tablespoons

1 16-ounce box elbow macaroni

1½ teaspoons kosher salt, plus 1 tablespoon for the pasta water

3 cups whole milk

½ onion, finely chopped

3 tablespoons all-purpose flour

1 teaspoon sweet paprika

Dash of cayenne pepper

2 slices American cheese, torn into small pieces

2 tablespoons cream cheese

1½ cups shredded Cheddar cheese

½ cup grated Parmesan cheese

1. Preheat the oven to 425°F. Grease a 3-quart casserole dish with the 1 tablespoon room-temperature butter and set aside. Bring a large pot of water to a boil. Add the macaroni and 1 tablespoon of the salt and cook according to the package instructions until the pasta is al dente. Drain and return the macaroni to the pot.

2. Warm the milk in the microwave and set aside. Melt the remaining 3 tablespoons butter in a large skillet over medium heat. Add the onion and cook until soft and just turning golden, about 6 minutes. Stir in the flour, paprika, and cayenne and cook for 2 minutes, stirring constantly. Raise the heat to medium and slowly whisk in the warm milk. Cook, stirring frequently with a wooden spoon, until the sauce is thick and coats the back of a spoon, about 10 minutes. Turn off the heat and let the sauce cool for 2 minutes.

3. Stir in the remaining 1½ teaspoons salt, the American cheese, and the cream cheese. Once the cream cheese is melted, stir in ½ cup of the Cheddar and all of the Parmesan. Stir the sauce into the macaroni and transfer it to the prepared baking dish. Sprinkle the remaining ½ cup Cheddar over the top of the macaroni and place it in the oven. Bake until the top is golden, 8 to 10 minutes. Serve warm.

dessert

A Sweet Last Impression

I have a real sweet tooth, which is why I can hardly imagine a meal that doesn't finish with at least a small nibble of dessert.

It can be as simple as a square of chocolate with an espresso (pour the espresso over ice cream and you have my standby quick company dessert, Affogato, on page 295) or a comforting, rich bread pudding heightened by raspberries and lemon cream. Making dessert can be a thrifty add-on to dinner plans, with the most economical being simple cakes and cookies that rely on inexpensive pantry staples such as flour, sugar, and eggs, while fancier desserts might call for pricier ingredients such as chocolate or cream to add that extra nudge of decadence. No matter what side you choose, the added value of desserts and baked goods remains the same: they make family and guests feel honored, welcomed, and special. Who would want to skip that?

Brûléed Mandarin Oranges and Sabayon

At its heart, sabayon is an easy three-ingredient egg custard sauce made using egg yolks, sugar, and wine (I add sour cream for extra creaminess and tang). It's also a snap to make if you remember these two tips: accept that you'll be attached to the stove and whisking for five minutes (you have to keep stirring or the custard can curdle), and once the mixture gets foamy and doubles in size, pull the custard off the stove. As an extra safeguard, you can even strain the custard through a fine-mesh sieve to ensure a smooth consistency before finishing the dessert under the broiler with the oranges.

serves 4

preparation time:
10 minutes

cooking time:
10 minutes

- 2 large egg yolks
- 3 tablespoons granulated sugar
- 2 tablespoons dessert wine, such as Marsala
- 1 tablespoon sour cream
- 2 15-ounce cans mandarin oranges, drained
- 2 tablespoons (packed) light brown sugar

1 Fill a saucepan with 1 inch of water and bring to a simmer over medium heat, then reduce the heat to low. Place the egg yolks, granulated sugar, and wine in a medium metal bowl and set over the simmering water (the bottom of the bowl shouldn't touch the water). Whisk the egg mixture constantly until it doubles in size, about 5 minutes (the mixture should be very warm but not boiling hot). Carefully remove the bowl from the saucepan and whisk the sour cream into the sabayon.

2 Adjust an oven rack to the top position and preheat the broiler to low. Place the oranges in a shallow oven-safe dish (or divide among 4 ramekins). Spoon the sabayon sauce over the top, sprinkle with the brown sugar, and place the dish on a baking sheet and broil until the oranges are golden brown (watch closely, as broiler intensity can vary), 1 to 2 minutes. Remove from the oven and serve immediately.

deals, dollars & sense: leftover egg whites

If you have leftover egg whites from a recipe, save them to use in omelets or other baking recipes, such as Strawberry Pavlovas with Apricot Sauce on page 287. Or freeze them to use another time. (Note: once frozen, they won't work in meringue.)

Strawberry Pavlovas with Apricot Sauce

My four girls love anything having to do with ballet, so of course they go crazy for pavlovas, a light and fruity dessert inspired by the billowy tulle skirt of famed ballerina Anna Pavlova. The meringue base is crisp and crackly on the outside and gives way to a tender and nearly marshmallow-like center. Whipped cream, fresh strawberries, and an easy apricot jam add soft and textural sweetness to these little edible pieces of art. The meringues can be made ahead of time and stored in an airtight container for several days before serving.

● ● ● ● ● ●

serves 4

preparation time:
15 minutes (plus at least 1 hour to cool)

cooking time:
1 hour

½ cup sugar

2 large egg whites

1 teaspoon cornstarch

½ teaspoon vanilla extract

½ teaspoon distilled white vinegar

½ cup heavy cream

1 cup sliced strawberries

¼ cup apricot jam

1 Preheat the oven to 275°F. Line a rimmed baking sheet with parchment and set aside. Place the sugar in the bowl of a food processor and pulse until it is very fine, about five 1-second pulses.

2 Place the egg whites in the bowl of a stand mixer (or in a medium bowl if using a hand mixer) and whip on medium speed until they're foamy. Begin sprinkling in half the sugar a little at a time, whipping until the egg whites form stiff peaks. Sift the remaining half of the sugar and all of the cornstarch into a small bowl and use a rubber spatula to gently fold into the beaten egg whites. Whisk in the vanilla and vinegar.

3 Divide the beaten egg whites into 4 equal mounds on the parchment-lined baking sheet. Use the curved side of a spoon to make a well in the center of each mound. Bake the meringues until they're dry and no longer tacky to touch, about 40 minutes. Turn off the oven and leave the meringues inside the oven for 20 minutes more. Remove from the oven and set aside to cool completely.

4 When you're ready to serve, whip the cream until it makes soft peaks. Divide the cream among the meringues and top with the strawberries. Place the jam in a small bowl and mix in 2 tablespoons hot water. Drizzle the apricot sauce over the pavlovas and serve.

Fruit Salad with Lemon-Mint Syrup

In this fruit salad I stretch one cup of strawberries into four servings by bulking them up with cheaper fruits such as bananas and oranges. Equal parts sugar and water plus some fresh mint and lemon become an elegant simple syrup that costs pennies to make. Simple syrup is a budget cook's secret weapon when you want to dress up something ordinary like winter fruit, plain pound cake, or iced tea.

● ● ○ ○ ○ ○

serves 4

preparation time:
20 minutes (plus 30 minutes to chill)

cooking time:
2 minutes (plus 20 minutes to steep)

¾ cup sugar

Zest and juice of ½ lemon

6 fresh mint sprigs

1 orange, peeled and segmented

1 banana, sliced

1 cup sliced strawberries (about ½ pint)

1. In a medium saucepan, add the sugar, ¾ cup water, and the lemon zest and bring to a simmer over medium-high heat, stirring occasionally, until the mixture is fragrant and the sugar is dissolved, about 2 minutes. Stir in the lemon juice, turn off the heat, cover the pan, and set aside for 20 minutes.

2. Strain the syrup through a fine-mesh sieve and into a medium bowl. Cover the bowl with plastic wrap and refrigerate until chilled, about 30 minutes.

3. Separate the mint leaves from the stems. Stack the mint leaves, roll into a tight cylinder, and slice crosswise into thin ribbons. Place the orange, banana, and strawberries in a medium bowl and toss with the mint (reserve some for garnish) and syrup. Serve in dessert bowls sprinkled with fresh mint.

deals, dollars & sense: overripe fruit

Turn overripe fruit into a quick fruit topping. Chop the fruit and add it to a pat of melted butter in a skillet on medium heat. Add a spoonful of granulated or brown sugar and cook just until the fruit is a little soft, anywhere from 30 seconds for soft fruits such as raspberries and blueberries to 3 minutes for apples or pears.

Classic Apple Tart

Apple tart is my family's favorite dessert. I love it because it makes the house smell amazing and the tart looks so polished and beautiful (taking a few extra minutes to fan out the apples makes it look like it came from a bakery!). This is a French-style apple tart, not an apple pie, meaning a wedge of the tart is thinner and neater than a slice of all-American apple pie. Try it topped with ice cream for that delicious à la mode taste. Rolling the dough for the tart makes for a finer-textured crust, but on many occasions I have simply pressed the crust into place with great results.

● ●

makes one 9- or 9½-inch tart

preparation time:
20 minutes (plus 15 minutes to chill the dough and 5 minutes to cool)

cooking time:
1 hour

1 stick unsalted butter, cut into 1-inch cubes, plus 1 tablespoon, melted

1½ cups all-purpose flour, plus extra for rolling dough

¼ teaspoon kosher salt

2 tablespoons sugar

3 Granny Smith apples

1 tablespoon fresh lemon juice

1 teaspoon ground cinnamon

1. Set the cubed butter on a plate and place it in the freezer for 15 minutes. Fill a cup with ice and water and set aside. Place 1½ cups of the flour, ⅛ teaspoon of the salt, and 1 tablespoon of the sugar in the bowl of a food processor and pulse to combine. Take the butter out of the freezer and add it to the flour. Pulse the mixture until it looks like wet sand, about 10 seconds. Add 2 to 3 tablespoons of the ice water and pulse until the dough comes together into a ball.

2. Lightly flour your work surface and place the dough on top. Then lightly flour the top of the dough and roll to about a 10- to 11-inch circle, sprinkling more flour under and on top of the dough as necessary. Gently drape the dough over the rolling pin and transfer it to a 9- or 9½-inch fluted tart pan (ideally one with a removable bottom). Fit the dough into the bottom and up the sides of the pan as evenly as possible and press off excess dough from the fluted rim. Set the tart pan on a baking sheet and place in the refrigerator for 15 minutes.

3. Preheat the oven to 350°F. Peel, core, and quarter the apples and then thinly slice them lengthwise. Place the apples in a large bowl and toss with the lemon juice, the cinnamon, and the remaining 1 tablespoon sugar and ⅛ teaspoon salt. Remove the baking sheet with the tart shell from the refrigerator. Arrange the apples in concentric circles so they overlap slightly. Brush the edges of the crust with the melted butter and then bake until the edges are golden and the apples have cooked down, about 1 hour. Cool for 15 minutes before slicing and serving.

Earl Grey Pots de Crème

A pot de crème is an extra-thick and luxuriously creamy pudding. The high fat content (thank you, heavy cream) allows you to offer smaller servings while still satisfying the craving for something sweet and decadent. These are extra cute portioned into mini shot glasses or espresso cups for parties! The Earl Grey tea adds a hint of floral citrus to the pudding, but it's delicious made with other flavor accents, too. One of my favorite variations is to melt 4 ounces good-quality chopped chocolate into the hot cream mixture instead of using the tea.

serves 4

preparation time:
10 minutes (plus time to cool and chill)

cooking time:
35 minutes

- ¾ cup whole milk
- ½ cup heavy cream
- 2 Earl Grey tea bags
- 2 tablespoons granulated sugar
- 2 tablespoons (packed) light brown sugar
- Pinch of kosher salt
- 1 large egg plus 2 large egg yolks
- Whipped cream for garnishing (optional)

1 Preheat the oven to 325°F. Heat the milk and cream in a medium saucepan over medium heat until it comes to a simmer. Turn off the heat, add the tea bags, steep for 5 minutes, and then remove the bags, pressing them against the side of the pan to extract as much liquid as possible.

2 Bring a kettle of water to a boil. Turn off the heat and set aside. Add the granulated sugar, brown sugar, and salt to the tea-infused cream mixture and return to a simmer. Remove from the heat and set aside.

3 Whisk the egg and egg yolks in a large glass measuring cup and pour in a few tablespoons of the tea-infused cream mixture. Whisk gently to combine (overwhisking will cause air bubbles). Continue adding until the bottom of the measuring cup is hot, then add all of the remaining liquid. Divide the mixture into four 3- to 4-ounce ramekins. Place them in a baking dish and fill the baking dish with enough hot water from the kettle to come up to the midway point of the ramekins (take care not to splash water into the ramekins). Bake until the edges are set and the center still jiggles when the side of the ramekin is tapped, 20 to 25 minutes.

4 Fill another baking dish half full with ice water. Use tongs to remove the ramekins from the hot-water bath and transfer to the ice-water bath to chill quickly. Once cool, place the ramekins in a baking dish and cover with plastic wrap. Refrigerate until ready to serve. Serve with a small dollop of whipped cream, if using.

Affogato

I am convinced that one evening a resourceful Italian woman found herself preparing for a dinner party and realized too late that she had only ice cream to serve for dessert. Quick on her feet, she tipped an obligatory cup of steamy espresso over a scoop of ice cream. How ingenious, tasty, and cheap! I like to doll it up with chocolate shavings, and if I'm using drip coffee instead of espresso, I brew it with a pinch of cinnamon or cardamom for a hint of spice.

● ○ ○ ○ ○

serves 4

preparation time:
5 minutes

cooking time:
none

Small block of bittersweet chocolate for making chocolate ribbons

2 cups vanilla ice cream

1 cup still-warm espresso or double-strength drip coffee brewed with a pinch of cinnamon or cardamom

deals, dollars & sense: ice cream

Every week at the supermarket there is usually one brand of ice cream marked down by 50 percent or locked in a buy-one-get-one-free promotion. If you are flexible on brand, pick up whatever ice cream is on sale for biggest savings. If you are brand loyal, wait a week or two and your favorite brand will probably be on sale. Don't forget to stock up!

Use a vegetable peeler to shave off about 1 tablespoon of chocolate shards from the block. Fill 4 cappuccino cups or small bowls with 3 melon ball–sized scoops of ice cream. Pour a little hot coffee over each serving and sprinkle with the chocolate shavings. Serve immediately.

Cardamom Caramel Sauce

Take sugar, simmer with water, and finish with a little butter and cream and you have a swoon-worthy caramel sauce in minutes. I add some cardamom for an exotic warm note. The possibilities for caramel sauce are limited only by your imagination—you can drizzle it over ice cream or baked fruit, or portion it into small ramekins and serve fondue-style with fresh fruit or cubes of pound cake. This is an inexpensive way to dress up even the plainest pound cake or vanilla ice cream for company.

makes about ¾ cup

preparation time:
3 minutes

cooking time:
10 minutes

⅔ cup sugar

1 tablespoon unsalted butter

½ cup heavy cream or half-and-half

1 teaspoon cardamom seeds, gently crushed

1 teaspoon vanilla extract

1 Place the sugar in a medium heavy-bottomed, tall-sided saucepan and cover with ¼ cup water. Give it a gentle stir, trying not to splash any water or sugar up on the sides of the pan. Place the saucepan over medium-high heat until it comes to a strong simmer (don't stir, though you can swirl the pan if it looks like the syrup is coloring more on one side). Continue to simmer until the sugar mixture is golden brown, about 7 minutes.

2 Watch the mixture closely, as sugar syrup can turn from deep brown to burned very quickly (once the sugar looks like ginger ale, you have about 1 minute to go).

3 Remove the pan from the heat and add the butter and cream (the mixture will hiss and bubble violently), whisking until smooth. Stir in the cardamom seeds and bring the mixture back to a boil over high heat. Turn off the heat and cool for 2 minutes before stirring in the vanilla and straining the sauce through a fine-mesh sieve. Cool slightly before serving. The caramel sauce keeps in an airtight container in the refrigerator for up to 1 week.

Peanut Butter–Chocolate Lava Sundaes

When I was a little girl, I spent summers at my grandparents' house in Villa Park, California. Without fail, every night we'd have hot fudge sundaes for dessert while watching the Disneyland fireworks from their front lawn. It became my favorite summertime tradition. The only possible improvement over Grandpa's sundaes is to add peanut butter to the chocolate. Peanut butter and chocolate are best friends in my book, and I can't think of a better way to celebrate them than bringing the two together over a big scoop of vanilla ice cream. This simple combination is pure magic.

● ● ○ ○ ○ ○

serves 4

preparation time:
5 minutes

cooking time:
1 minute

½ cup semisweet chocolate chips

2 tablespoons peanut butter

3 to 5 tablespoons whole milk

1 teaspoon light corn syrup (optional)

1 pint vanilla ice cream

Chopped roasted peanuts (optional)

Place the chocolate chips in a medium heatproof bowl and microwave them until they start to melt, 30 seconds to 1 minute. Use a rubber spatula to stir the chocolate and add the peanut butter and 3 tablespoons of the milk. Microwave until the milk is bubbling, 15 to 30 seconds. Remove from the microwave and stir until smooth (add more milk for a thinner sauce). Mix in the corn syrup (if using). Serve over ice cream and sprinkled with peanuts, if you like.

deals, dollars & sense: affordable desserts

Dessert can be as small or big as you like. Even a tiny portion of ice cream presented elegantly (like with Cardamom Caramel Sauce, page 296, or Peanut Butter–Chocolate Lava sauce, above) and served with a beautiful coffee and tea service will make your guests feel special. If you're looking for more of a statement dessert but want to keep the cost in check, focus on recipes that use flour and sugar as their main ingredients (instead of pricier chocolate, fruits, nuts, and other specialty ingredients).

Lemon-Ginger Pudding

When my sister and I were young, we used to have weekend "pudding parties." We'd make pudding from a box, set our hair in pink foam rollers, and watch Love Boat *and* Fantasy Island. *If only we had known how easy it is to make pudding from scratch! When making pudding, I have a strong lead flavor that gets supported by a secondary flavor—in this case, lemon takes the lead while ginger offers a little punch. Other great combos are butterscotch pudding made with brown sugar (instead of granulated), cinnamon, and cloves, or hot chocolate pudding made with a handful of chocolate chips and a pinch of cayenne.*

● ● ● ● ● ●

serves 4

preparation time:
10 minutes (plus 10 minutes to cool and 1 hour to chill)

cooking time:
10 minutes

2-inch piece fresh ginger, peeled

Zest of 1 lemon, plus juice of 1½ lemons

½ cup sugar

2 tablespoons cornstarch

Pinch of kosher salt

1 cup whole milk

¾ cup half-and-half

1 tablespoon unsalted butter

1 Grate the ginger into a medium bowl. Add the lemon zest and juice and set aside.

2 Whisk the sugar, cornstarch, and salt together in a medium saucepan. Add the milk and half-and-half and whisk to combine. Bring the ingredients to a simmer over medium-high heat while whisking constantly, until the mixture is thick and starts to bubble, 6 to 8 minutes. Turn off the heat and use a wooden spoon to stir in the ginger-lemon mixture and the butter, slowly stirring until the butter is completely melted. Pour the mixture through a fine-mesh sieve and into a medium bowl.

3 Cool for 10 minutes before covering flush with plastic wrap and refrigerating (at this point you can also divide the pudding into 4 dessert bowls and cover each flush with plastic wrap). Refrigerate for at least 1 hour before serving.

Raspberry-Vanilla Bread Pudding with Lemon Cream

Bread pudding is my ultimate comfort dessert, and when it's paired with my favorite fruit, raspberries, I am in dessert heaven! Although fresh raspberries are reasonably priced only a few weeks of the year, raspberry jam is a cheap alternative that offers the same bright berry flavor. To add a little extra tang, I add a squirt of fresh lemon juice. Cherry jam is another smart way to satisfy a cherry craving without having to buy expensive fresh cherries.

● ● ●

makes one 8-inch pudding

preparation time:
10 minutes (plus 15 minutes to soak the bread and 10 minutes to cool)

cooking time:
30 minutes

1 tablespoon unsalted butter, at room temperature

½ cup raspberry jam

Zest and juice of ¼ lemon

3 large eggs

½ cup whole milk

½ cup heavy cream

¼ cup plus 1 tablespoon sugar

2 teaspoons vanilla extract

7 slices white sandwich bread

deals, dollars & sense: using jam instead of fresh fruit

If a recipe calls for a fruit that may be available at a reasonable price only a few months of the year, such as fresh berries, cherries, and peaches, go for jam instead. Jam delivers the essence of the fresh fruit in a much more economical package. If fresh fruit is called for as a topping, dilute jam with a little hot water or the lemon-mint syrup on page 288, and serve as a fruit sauce. For muffin or cake batters, swirl in small dollops of jam.

1 Preheat the oven to 350°F. Grease an 8-inch baking dish with the butter and set aside. Place the raspberry jam in a small bowl. Add 1 tablespoon hot water and whisk, then stir in the lemon juice. The consistency should be thick, yet thin enough to pour; if it is too thick, stir in 1 more tablespoon hot water. Set aside.

2 Whisk the eggs with the milk, ¼ cup of the cream, ¼ cup of the sugar, and the vanilla in a medium bowl. Slice the bread into large cubes and place half of them in the buttered baking dish. Pour half of the egg mixture over the bread and then drizzle half of the raspberry sauce over the top. Repeat with the remaining bread cubes, egg mixture, and raspberry sauce. Set aside for 15 minutes.

3 Bake the bread pudding until it is set and no longer wet looking and is golden on top, about 30 minutes. Meanwhile, using a stand mixer or a hand mixer, whip the remaining ¼ cup cream and remaining 1 tablespoon sugar into soft peaks. Add the lemon zest and whip just enough to incorporate. Remove the bread pudding from the oven, let cool for 10 minutes, and then serve with a dollop of lemon cream. Refrigerate leftovers for up to 3 days; warm before serving.

Chocolate Pain Perdu

Pain perdu (French toast) means "lost bread," and it is one of the ingenious ways that the French lend new life to dried-out bread. Here I take a few liberties; instead of cooking the egg-and-cream-soaked bread slices in a skillet, I soak them in a baking dish bread pudding–style for a chocoholic's dream come true. This is wonderfully decadent, making it a fantastic end to any meal. Or, follow in the footsteps of many of my fans and serve it for a special breakfast instead!

● ●

serves 4

preparation time:
20 minutes (plus 2 hours to chill)

cooking time:
35 minutes

- 4 tablespoons unsalted butter, at room temperature
- ½ cup heavy cream
- ½ cup whole milk
- 2 tablespoons sugar
- 1 teaspoon vanilla extract
  Pinch of kosher salt
- ½ cup semisweet chocolate chips
- 2 large eggs, lightly beaten
- 6 slices white bread, crusts removed, halved diagonally into triangles

1 Grease a 9 × 5-inch loaf pan with 1 tablespoon of the butter and set aside. Bring ¼ cup of the cream, all of the milk and sugar, the remaining 3 tablespoons butter, the vanilla, and the salt to a simmer in a small pot over low heat. Turn off the heat. Place the chocolate in a medium bowl and pour the hot cream mixture over it. Set aside for 5 minutes and then add the eggs and gently whisk to combine. Line the bottom of the baking dish with the bread triangles, overlapping them slightly, and then pour the chocolate mixture over the bread, making sure to coat all exposed surfaces of the bread. With your fingertips, push down on the bread to submerge the bread in the chocolate. Cover with plastic wrap and refrigerate for 2 hours.

2 Remove the baking dish from the refrigerator and let it sit on the counter for 30 minutes while you preheat the oven to 375°F. Bake the French toast until the custard is set and the bread turns golden around the edges, about 30 minutes. Remove from the oven and set aside to cool slightly. Whip the remaining ¼ cup cream on medium speed until it forms soft peaks. Serve the French toast with a dollop of the whipped cream.

Double Chocolate Pound Cake

When I eat a chocolate dessert, I want it to scream chocolate! This cake is perfect for people like me—it's incredibly rich thanks to a generous amount of butter (it is a pound cake, after all) and it gets a double whammy of chocolate from cocoa powder and chocolate chips. Dark brown sugar lends extra moistness and an even deeper, molasses-y richness. This dessert is a little pricier to make but a thin slice goes a long way. For an extra-rich treat, spend another dollar and top with a ganache frosting (see box).

● ● ● ● ○

makes one 9 × 5-inch loaf

preparation time:
30 minutes (plus 1½ hours to cool)

cooking time:
1 hour

⅔ cup unsweetened Dutch-processed cocoa powder

2 sticks plus 1 tablespoon unsalted butter, at room temperature

1½ cups all-purpose flour

1½ teaspoons baking powder

½ teaspoon baking soda

½ teaspoon kosher salt

3 large eggs

1½ teaspoons vanilla extract

1¼ cups (packed) dark brown sugar

¾ cup semisweet chocolate chips

Confectioners' sugar, for dusting (optional)

deals, dollars & sense: quick ganache frosting

Chocolate and cream mixed together until melted, smooth, and glossy is called ganache. Place some chopped chocolate (or chocolate chips) in a heat-safe bowl and pour half as much hot cream (or half-and-half) over the chocolate (so if you have ½ cup of chocolate in the bowl, you pour ¼ cup of hot cream over it). Set aside for 5 minutes and then stir until smooth. Drizzle over pound cake (or any other cake) or let cool a bit to thicken and spread using a knife.

1 Preheat the oven to 350°F. Place the cocoa in a small bowl. Bring a kettle of water to a boil, pour ⅔ cup boiling water over the cocoa, stir to combine, and set aside. Grease a 9 × 5-inch loaf pan with 1 tablespoon of the butter and set aside. Whisk the flour, baking powder, baking soda, and salt together in a large bowl and set aside. Whisk the eggs and vanilla together in a small bowl and set aside.

2 Place the remaining 2 sticks butter and the sugar in the bowl of a stand mixer (or in a large bowl if using a hand mixer) and beat on medium-high speed until light and airy, about 2 minutes. Reduce the speed to low and add the cocoa mixture, using a rubber spatula to scrape down the sides of the bowl as necessary. Raise the speed to medium and slowly add the egg mixture. Once all of the eggs are added, add the flour mixture in two parts, stirring and scraping the sides of the

bowl after each addition. Mix in the chocolate chips and scrape the batter into the prepared loaf pan, evening it out with the top of the spatula before placing it in the oven.

3 Bake the cake until it springs back to light pressure and a cake tester comes out without any batter attached (melted chocolate from the chocolate chips is okay), 55 minutes to 1 hour. Remove the cake from the oven and set aside to cool completely, about 1½ hours. Run a paring knife around the edges of the cake to release it from the pan and turn it out onto a plate or platter. Once the cake is completely cool, dust the top with confectioners' sugar (if using), slice, and serve.

Muriel's Yogurt Cake with Chocolate Chips

Muriel is my French mother-in-law, and she makes this cake for us whenever she comes to our house for a visit. She uses a six-ounce plastic yogurt container to measure out the ingredients—the girls think it's hilarious that she uses the plastic cup instead of measuring cups (which is why I included the yogurt container measurements in the recipe)! It's a basic yet lovely cake that is quick to make and easy to love.

● ● ● ● ●

makes **1** Bundt cake

preparation time:
20 minutes (plus time to cool)

cooking time:
40 minutes

- 1½ cups all-purpose flour (two 6-ounce yogurt cups full)
- 1 teaspoon baking powder
- ½ teaspoon baking soda
- ¼ teaspoon kosher salt
- 4 tablespoons unsalted butter, at room temperature
- ¾ cup granulated sugar (one 6-ounce yogurt cup full)
- 2 large eggs
- ¾ cup plain yogurt (one 6-ounce yogurt cup full)
- 1 teaspoon vanilla extract
- 3 tablespoons mini semisweet chocolate chips
- Confectioners' sugar, for dusting

1 Preheat the oven to 375°F. Lightly coat a nonstick Bundt pan with neutral-flavored pan spray and set aside. Whisk the flour, baking powder, baking soda, and salt together in a medium bowl and set aside.

2 In the bowl of a stand mixer (or in a large bowl if using a hand mixer) cream the butter and granulated sugar together on high speed until pale yellow, about 3 minutes. Add the eggs one at a time, mixing well between additions; scrape down the sides and bottom of the bowl as necessary. In a medium bowl, whisk the yogurt and vanilla together and set aside. Add one third of the flour mixture to the butter-sugar mixture, mixing until no dry streaks remain, followed by half of the yogurt mixture. Repeat, ending with the last one third of the flour mixture. Use a wooden spoon or rubber spatula to stir in the chocolate chips and then scrape the batter into the prepared pan. Bake until golden brown and a cake tester comes out clean, 30 to 35 minutes.

3 Remove the cake from the oven and cool 15 minutes before inverting the cake onto a wire rack to cool completely. Place some confectioners' sugar in a fine-mesh sieve and dust over the top of the cake. Slice and serve.

VARIATION: Yogurt Upside-Down Cake

Sauté a chopped apple in a medium skillet with butter until it begins to soften (or use canned crushed pineapple, drained) and set aside. After coating the Bundt pan with pan spray, smear 1 tablespoon unsalted butter around the bottom of the pan and all of the grooves. Sprinkle 2 to 3 tablespoons (packed) dark brown sugar over the butter. Add an even layer of apples (or pineapple) to the pan and make the cake batter as described on page 306. After baking, let the cake cool for 5 minutes before inverting it onto a wire rack to cool. If there is any brown sugar–butter mixture still in the pan, use a wooden skewer or wooden spoon to scrape it up and place it on top of the cake.

Olive Oil and Orange Cake

My lightly sweetened and citrusy olive oil cake is a great recipe to have in your baking arsenal for a few reasons. It relies on pantry ingredients you probably already have on hand, meaning you can bake it without making a special trip to the store, plus it's incredibly tasty, of course. Its best attribute, however, is that it puts forward a sophisticated presentation while costing just over a buck to make. What's the trick? Desserts that count on pantry ingredients like flour, oil, and eggs are always the thriftiest to pull off, and when presented in such an elegant manner, no one will ever be the wiser.

● ▢ ▢ ▢ ▢

makes one 8-inch cake

preparation time:
10 minutes (plus 2 hours to cool)

cooking time:
35 minutes

1¼ cups all-purpose flour

 1 teaspoon baking powder

½ teaspoon baking soda

 1 teaspoon table salt

 2 large eggs

¾ cup granulated sugar

⅓ cup olive oil

 1 teaspoon vanilla extract

Zest and juice of 1 orange

Confectioners' sugar, for dusting

1 Preheat the oven to 350°F. Lightly coat an 8-inch round cake pan with unflavored pan spray and set aside. Sift the flour, baking powder, baking soda, and salt into a medium bowl and set aside.

2 In the bowl of a stand mixer (or in a medium bowl if using a hand mixer) whip the eggs and granulated sugar together on medium speed until they're well blended, somewhat thick, and pale yellow, 1½ to 2 minutes. While mixing, pour in the oil and vanilla, beat until smooth, and then mix in the orange zest and juice. Reduce the mixer speed to low and add half the flour mixture. Once it is mostly incorporated, add the remaining flour mixture just until the dry ingredients are incorporated. Turn off the mixer and use a rubber spatula to scrape the batter into the prepared cake pan.

3 Bake until the center of the cake springs back to light pressure and a cake tester inserted into the middle of the cake comes out with just a crumb or two attached, 30 to 35 minutes. Remove the cake from the oven and set aside to cool completely in the pan, about 2 hours. Run a paring knife around the edges of the pan and turn the cake out onto a cake stand or platter. Sift confectioners' sugar over the cake, slice, and serve.

Buttery Shortbread

It is great to have a no-fail tried-and-true butter cookie recipe up your sleeve that you can make without much of a fuss. Shortbread is a great cookie, as its buttery flavor can fly solo or provide a canvas for all kinds of flavors, such as sweet vanilla, fresh orange zest, or savory rosemary. This isn't an all-day project cookie—it's a make, bake, and enjoy cookie (my favorite kind!).

● ● ● ● ● ●

makes 16 cookies

preparation time:
20 minutes (plus time to cool)

cooking time:
25 minutes

- 1 stick unsalted butter, at room temperature
- ¼ cup sugar
- ½ teaspoon kosher salt
- 1 cup all-purpose flour, plus extra for flouring work surface

1 Preheat the oven to 300°F. Place the butter and sugar in the bowl of a stand mixer (or in a medium bowl if using a hand mixer) and cream until light and airy, about 1 minute. Mix in the salt and then add the flour in four ¼-cup increments, mixing after each addition. Gather the dough into a ball, wrap in plastic wrap, and refrigerate for 15 minutes.

2 Lightly flour the work surface and roll the dough into an 8 × 2-inch rectangle ½ inch thick. Trim the slightly ragged edges and slice the rectangle into 4 equal strips lengthwise. Repeat crosswise to yield 16 rectangles. Use a spatula to transfer the shortbread to a cold, ungreased rimmed baking sheet. Prick the tops of the squares with a fork and bake until the cookies are golden, about 25 minutes. Remove the pan from the oven and cool completely on a wire rack.

Chocolate-Drizzled Mandarin Orange Napoleons

Store-bought puff pastry, melted chocolate, and some sliced fruit become an impressive dinner-party-worthy napoleon in hardly any time at all. I often make this with fresh, sliced fruits such as bananas, berries, and kiwi, but when they're not on sale (or I don't have time to shop) I use a can of mandarin oranges. Puff pastry is a bit of a splurge, but the extra dollar or two you spend for it gets evened out by the inexpensive oranges.

● ● ●

serves 4

preparation time:
20 minutes

cooking time:
16 minutes

for the napoleons

All-purpose flour, for dusting

1 sheet thawed puff pastry, from a 17.3-ounce box

3 tablespoons sugar

½ teaspoon orange zest

½ cup heavy cream

1 cup canned mandarin oranges, drained

for the chocolate drizzle

¼ cup semisweet chocolate chips

2 teaspoons whole milk

1 **To make the napoleons:** Preheat the oven to 400°F. Line a rimmed baking sheet with parchment paper and set aside. Lightly flour a work surface with flour and place the sheet of puff pastry on top. Unfold and press flat. Sprinkle with a little flour and use a rolling pin to roll into a slightly wider rectangle. Slice the dough into 4 strips lengthwise, then slice crosswise in half. Use an offset spatula to transfer the dough to the prepared baking sheet and use a fork to prick a few holes in each rectangle. Bake the pastry until it is golden brown, about 15 minutes. Remove from the oven and set aside to cool.

2 Rub the sugar and orange zest together in a small bowl until the sugar is very fragrant and pale orange. Pour the cream into the bowl of a stand mixer (or in a medium bowl if using a hand mixer) and whip on medium-high speed until it makes soft peaks. While whipping the cream, sprinkle in the sugar mixture and continue to beat until you have stiff peaks.

3 **To make the chocolate drizzle:** Place the chocolate chips and milk in a small heatproof bowl and microwave in 15-second increments, stirring between each, until melted.

4 To assemble the napoleons, place a puff pastry rectangle on each of 4 plates. Divide half of the whipped cream among the pastry rectangles and top with mandarin oranges. Cover with the remaining 4 pastry rectangles, top with the remaining whipped cream, drizzle with chocolate, and serve.

Citrus Butter Cookies

My girls and I make these butter cookies in the wintertime and dunk them into small bowls of hot chocolate. What a treat! They're also tasty dipped into melted chocolate or caramel sauce. When I have a lemon, a lime, and an orange in the house, I like to double the ingredients and then divide the dough into thirds. If you add a different type of zest to each batch, you get three different flavors for the effort of one.

makes 2½ dozen cookies

preparation time:
30 minutes

cooking time:
50 minutes

1 stick unsalted butter, at room temperature

¼ cup cream cheese, at room temperature

½ cup sugar

1 teaspoon vanilla extract

1 cup all-purpose flour

⅛ teaspoon baking powder

Pinch of salt

Zest from 1 citrus fruit (lemon, lime, or orange)

1. Preheat the oven to 350°F. Place the butter, cream cheese, sugar, and vanilla in the bowl of a stand mixer (or in a large bowl if using a hand mixer) and beat on medium speed until light and creamy, about 1 minute. Whisk the flour, baking powder, and salt together in a medium bowl. While mixing on low speed, gradually add the flour mixture to the butter mixture, mixing just until blended. Remove the bowl from the mixer and use a wooden spoon to stir in the zest.

2. Fill a quart-sized resealable bag with the batter. Seal the bag and press the batter down to the bottom. Snip off a corner of the bag (low enough on the bag to yield a ¼-inch-wide opening) and pipe 2-inch-long strips 2 inches apart on an unlined rimmed baking sheet (you will probably have to bake the cookies in 2 or 3 batches). Bake until golden brown, 12 to 14 minutes.

3. Remove the cookies from the oven and cool on the baking sheet for 3 minutes before using a spatula to transfer them to a cooling rack. Repeat with the remaining dough.

Orange Marmalade and Raspberry Jam Pochette Cookies

These filled cookies exist in a middle ground between a cookie and a pastry, making them perfect for many occasions: weeknight dessert, PTA coffee, hosting teatime, greeting new neighbors, or (I'm thinking of my husband) breakfast. The simple butter and cream cheese pastry is rich and flaky without being overly sweet. (Pictured here with Buttery Shortbread and Citrus Butter Cookies, pages 309 and 311.)

● ●

makes **3** dozen

preparation time:
25 minutes (plus 30 minutes to chill and time to cool)

cooking time:
22 minutes (plus time to cool)

- 2 cups all-purpose flour, plus more for rolling
- ¼ teaspoon kosher salt
- 2 sticks unsalted butter, at room temperature
- 8 ounces cream cheese, at room temperature
- ¼ cup orange marmalade
- ¼ cup raspberry jam
- Confectioners' sugar, for dusting

1 Stir the flour and salt together in a medium bowl and set aside. Place the butter and cream cheese in the bowl of a stand mixer (or in a large bowl if using a hand mixer) and beat until light and creamy, about 1 minute. Reduce the speed to medium-low and add the flour mixture ¼ cup at a time until the dough comes together. Divide the dough in half and shape each portion into a disk. Wrap in plastic wrap and refrigerate until slightly firm, about 30 minutes.

2 Set a small bowl of water and 2 rimmed baking sheets on the counter. Adjust an oven rack to the upper-middle position and another rack to the lower-middle position. Preheat the oven to 375°F. Lightly flour a work surface and, using a rolling pin, roll one dough disk into an ⅛-inch-thick circle. Use a 3-inch round fluted cookie cutter to stamp out as many rounds as you can. Top each with ½ teaspoon orange marmalade. Brush the edges of one side of the dough with water and fold one side over the jam to meet the opposite edge (for a half-moon shape). Press the seam together to seal, and place on an ungreased rimmed baking sheet. Reroll the remaining scraps on the counter and fill with more marmalade. Repeat with the remaining dough disk and the raspberry jam.

3 Bake the cookies until golden, 20 to 22 minutes, rotating the sheets from the upper-middle rack to the lower-middle rack and vice versa midway through baking. Remove from the oven and use a spatula to transfer the cookies to a cooling rack to cool completely. Dust with confectioners' sugar and serve.

Black Bean Brownies

Black beans add a velvety texture and incredible moistness to these rich, chocolaty brownies. Because of the grounding protein and fiber they sneak into dessert, the brownies don't send kids into a total sugar rush after they eat them, which to me is a huge win. For a pretty finish, I sprinkle them with powdered sugar before serving, or, if I'm feeling extra snazzy, I'll place a stencil on top of the pan of brownies and sprinkle the sugar over it to get a fun design.

● ●

makes **12** brownies

preparation time:
20 minutes (plus 15 minutes to cool)

cooking time:
20 minutes

1 tablespoon unsalted butter, at room temperature

½ cup mini semisweet chocolate chips

⅓ cup all-purpose flour

½ teaspoon baking powder

½ teaspoon kosher salt

¾ cup cooked black beans

½ cup vegetable oil

2 large eggs

¼ cup unsweetened natural cocoa powder

⅔ cup granulated sugar

1 teaspoon instant coffee or espresso

1 teaspoon vanilla extract

Confectioners' sugar, for dusting

deals, dollars & sense: confectioners' sugar
Want to dress up cakes, cookies, or bar cookies while barely spending a cent? Dust them with confectioners' sugar. There's something about a final sprinkle of powdered sugar that gives sweet treats that special fresh-from-the-bakery look. I even shower bran muffins with a shake or two of powdered sugar to make them look extra enticing for breakfast.

1 Preheat the oven to 350°F. Grease a 9-inch square baking dish with the butter and set aside. Place ¼ cup of the chocolate chips in a heatproof bowl and microwave in 30-second increments, stirring after each, until the chocolate is melted.

2 Whisk the flour, baking powder, and salt together in a small bowl and set aside. Purée the beans with the oil in a blender. Add the eggs, cocoa, granulated sugar, coffee, vanilla, and melted chocolate and purée until smooth. Add the flour mixture and pulse just until incorporated. Scrape the mixture into a medium bowl and stir in the remaining ¼ cup chocolate chips. Transfer the batter to the prepared pan and bake until the surface is somewhat matte around the edges and still glossy in the center, about 20 minutes. Remove from the oven and cool for at least 15 minutes before slicing into 12 squares. Dust with confectioners' sugar and serve.

// 11 //

breakfast

Bonus Chapter!

There are ample opportunities to save money when it comes to breakfast, making breakfast a real treasure for budget-savvy cooks.

One secret I swear by is to entertain at breakfast time. I find friends and family have much more flexible weekend morning schedules than later in the day, meaning impromptu get-togethers are easier to organize, even with only a few days' notice. Breakfast basics, such as flour, butter, and eggs, are always in the house, too, so whipping up a quick batch of scones or a scramble for unplanned gatherings is a snap. And cooking breakfast is so affordable, plus kids are almost always happiest in the morning, so why not take advantage?

Breakfast is also fantastic for dinner. When fancy wild mushrooms are scrambled into eggs and the dish is paired with a simple green salad, this breakfast standard is instantly transformed into chic bistro-worthy fare. Dishes such as huevos rancheros and croque madames are some ways to slide breakfast recipes into dinnertime slots.

Honey-Maple Granola with Pecans

One of the best arguments for making your own granola (besides saving big bucks) is that you are in control of what goes in it and how sweet it is. Check the nutritional labels of the granola you buy at the store—you may be surprised by how much sugar is added. This granola is excellent sprinkled over yogurt for breakfast, eaten like cereal with milk, or with dried fruits and nuts for an energizing trail mix.

● ● ● ○ ○ ○

makes **3** cups

preparation time:
10 minutes (plus 30 minutes to cool)

cooking time:
35 minutes

2 cups old-fashioned rolled oats (not instant)

½ cup chopped pecans

½ cup crisped rice cereal

¼ cup wheat germ or milled flax seeds

2 teaspoons ground cinnamon

½ teaspoon ground ginger

¼ teaspoon kosher salt

2 tablespoons vegetable oil

3 tablespoons honey

2 tablespoons maple syrup

1 teaspoon vanilla extract

1 Preheat the oven to 300°F. Stir the oats, pecans, rice cereal, wheat germ, cinnamon, ginger, and salt together in a large bowl. Whisk the oil, honey, maple syrup, vanilla, and 2 tablespoons water together in a small bowl. Pour the honey mixture over the oat mixture and use a wooden spoon to stir it all together, using your fingers to thoroughly coat the ingredients.

2 Spread out the granola onto a rimmed baking sheet and bake until dry, crisp, and golden, 30 to 35 minutes, using a spatula to push the granola around the pan every 10 minutes or so. Remove from the oven and cool completely before transferring to an airtight container (the granola can be stored for up to 1 week).

breakfast parfaits Layering yogurt with granola and some caramelized pan-seared fruit turns simple granola and yogurt into a special breakfast dish. My favorite parfait fruit is bananas, but you can also use apples, pears, or pineapple. Simply melt 1 tablespoon butter in a skillet, then add the fruit (I use about 2 cups to make four servings) and cook until it begins to brown. Add a sprinkle of sugar, a pinch of salt, and the juice of an orange. Cook just a few minutes until the fruit looks sweet and glazed, cool for a minute or two, and then layer with yogurt and granola.

Homemade Yogurt

When I lived in Dallas, I taught money-saving tactics to women's groups. The topic that everyone responded to the most was how I made my own yogurt using just a few everyday ingredients: milk, a spoonful of yogurt as a "starter," sweetener, dry milk powder (a supermarket staple), and the heat of my garage! With four small children, we were going through a quart of yogurt a day. Once I started making my own, the savings came to more than a hundred bucks a month! I made a video of myself making yogurt, which got me on The Next Food Network Star. *(Note that because commercial yogurts use thickening agents and stabilizers, homemade yogurts aren't as thick.)*

serves 4

preparation time:
10 minutes (plus 20 to 26 hours to ferment and chill)

cooking time:
10 minutes

- 4 cups whole milk
- ¼ cup nonfat dry milk powder
- 2 tablespoons maple syrup
- ¼ cup whole milk, low-fat, or fat-free plain yogurt with active cultures

1 Heat the milk in a large saucepan over medium-low heat until you see the first swirls of steam come off the surface of the milk and an instant-read thermometer is at 160°F., 2 to 3 minutes. Turn off the heat and whisk in the milk powder and the maple syrup. Cool until the temperature of the milk is 120°F., 12 to 15 minutes. Whisk in the starter yogurt and pour the mixture into a large glass jar (a mason jar with a screw-top lid works nicely) or bowl.

2 Cover with a clean kitchen towel and set aside in a warm place between 90°F. and 105°F. (such as a warm garage in the summer; near a heater; in a cooler alongside a thermos wrapped in a kitchen towel and filled with hot water—replace the water after 5 hours; in an oven preheated for 3 minutes and then turned off; in a slow cooker preheated to low and then turned off; or in a warm car sitting in the sun), for 10 to 12 hours. The yogurt gets tangier and thicker the longer it sits.

3 Place the yogurt in the refrigerator and chill for a few hours. It will stay fresh for up to a couple of weeks—if it lasts that long!

Black Bean, Chocolate, and Banana Smoothies

One of my favorite ways to start the day is with a breakfast smoothie. When I'm craving a bit of chocolate in the morning, this is the smoothie I make. Chocolate and black beans are great pals—the beans give the smoothie filling protein, fiber, and a nice creaminess while the cocoa powder adds a deep and toasty chocolate taste. I like the light, nutty sweetness of chocolate-flavored almond milk, but other milks work great, too, such as soy milk, rice milk, or coconut milk. If using cow's milk, you may want to add an extra teaspoon of cocoa.

makes **2** smoothies

preparation time:
5 minutes

cooking time:
none

1½ cups unsweetened chocolate almond milk (or soy, coconut, or rice milk)

¼ cup cooked black beans, rinsed under water

1 banana, peeled

1 tablespoon honey

2 teaspoons unsweetened cocoa powder

1 teaspoon instant coffee (optional)

1 teaspoon vanilla extract

¾ cup ice cubes

½ cup loosely packed baby spinach

Pour the almond milk into a blender jar. Add the black beans, banana, and honey and blend on high for 15 seconds. Add the cocoa powder, instant coffee (if using), and vanilla, then the ice cubes, and then the spinach. Blend on high until smooth, about 45 seconds. Drink immediately.

Green Morning Smoothies

I've been known to throw everything into the blender: cabbage, beans, even raw oats! Green smoothies are one of my favorite smoothie blends and they also happen to be one of my kids' favorites. I'm thrilled when my kids eat raw vegetables in the morning! The trick to pleasing young palates is to add a banana for creaminess and sweetness and just enough light-colored fruits to give the vegetables a sweet profile. Stay away from red fruits, though (red plus green equals gray). I sometimes even add white beans for an extra protein boost. If you're new to green smoothies, start with ½ cup spinach and work your way up to 1 cup.

●●

makes 2 smoothies

preparation time:
5 minutes

cooking time:
none

- 1½ cups unsweetened vanilla soy milk (or almond, coconut, or rice milk)
- ¼ cup whole oats
- 1 banana, peeled and halved
- 1 cup fresh or frozen chopped peaches (or any light-colored fruit; see sidebar on opposite page)
- 1 tablespoon honey or maple syrup
- 1 teaspoon vanilla extract
- ¾ cup ice cubes
- 1 cup fresh or frozen baby spinach (or ¾ cup spinach plus 2 or 3 cabbage leaves or other leafy greens, chopped)

Pour the milk into a blender jar. Add the oats and banana and blend on high for 15 seconds. Add the peaches, honey, and vanilla followed by the ice cubes and then the spinach. Blend on high until smooth, about 45 seconds. Drink immediately.

Green Smoothie Mix-and-Match Mash-Up! There are endless possibilities as to what fruits and veggies can get tossed into a blender to make a green smoothie. Remember to keep the proportions of fruits to vegetables in check for a sweet flavor profile that even kids will love.

LIGHT-COLORED (NOT RED) FRUITS

- Apples
- Avocados
- Bananas
- Grapefruit
- Green grapes
- Kiwis
- Nectarines, frozen or fresh (peeled)
- Oranges
- Peaches, frozen or fresh (peeled)
- Pears
- Pineapple

GREEN VEGETABLES

- Carrots (they're not green but are a sweet addition)
- Celery
- Cucumbers
- Green cabbage
- Kale
- Parsley
- Spinach
- Swiss chard

EXTRAS!

- Bran cereal (be sure to blend the smoothie really well)
- Fresh ginger (just a touch)
- Honey
- Maple syrup
- Peanut butter or almond butter
- Raw oats
- Vanilla extract
- White beans

Croque Madames

Traditionally a lunch meal, croque madames are fair game for breakfast (or brunch or dinner!) at my house. The deliciously decadent French version of a ham and cheese sandwich is classically made with a somewhat time-consuming Mornay sauce (a cheesy béchamel sauce), but I often use sour cream instead. It's about 90 percent as good yet takes half as much time, making a fantastically rich croque madame doable even on busy days. The secret is to start with great ham. Ask your deli for only four slices, so you can splurge on the good stuff without breaking your budget.

● ● ● ○ ○

serves 4

preparation time:
15 minutes

cooking time:
10 minutes

4 large slices country-style bread

1½ cups grated Swiss cheese

2 tablespoons dry white wine

¼ cup sour cream

1 teaspoon Dijon mustard

1 teaspoon granulated garlic

½ teaspoon kosher salt, plus extra for seasoning

¼ teaspoon ground black pepper, plus extra for seasoning

4 large slices good-quality ham

1 tablespoon unsalted butter

4 large eggs

1 Toast the bread on the lowest setting until it is just dry but not browned. Place on an aluminum foil–lined rimmed baking sheet and set aside.

2 Stir the cheese and wine together in a small bowl and set aside. In another small bowl, stir together the sour cream, mustard, garlic, salt, and pepper. Scoop out about 1 tablespoon of the sour cream mixture from the bowl and spread a thin layer on top of each bread slice, and then cover each with 1 slice of ham. Divide the remaining sour cream mixture over the ham slices. Use a paper towel to lightly blot the grated cheese (to absorb any extra wine) and then sprinkle over the sour cream.

3 Adjust an oven rack to the upper-middle position, 5 to 6 inches from the heating element, and preheat the broiler to low. Place the baking sheet with the bread under the broiler and cook until the cheese-topped bread slices are bubbly and lightly browned, about 3 minutes (broiler intensity varies, so keep an eye on it).

4 Melt the butter in a large nonstick skillet over medium heat. Crack the eggs into the pan and cook them to your liking, either sunny side up or over easy.

5 Remove the bread from the oven and transfer to 4 plates. Top with an egg, season with salt and pepper, and serve.

Fried Brown Rice and Eggs with Garlic-Soy Vinaigrette

I love to make this for breakfast when I have leftover rice in the fridge. It's quick to pull together and offers a nice change of pace from the usual breakfasts. Plus it's a great brunch dish for company, as it's unexpected and rustically elegant (and cheap!). The fried egg is served on top of the rice, ready to be mixed into the rice for a garlicky-gingery dish that is just as tasty for dinner as it is for breakfast. If you have other grains left over in the refrigerator, use them in place of some or all of the rice. Quinoa is especially nice for its great toothsome texture and pop (and white rice works just fine, too).

serves 4

preparation time:
15 minutes

cooking time:
15 minutes

for the vinaigrette

2 tablespoons soy sauce

2 teaspoons rice vinegar

1 tablespoon sesame oil

for the fried rice and eggs

2½ tablespoons vegetable oil

1 onion, halved and thinly sliced lengthwise with the grain

3 garlic cloves, finely minced or pressed through a garlic press

2 tablespoons grated fresh ginger

2½ cups cooked brown rice

2 teaspoons chili powder

4 large eggs

2 scallions (white and green parts), finely chopped

1 **To make the vinaigrette:** Whisk the soy sauce, vinegar, and sesame oil together in a small bowl and set aside.

2 **To make the fried rice and eggs:** Heat 2 tablespoons of the vegetable oil in a large skillet over medium-high heat. Add the onion and cook, stirring often, until soft and golden, about 5 minutes. Stir in the garlic and ginger and cook until crisp and fragrant, about 2 minutes. Mix in the rice and chili powder and cook until the rice is warmed through and starting to brown, about 5 minutes. Turn off the heat and set aside.

3 Heat the remaining ½ tablespoon vegetable oil in a medium nonstick skillet over medium heat. Fry the eggs to your liking, either sunny side up or over easy. Divide the rice among 4 bowls, top each with an egg, some scallions, and some of the soy vinaigrette, and serve.

Baked Huevos Rancheros in Crispy Tortilla Cups

I grew up eating Mexican food in Tucson, Arizona, where huevos rancheros are as everyday as omelets and pancakes. I make mine into cute individual cup-sized servings, with a tortilla acting as a crispy edible bowl for the beans, salsa, and a soft-baked egg topped with melted Jack cheese. Since the eggs are baked in the oven at once, this is perfect brunch fare for a crowd (you can easily increase the recipe to feed a crowd or scale it down to one or two portions to make yourself a solo dinner, as I used to do in grad school). These are great arranged on a platter for buffets, too.

●●

serves 4

preparation time:
20 minutes

cooking time:
15 minutes

- 8 6-inch flour tortillas, trimmed to 5-inch circles
- 3 tablespoons unsalted butter, melted
- ½ teaspoon kosher salt
- 1 cup store-bought salsa
- ¾ cup cooked black beans
- ¼ teaspoon ground black pepper
- 8 large eggs
- ½ cup grated pepper Jack cheese
- ½ cup sour cream
- Cilantro leaves, for garnish (optional)

1 Preheat the oven to 400°F. Brush both sides of the tortillas with melted butter and sprinkle with some of the salt. Fit the tortillas into 8 cups of a 12-cup muffin tin (they should look like little cups).

2 Using a wooden spoon, mix ½ cup of the salsa with the black beans, a pinch of salt, and the pepper. Divide the bean mixture among the tortilla cups. Crack an egg into each cup and place the muffin pan in the oven. Bake until the eggs are barely set, about 8 minutes. Remove from the oven and top each egg with 1 tablespoon of the cheese. Loosely tent with aluminum foil and continue baking until the cheese is melted, 6 to 7 minutes longer. Remove the pan from the oven and gently use the corners of the tortilla to lift it out of the muffin cup. Sprinkle with cilantro leaves, if using, top with the sour cream and the remaining ½ cup salsa, and serve.

deals, dollars & sense: personalized portions

A single-serving portion does two things: one, it is what I like to call "elegant" portion control (personalized portions don't look cheap, they look special); and two, kids love anything that comes in a small package. This recipe is a win-win all around.

Scrambled Eggs with Wild Mushrooms

A few humble eggs turn creamy, decadent, and downright elegant when you scramble them right. The keys to beautifully made scrambled eggs are to cook them in butter, over a lower heat than you think you should; to stop cooking them just before you think they're done; and to halt the cooking with a splash of milk or cream at the end. Wild mushrooms are what I call a smart splurge because you need only very few to add a sophisticated flavor to the eggs. At less than a buck for a handful, it's a small price to pay to feel like you're treating yourself to something really special.

● ●

serves 4

preparation time:
15 minutes

cooking time:
18 minutes

3 tablespoons unsalted butter

½ small onion, finely chopped

½ teaspoon kosher salt

6 wild mushrooms, chopped
  (about ¾ cup; creminis, oyster
  mushrooms, and/or shiitakes)

9 large eggs

¼ cup plus 1 teaspoon milk or
  heavy cream

1 scallion (white and green
  parts), finely chopped

2 tablespoons grated Pecorino
  cheese

¼ teaspoon ground black pepper

1 Melt 1 tablespoon of the butter in a medium nonstick skillet over medium heat. Add the onion and ¼ teaspoon of the salt, and cook, stirring often, until soft and translucent, about 3 minutes. Add the mushrooms and cook, stirring occasionally, until lightly browned and soft, 4 to 6 minutes. Transfer to a small bowl and set aside. Use paper towels to wipe the pan clean.

2 Vigorously whisk the eggs and ¼ cup of the milk together in a medium bowl until the eggs are an even yellow color and foamy on the surface, about 30 seconds. Over medium-low heat, melt the remaining 2 tablespoons butter in the pan used for the onion mixture. Pour in the egg mixture, reduce the heat to low, and, using a wooden spoon or a rubber spatula, gently stir the eggs until they turn creamy with soft curds and are still slightly runny, about 6 minutes. Stir in the mushroom mixture, scallion, Pecorino, the remaining ¼ teaspoon salt, and the pepper. Continue to stir the eggs until they aren't runny but are still wet looking, 1 to 2 minutes longer. Then splash the top of the eggs with the remaining 1 teaspoon milk to stop the cooking. Serve immediately.

Poached Eggs with Roasted Asparagus and Browned Butter

An entire season of Ten Dollar Dinners is filmed over one several-week period. This means I have entire weekends to myself in New York City to wander, eat, and get inspired. On one particularly chilly day, I found myself in Brooklyn and hungry. I ducked into a little restaurant where I ate incredible poached eggs drizzled with nutty browned butter and served with perfectly crusty toast points. I was in egg-dunking heaven! Ever since, I have made my own version at home. In the winter, when asparagus is pricey, I'll substitute roasted vegetables such as cauliflower, broccoli, or potatoes instead.

serves **4**

preparation time:
15 minutes

cooking time:
35 minutes

- 12 asparagus spears, tough ends snapped off (if thick, use a vegetable peeler to shave the stalks)
- 1 teaspoon olive oil
- ½ teaspoon kosher salt, plus 2 teaspoons for poaching the eggs
- ½ teaspoon ground black pepper
- 1 teaspoon fresh lemon juice
- 1 tablespoon white vinegar
- 8 large eggs
- 1 stick unsalted butter
- ½ baguette, thinly sliced on a bias into 8 pieces
- Wedge of Parmesan cheese

1 Preheat the oven to 425°F. Place the asparagus on an aluminum foil–lined rimmed baking sheet. Drizzle the olive oil over the spears and roll them to evenly coat. Season with ¼ teaspoon of the salt and ¼ teaspoon of the pepper and then roast until browned and tender (not too soft), 10 to 12 minutes, turning the spears halfway through cooking. Remove from the oven, sprinkle with the lemon juice, and set aside.

2 To poach the eggs, fill a medium saucepan two thirds full with water. Add the vinegar and bring the water to a bare simmer over medium heat (it should look like fizzy soda water). Crack an egg into a ramekin and tip the ramekin over the water (the ramekin should be just barely above the water but not touching it) so the egg gently slides into the water. Repeat with another egg. Gently simmer for 3½ minutes (keep the water at a fizzy simmering state, raising or reducing the heat as necessary) and then use a slotted spoon to transfer them to a paper towel–lined plate. Repeat in 3 batches with the remaining 6 eggs. (For perfect timing, start browning the butter after the first batch of eggs is poached.)

recipe continues

3 To brown the butter, melt it in a small heavy-bottomed saucepan (preferably one with a light-colored interior) over medium heat. Let the butter bubble and foam, swirling it in the pan frequently. After a few minutes the foam will subside. Once the butter bits in the bottom of the pan are brown and the butter smells like toasted hazelnuts, 2 to 3 minutes longer, turn off the heat and set the pan aside.

4 Toast the baguette slices in the toaster (or under a broiler) and place 2 pieces on each plate. Slide a thin spatula under each poached egg and place it on top of a toasted piece of bread. Repeat with the remaining eggs. Place the asparagus spears alongside the bread and drizzle with the browned butter. Season with the remaining ¼ teaspoon salt and the remaining ¼ teaspoon pepper. Then use a vegetable peeler to shave Parmesan ribbons over the eggs. Serve immediately.

Easy Scones

This is my go-to quick scone recipe for bake sales, teacher appreciation days, and morning breakfast parties—anytime I need a homemade treat but don't have a lot of time. They're infinitely versatile (see my favorite flavor combinations on page 341) and such a breeze to throw together since I skip cutting butter into the dough and use heavy cream instead. Unbaked scones freeze beautifully, making them a great impromptu fresh-from-the-freezer start to a lazy Sunday. Semifreeze them on a baking sheet, and then transfer to gallon-sized resealable freezer bags (label the scone flavor!). When you bake frozen scones, add 4 to 5 minutes to the baking time.

makes **16** scones

preparation time:
30 minutes

cooking time:
12 minutes

- 2 cups all-purpose flour, plus extra for shaping
- 7 tablespoons sugar
- 2 tablespoons dry buttermilk powder (or 1 tablespoon lemon juice added with the cream)
- 2 teaspoons baking powder
- ½ teaspoon baking soda
- ½ teaspoon kosher salt
- 1 cup plus 2 tablespoons heavy cream
- 2 tablespoons unsalted butter, melted
- 1 teaspoon vanilla extract

deals, dollars & sense: dry buttermilk powder

Dry buttermilk powder is a convenient item to have in the house to make Easy Scones, pancakes, or a quick brine for fried chicken. You can find it in the baking aisle of most supermarkets (be sure to refrigerate after opening).

1 Preheat the oven to 425°F. Line a rimmed baking sheet with parchment paper and set aside. Whisk the flour, 6 tablespoons of the sugar, the buttermilk powder, baking powder, baking soda, and salt together in a large bowl.

2 Whisk 1 cup of the cream, the melted butter, and the vanilla together in a liquid measuring cup and pour over the sugar mixture. Use a wooden spoon to stir together until the mixture is rough textured and very few dry patches remain.

3 Turn the scone dough out onto a lightly floured work surface and knead the dough just until it is smooth, about 1 minute. Divide the dough in half, shape into 2 disks, and flatten each disk into a 6- to 7-inch-thick circle. Slice each circle into 8 wedges and transfer to the prepared baking sheet. Brush the tops with the remaining cream, sprinkle with the remaining 1 tablespoon sugar, and bake until golden brown, about 12 minutes. Remove the scones from the oven and set aside to cool for 5 minutes before serving warm or at room temperature.

Creative Scone Mix-Ins and Tasty Sweet Butters

Plain scones are delicious, but sometimes I like to get more creative and add unexpected mix-ins, such as citrus zest or dried herbs, to the scone dough. If I'm hosting a brunch, I'll bake a few of each kind so everyone can have fun tasting the different combinations.

- **Rosemary–Chocolate Chip Scones:** Whisk ¼ cup mini semisweet chocolate chips and 1 teaspoon dried rosemary into the sugar mixture. Add the cream mixture and proceed with the recipe as instructed.

- **Orange–White Chocolate–Basil Scones:** Whisk ¼ cup white chocolate chips, 1 tablespoon orange zest, and 1 teaspoon dried basil into the sugar mixture. Add the cream mixture and proceed with the recipe as instructed.

As an extra-special treat, I'll often add a flavored butter or cream cheese to the scone spread. It takes two seconds to make but often steals the show!

- **Spiced Caramel-Vanilla Butter:** Cream together 1 stick room-temperature unsalted butter, 2 tablespoons store-bought caramel sauce, 1 teaspoon ground cinnamon, ½ teaspoon ground cardamom, and the seeds from ½ vanilla bean. Chill before serving.

- **White Chocolate Butter:** Melt ¼ cup white chocolate chips and 2 teaspoons vegetable oil together in the microwave. Stir until smooth, then set aside to cool before mixing in 1 stick room-temperature unsalted butter and 3 tablespoons room-temperature cream cheese. Chill before serving.

- **Lemon Cream Cheese:** Stir together 8 ounces room-temperature cream cheese, ⅓ cup sour cream, 1 tablespoon (packed) light brown sugar, and 1 tablespoon lemon zest. Chill before serving.

Apple-Carrot Mini Muffins

Mini muffins are an anytime treat at my house, especially when they're packed with fiber and nutrients. My girls love them for breakfast on the run or as an after-school snack, and I love them because they're loaded with bran flakes, flax seeds, and fruit (apples and pears are my favorites) and vegetables (carrots, parsnips, and zucchini work best). For even more protein, swap out a tablespoon or two of the flour for soy flour.

● ● ○ ○ ○

makes 24 mini muffins

preparation time:
25 minutes

cooking time:
25 minutes

½ cup all-purpose flour

½ cup whole-wheat flour

½ cup bran flake cereal or
old-fashioned rolled oats
(or a combination of the two)

¼ cup ground flax seeds

2 tablespoons wheat germ

1 teaspoon baking powder

1 teaspoon baking soda

1 teaspoon ground cinnamon
Pinch of kosher salt

1 large egg

¼ cup (packed) light brown
sugar, plus extra for topping
(optional)

2 tablespoons olive oil

1 teaspoon vanilla extract

⅔ cup plus 1 tablespoon
whole milk

deals, dollars & sense: mini muffins

Compact mini muffins are a tasty way to pack fiber into a friendly package. Since they're so small, they can be frozen and then thawed in minutes, making them an excellent on-the-go, healthy snack. While the heft from bran, flax, and whole-wheat flour makes them too dense and heavy as regular-sized muffins, as minis they totally work while still retaining a cupcake-y charm.

1 Preheat the oven to 350°F. Spray a 24-cup mini muffin pan with nonstick pan spray or line with mini muffin liners.

2 Whisk the all-purpose flour, whole-wheat flour, bran flakes, flax seeds, wheat germ, baking powder, baking soda, cinnamon, and salt together in a large bowl.

3 Whisk the egg and the ¼ cup sugar together in a medium bowl. Mix in the olive oil and vanilla, then whisk in the milk. Use a wooden spoon to stir in the vegetables and fruit, then pour the egg mixture over the flour mixture. Stir just until combined (a few lumps are fine).

4 Divide the batter among the prepared muffin cups, filling each one about three quarters full. If you'd like, sprinkle a little sugar over each muffin. Bake until the center of the muffins spring back to light pressure, 20 to 25 minutes (muffins made with dried fruit take about 5 minutes less to bake). Remove from the oven and cool for a few minutes in the pan before transferring to a rack to cool completely.

¾ cup grated vegetables, such as carrots, parsnips, spinach, and/or zucchini

¾ cup very finely chopped fresh or dried fruit, such as apples, pears, pineapple, and/or raisins

Cinnamon Buns

One year, as I was putting the finishing touches on the brunch buffet table for my daughter Valentine's birthday party, she announced to me that she had promised all of her little friends (and parents) my famous cinnamon buns. She was so excited about the mysteriously "famous" cinnamon buns that I couldn't bear to let her down. With no time to make a yeast dough, I pulled some bread dough out of the fridge and whipped up these cinnamon buns. In no time flat, the house smelled of welcoming cinnamon, and not long after that our guests were pulling apart still-warm, sweet, and maple-glazed cinnamon buns. And Valentine was beaming.

● ● ● ○ ○ ○

makes 6 buns

preparation time:
20 minutes (plus 20 minutes to rest and 5 minutes to cool)

cooking time:
24 minutes

for the cinnamon buns

All-purpose flour, for rolling the dough

1 pound store-bought bread dough

¼ cup (packed) dark brown sugar

1½ teaspoons ground cinnamon

Pinch of kosher salt

4 tablespoons unsalted butter, at room temperature, plus 1 tablespoon melted

for the maple glaze

2 tablespoons cream cheese, at room temperature

¼ cup confectioners' sugar

3 tablespoons maple syrup

1 To make the cinnamon buns: Dust a cutting board with the flour. Place the bread dough on the floured cutting board, cover with a kitchen towel or a sheet of plastic wrap, and set aside for 20 minutes. Stir the brown sugar, cinnamon, and salt together in a small bowl and set aside.

2 Preheat the oven to 375°F. Grease an 8- or 9-inch baking dish with 1 tablespoon of the room-temperature butter and set aside.

3 Turn the bread dough over on the cutting board to dust the other side and then use a rolling pin to roll it to an 11- to 12-inch × 7- to 8-inch rectangle that is about ⅛ inch thick. Mash the remaining 3 tablespoons room-temperature butter in a small bowl and use your fingers to smear it all over the bread dough. Sprinkle the brown sugar mixture over the dough, using your hand to evenly cover it. Starting at the bottom, roll the dough into a tight cylinder that is about 12 inches long. Pinch the seam to seal and then cut the log crosswise into 6 equal pieces.

4 Transfer the cinnamon buns, cut side down, to the baking dish, gently pressing them down into the pan. Brush the melted butter over the rolls and bake until golden brown, 22 to 24 minutes. Remove from the oven and set aside to cool for 5 minutes before glazing.

recipe continues

5 To make the maple glaze: While the cinnamon buns cool, whisk the cream cheese and confectioners' sugar together in a small bowl. Add the maple syrup and stir to combine. Spoon about 1 tablespoon of the mixture over each cinnamon bun. Serve warm or at room temperature. The cinnamon buns are best eaten within a few hours of baking.

Philippe's Sunday Morning Waffles

My husband and I have a weekend morning ritual: one of us gets to sleep in (at least past sunrise!) while the other makes breakfast with our daughters. On Philippe's days he always makes his "famous" crisp and buttery waffles. The girls love cooking with their dad, who doesn't miss a chance to get silly with the girls on those lazy mornings. On weekday mornings, I'm bustling around the kitchen making breakfast and packing lunches, so on Philippe's weekend morning I take in the sweet smell of waffles and wait for the sound of eight little girl feet running down the hall to wake me up for breakfast. It's my favorite moment of the week.

makes 16 small (or 8 large) waffles

preparation time:
25 minutes

cooking time:
20 minutes

6 large eggs, separated

1½ cups whole milk

1 teaspoon vanilla extract

4 tablespoons unsalted butter, melted

1 cup all-purpose flour

½ cup whole-wheat flour

1 tablespoon sugar

½ teaspoon kosher salt

1 tablespoon orange zest

Warm maple syrup, for serving

1 Preheat a waffle iron. Pour the egg whites into the bowl of a stand mixer (or a large bowl if using a hand mixer) and beat on medium-high speed until they hold stiff peaks.

2 Whisk the egg yolks, milk, and vanilla together in a large bowl until smooth. Whisk in the butter. In another medium bowl, whisk together the all-purpose flour, whole-wheat flour, sugar, salt, and orange zest. Whisk the flour mixture into the milk mixture and then whisk one third of the egg whites into the batter. Use a rubber spatula to gently fold in the remaining egg whites until no white streaks remain.

3 Add enough waffle batter to the iron to fill in all of the squares and cook until golden and crisp, 4 to 5 minutes. Serve immediately with warm maple syrup. (Or place the waffles on a wire rack set on top of a baking sheet and keep them warm in a 250°F. oven until they're ready to serve at once.)

Potato-Bacon Torte

This is not just my signature dish, but may actually be the recipe on The Next Food Network Star *that won me my own cooking show. The contestants were challenged to cook the ultimate dinner party meal for an incredibly esteemed group of chef-judges including Bobby Flay, Masaharu Morimoto, and François Payard. There were three finalists remaining and we had a sky-high budget to execute our menu. What did I make? My humble fifty-cents-a-serving Potato-Bacon Torte! It proved definitively that you can create something special enough to serve the country's finest chefs while not spending an arm and a leg to make it.*

● ● ● ○ ○ ○

serves 8

preparation time:
30 minutes (plus 30 minutes to rest and 30 minutes to cool)

cooking time:
1 hour

for the crust

2¼ cups all-purpose flour, plus extra for rolling

1 teaspoon kosher salt

2 sticks unsalted butter, cut into small cubes and chilled

8 to 10 tablespoons ice water

for the torte

2 large russet potatoes

2 teaspoons dried tarragon

¾ teaspoon kosher salt

½ teaspoon ground black pepper

4 bacon strips, halved crosswise

½ to ⅔ cup heavy cream, plus 1 tablespoon for the crust

1 **To make the crust:** Place the flour and salt in the bowl of a food processor and pulse to combine. Add the butter and process just until the mixture resembles wet sand, about 6 seconds. Add the ice water, 1 tablespoon at a time, pulsing after each addition, until the dough begins to come together in large clumps. Divide the dough evenly between two quart-sized resealable bags, seal, and gently knead and pat each into a flat disk. Refrigerate the dough disks for at least 30 minutes or overnight.

2 Preheat the oven to 375°F. Lightly dust your work surface with some flour. Remove one dough disk from the refrigerator, take it out of the bag, and set it on the floured surface. Roll the dough into a 10-inch circle that's between ⅛ and ¼ inch thick. Gently drape the dough over the rolling pin and lift it over and into a 9-inch pie plate. Fit the dough into the edges of the pan and set aside.

recipe continues

mom's pie trick A few slits in the top crust of a pie or torte helps allow steam to escape so the hot filling doesn't elbow through the top crust and leak out the sides. My mom used to carve steam vents in the shape of a guest's initials into the top crust of her pies and tortes. It's a heartfelt tradition that I proudly carry forth in my kitchen and you may want to adopt it, too.

3 To make the torte: Place the potatoes on a cutting board, peel them and halve them lengthwise, and then slice into ⅛- to ¼-inch-thick half moons. Begin arranging the potatoes in the pie crust, rounded edges facing out, until you have a single layer of potatoes around the edges of the crust. Add another circle of potatoes in the center of the crust so you end up with a single layer of sliced potatoes that completely covers the bottom of the crust. Season the potatoes with one third of the tarragon, one third of the salt, and one third of the pepper. Repeat, seasoning between each layer, until you use all of the potatoes (you'll probably have about 3 layers of potatoes). Season the top layer with the remaining tarragon, salt, and pepper and lay the bacon strips over the final layer of potatoes. Slowly drizzle ½ cup of the cream evenly over the top layer, letting it seep down before adding more, if needed (add enough cream so the liquid nears the top of the potatoes—you don't want it to overflow). Set aside.

4 Roll the second dough disk into a 10-inch circle that's between ⅛ and ¼ inch thick, drape it over the rolling pin, and gently lay it over the top of the torte. Press down on the edges to seal and then crimp the edges by pinching them with your thumb and forefinger. Use a paring knife to make two or three small slits at the center of the top crust and place the torte on a rimmed baking sheet.

5 Brush the top crust with the remaining 1 tablespoon cream. Bake until the top crust is golden brown, about 1 hour, tenting the torte with a sheet of aluminum foil if it looks like it's getting too dark. Remove the baking sheet from the oven and place the torte on a wire rack to cool for at least 30 minutes before slicing. Serve warm or at room temperature.

in a pinch, go premade

While my buttery and easy-to-make double crust makes pies, tarts, and tortes super special, I want to assure you that there is no shame in using a premade store-bought crust to make pies and tortes. Shortly after I had my twins, I made potato-bacon tortes for all of my neighbors as a holiday gift. I must have baked more than two dozen of them! I had four babies, all in diapers, and you know what? I bought my crusts premade. I won't lie: the homemade butter crust really makes this torte sing. But even with a store-bought crust this savory pie is fantastic. Just be sure to buy an unsweetened crust when using it to make a savory pie or torte.

acknowledgments

Creating a book is such a collaborative process.
Readers, please know that these acknowledgments are
a too-brief expression of a richer and deeper gratitude.

This book wouldn't have happened without the team at Clarkson Potter: Jane Treuhaft, your eye for aesthetic detail is amazing. Ashley Tucker, thank you for making the book's design look so beautiful. Emily Takoudes, I have rarely felt so *listened to*. Not a word gets by you unnoticed. The only thing I love more than having you as my editor is sharing our lives and family stories. Thank you from the bottom of my heart. And thank you for bringing Raquel Pelzel into my life; she is a wonderful collaborator and partner who became a fast friend. Thank you, Raquel, for saving me and my sanity (and my orange dress). Ben Fink and Dahlia Warner, you made the pictures beautiful. Thank you for making so many lovely memories for my entire family. My kids and I want to spend holidays with you. (But don't worry, we won't.)

I would like to thank my entire Food Network family, and in particular Susie Fogelson and Bob Tuschman, who took an incredible gamble on giving me my job. You will always have a place at my table, both food and conference. Bobby Flay, thank you for never phoning it in, and for keeping the bar high. I treasure that in a mentor and friend.

Mark Dissin, thank you for turning my ideas into a TV show and me into a host. Sarah Paulsen, I couldn't have picked a better culinary producer. Bonus: I just adore you and our friendship. Michelle Betrock, my professional regard and appreciation for you is surpassed only by the profound friendship that has resulted from our work together.

Thank you to the William Morris Endeavor team. Josh, a day isn't the same if we haven't talked. I smile each time my kids call you Uncle Joshy (and each time that you let them). Jon and Jeff, I love working with you and counting you among my friends. A huge thank you to Andy McNicol for your guidance along the way with my first book. Ross and Bradley, without you, I would probably still be at JFK trying to go standby somewhere.

I couldn't keep the crazy schedule I keep if it weren't for an incredibly supportive extended family, particularly my sister Stacy, who has been in charge of all nine of our collective kids on many a day, and the "cousins" who inspire, play with, and babysit my children. Thank you to my mother-in-law, Muriel, who not only hops on ridiculously long plane rides routinely to come help us with the kids, but loves them as much as we do (not to mention raising the finest man I've met anywhere, and then entrusting him to me). *Tu es la meilleure; merci.*

I would like to thank my mom. Without you, all my dreams would just dance in my head. I wish you could share this, and I know you do, too.

Last, and definitely most, I want to thank my husband and my four sweet girls. You are in every word, crumb, and drop in this book. Thank you for who we are behind the closed doors of our home. I cherish our family.

recipe cost index

●●●

index